S0-AFN-044

# Learn PHP 7

Object-Oriented Modular Programming
using HTML5, CSS3, JavaScript, XML,
JSON, and MySQL

Steve Prettyman

Apress®

*Learn PHP 7: Object-Oriented Modular Programming using HTML5, CSS3, JavaScript, XML, JSON, and MySQL*

Steve Prettyman
Stone Mountain, Georgia USA

ISBN-13 (pbk): 978-1-4842-1729-0        ISBN-13 (electronic): 978-1-4842-1730-6
DOI 10.1007/978-1-4842-1730-6

Library of Congress Control Number: 2015960461

Managing Director: Welmoed Spahr
Lead Editor: Steve Anglin
Editorial Board: Steve Anglin, Louise Corrigan, Jonathan Gennick, Robert Hutchinson, Michelle Lowman, James Markham, Susan McDermott, Matthew Moodie, Jeffrey Pepper, Douglas Pundick, Ben Renow-Clarke, Gwenan Spearing
Coordinating Editor: Mark Powers
Copy Editor: Kezia Endsley
Compositor: SPi Global
Indexer: SPi Global
Artist: SPi Global

Distributed to the book trade worldwide by Springer Science+Business Media New York, 233 Spring Street, 6th Floor, New York, NY 10013. Phone 1-800-SPRINGER, fax (201) 348-4505, e-mail orders-ny@springer-sbm.com, or visit www.springeronline.com. Apress Media, LLC is a California LLC and the sole member (owner) is Springer Science + Business Media Finance Inc (SSBM Finance Inc). SSBM Finance Inc is a Delaware corporation.

For information on translations, please e-mail rights@apress.com, or visit www.apress.com.

Apress and friends of ED books may be purchased in bulk for academic, corporate, or promotional use. eBook versions and licenses are also available for most titles. For more information, reference our Special Bulk Sales–eBook Licensing web page at www.apress.com/bulk-sales.

Any source code or other supplementary material referenced by the author in this text is available to readers at www.apress.com. For additional information about how to locate and download your book's source code, go to www.apress.com/source-code/. Readers can also access source code at SpringerLink in the Supplementary Material section for each chapter.

Printed on acid-free paper

# Contents at a Glance

# Contents

# About the Author

**Steve Prettyman** earned his Bachelor's of Arts Degree in education from Oglethorpe University in 1979. He quickly began his teaching career as a high school mathematics instructor while continuing his education by earning a Master's Degree in business information systems from Georgia State University (1985). Since then, Steve has spent over 30 years in the IT industry. He has been an instructor at Chattahoochee Technical College, Kennesaw State University, and Southern Polytechnic State University for almost 20 years. His primary teaching responsibilities include programming, web design, and web application development.

# Acknowledgments

Thank you to everyone who has helped put this book together. Special thanks to the Introduction to PHP classes that have been the true testers and debuggers for this journey.

Special acknowledgement to all the open source developers and providers of free tutorials and training to every Internet user who wants to learn more about programming, especially w3schools and The New Boston.

# Introduction

*Learn PHP 7: Object-Oriented Modular Programming using HTML5, CSS3, JavaScript, XML, JSON, and MySQL* is intended for use as a beginning level programming book. It is not the goal of this book to cover advanced techniques in the current versions of the PHP programming language. Some knowledge of general programming concepts is expected but no actual programming experience or education is assumed.

All code examples in this book are compatible with PHP 7. Most examples are compatible with PHP 5.6. The newest (as of the publication date) methods (functions) available in PHP have been used to provide the reader with the most current coding techniques. The examples use core methods provided in the PHP language. PHP includes many additional methods to accomplish similar tasks. The reader may, and should, research additional ways of improving security, performance, and other techniques. It is the goal of this book to prompt users to always consider using the most secure and efficient methods of program development. The code in this book provides some examples of using these techniques. The user should remember that *no program is 100% secure*. The programmer can only strive to make an application as secure as possible. It takes a team of developers, network personnel, security administrators, data center personnel, and others working together to provide the safest environment.

## A Different Approach

There are quite a number of PHP books on the market today. What makes this book any different than any other?

- This book uses the concept of "learning by doing," which shows the reader how to develop applications with conditional statements, loops, arrays, and methods. Over 70 PHP methods (functions) are introduced and demonstrated in coding examples.

- From the very first examples, the reader is introduced to object-oriented programming techniques. Many other books only briefly cover OO programming (if at all) in the final chapters.

- Object-oriented set methods are used to verify and filter user input. Many other books simply show a set method accepting data and storing it.

- A major objective of the book is to convince the reader to create all programs as secure and efficient as possible. The newest password encryption techniques (password_hash) are demonstrated.

- The try and catch methods are introduced to capture exceptions and some errors. The newest versions of PHP have been created to handle exceptions and errors using this approach. Many other books use die or other techniques to shut down a program.

- Multi-tier program design is introduced in the early chapters. This allows the reader to discover what logic and coding should take place in each tier. Many PHP books do not even cover this topic.

- The majority of the examples in the book are used to develop one main application (ABC Canine Shelter Reservation System). As the book progresses, the application is built from the beginning, in stages, showing the reader that application development should be broken into stages. Only after each stage is completed and tested, can the next stage begin. This approach works hand in hand with multi-tier design. Additional programming exercises and a term project are provided to enhance the understanding of development.

- The creation of user, change, and error logs are introduced. This allows the reader to gain an understanding of how to provide backup and recovery ability to keep an application functioning properly when security breaches or exceptions occur.

- The introduction of data objects and the data tier demonstrates to the reader the importance of creating an application that provides the ability to change data storage techniques and data storage location without requiring a major rewrite of the application. XML, JSON, and MySQL examples are provided.

- A natural relationship between PHP, HTML5, CSS3, and JavaScript is demonstrated throughout the book. This relationship is one of the major strengths of PHP.

- Throughout the book, web links are provided to point the user to additional resources to help understand the material or to dig deeper into the subject matter. Updates to link locations are provided on the book's web site.

## Special Note for Teachers

The design of the content of this book provides flexibility in teaching styles and approaches. Each college and university approaches the initial education of programming concepts in different ways. This book provides three different types of programming exercises, which allow teachers to pick and choose what would work best in their environment. "Do It" exercises are provided in each chapter to allow the student to gain hands-on experience with techniques shown by modifying existing examples to produce the desired results. These exercises provide a level of confidence before the student attempts to program exercises at the end of the chapters. In addition, a Term Project is provided that builds an application that uses the same types of algorithms and programming techniques shown in the book.

Teaching tools, including test banks, course outline, and PowerPoint slides are available for use from the book's web site and from `apress.com`.

## Code Examples, Images, and Links

Every effort has been made to catch any errors in code (and grammar). Please let us know if/when you discover problems in this book. Please send all corrections to Steve Prettyman (`steve_prettyman@hotmail.com`).

All code examples, images, and links are available for download from `apress.com` and the following location. You can download code examples from either web site. Copying code from the book may cause errors due to format requirements for publishing.

Book's web site: `www.littleoceanwaves.com/securephp/`

# Chapter Overview
## Chapter 1: An Introduction to PHP 7

After completing this chapter, the student will be able to:

- Understand the difference between LAMP, WAMP, and MAMP
- Successfully install a version of LAMP, WAMP, or MAMP
- Search the Internet for troubleshooting problems
- Explain the difference between a programming language and a scripting language
- Create an error-free simple PHP program

## Chapter 2: Interfaces, Platforms, Containers, Three Tier Programming

After completing this chapter, the student will be able to:

- Give examples of platforms or containers that can host PHP programs
- Create a simple, dynamic web application using PHP
- Explain three-tier design and determine what is contained in each tier
- Design a three-tier application
- Explain each step of the program development life cycle (PDLC)
- Define and explain MVC and dependency injection

## Chapter 3: Modular Programming

After completing this chapter, the student will be able to:

- Create an error-free simple objected-oriented (OO) modular PHP program
- Create a PHP class and make an instance of the class (object)
- Create an OO PHP encapsulated program, including get and set methods
- Create PHP methods (functions) that accept parameters and return information
- Create PHP public and private properties (variables)
- Import existing PHP code from another file or library into a program
- Validate information received using ternary (conditional) operators

# Chapter 4: Secure User Interfaces

After completing this chapter, the student will be able to:

- Explain why user input must be validated in the interface and business rules tiers
- Explain why user input must be filtered in the business rules tier
- Use HTML5 code to validate user input
- Use JavaScript code to validate user input
- Use PHP `if` statements (conditional statements) to validate and filter input
- Use `foreach` loops to dynamically create an HTML select box from an XML file
- Use simple arrays for filtering and validation
- Pass simple arrays into methods (functions)
- Understand how to use dependency injection to control code version changes

# Chapter 5: Handling and Logging Exceptions

After completing this chapter, the student will be able to:

- Explain the difference between errors and exceptions
- Create a PHP program that can handle general exceptions
- Create a PHP program that can create, raise, and handle user exceptions
- Explain and use a `switch` and/or embedded `if/else` statement
- Create a PHP program that uses the `while` loop and/or the `for` loop
- Create a program that reads/updates a text file using a two-dimensional array
- Create a PHP program that logs exceptions and e-mails support personnel

# Chapter 6: Data Objects

After completing this chapter, the student will be able to:

- Create a data class that inserts, updates, and deletes XML or JSON data
- Explain how to create a data class that updates MySQL Data using a SQL Script
- Create a PHP program that creates a change backup log
- Create a PHP program that can recover data from a previous backup
- Apply changes to create up-to-date valid information
- Use dependency injection to attach a data class to another class in the BR tier
- Create a three-tier PHP application

# Chapter 7: Authentication

After completing this chapter, the student will be able to:

- Define sessions and explain how sessions are used for authentication
- Create a PHP program that authenticates user logon
- Create a PHP program that register users
- Create a PHP program that will allow users to change passwords
- Create a PHP program that logs invalid login attempts

# Chapter 8: Multifunctional Interfaces

After completing this chapter, the student will be able to:

- Create a complete PHP application that deletes, updates, and inserts data
- Create a professional look to a completed application using CSS
- Use JavaScript to accept and manipulate data from another program
- Secure all programs within an application requiring user IDs/passwords
- Populate HTML objects with values from a JSON object

# CHAPTER 1

# An Introduction to PHP 7

*"PHP is a popular general-purpose scripting language that is especially suited to web development. Fast, flexible, and pragmatic, PHP powers everything from your blog to the most popular web sites in the world." —www.php.net*

## Chapter Objectives/Student Learning Outcomes

After completing this chapter, the student will be able to:

- Understand the differences between LAMP, WAMP, and MAMP

- Successfully install a version of LAMP, WAMP, or MAMP

- Search the Internet for troubleshooting problems

- Explain the difference between a programming language and a scripting language

- Create an error-free simple PHP program

## PHP 5.5+, PHP 7+, and PHP.NET

Today, **PHP** (Hypertext Preprocessor) is one of the most popular languages used for web application development. The language has evolved to allow the programmer to quickly develop well-formed error-free programs using both **procedural** and **objected-oriented** programming techniques. It provides the ability to use many preexisting libraries of code that either come with the basic installation or can be installed within the PHP environment. This gives you multiple ways to complete a particular task. It provides more flexibility than many other languages. The ease with which additional libraries of code can be added to the environment is one of the many driving forces in its popularity.

> *Procedural language—A procedural programming language includes functions/methods that can be called from the main flow of the program. The flow of the program jumps to the function/method, executes the code within the module, and then returns to the next statement in the main flow of the program. Some Procedural languages include a main function/method that automatically is called when the program is executed.*

---

**Electronic supplementary material**  The online version of this chapter (doi:10.1007/978-1-4842-1730-6_1) contains supplementary material, which is available to authorized users.

© Steve Prettyman 2015
S. Prettyman, *Learn PHP 7*, DOI 10.1007/978-1-4842-1730-6_1

*Object-oriented language—An object-oriented language uses classes and objects. Classes are similar to blue prints. A class describes what an object can contain, including properties/variables and functions/methods. An object is an instance of a class (like a building that has been created from a blueprint). Object-oriented languages provide polymorphism, encapsulation, and inheritance. Objects are naturally encapsulated by containing all related functions/methods and properties/variables within the object itself. Polymorphism allows duplicate method/function names within object-oriented objects. However, the "signature" must be different. The "signature" is the combination of the types of variables (numbers and characters) passed into the method/function and the type of information passed out of a method/function. For example, several add methods could be created—one that only accepts integers (whole numbers), one that only accepts floating point numbers (numbers with decimals), and one that accepts a combination. The program will determine which method/function to call by what has been passed into the method/function. Inheritance in object-oriented programming allows an object to inherit properties/variables and functions/methods from another object. The object can also override those items inherited. This is similar to a child inheriting characteristics from the parents. Object-oriented languages can also be event-driven. An event-driven program will "sleep" until an event occurs. This is similar to an ATM machine program waiting for a user to input an ATM card.*

PHP is an **open source** language. As such, each version of the language is created using input from the individuals who use it—the programmers themselves. This allows the language, over time, to evolve and float into the direction that is driven by the users. From its first release in 1995 as a Personal Home Page Tool (PHP) by Rasmus Lerdorf, the versions have been released on the Internet with forums to provide users the ability to make suggestions and even provide code changes and additions. Today `www.php.net` is the official PHP web site.

*Open source language—An open source programming language is developed by a community of interested parties. The community accepts input from fellow programmers for suggested upgrades and corrections. Several members of the community work together to present proposals and to make changes to the language. Open source languages are "free". A non-open source language (such as Microsoft C#) is created and updated by a company or major organization. Non-open source languages are not usually "free".*

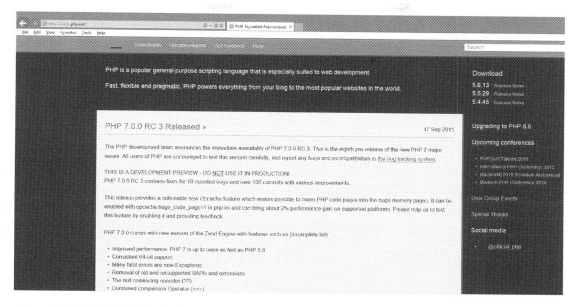

**Figure 1-1.** *PHP.NET (09/24/15)*

The `www.php.net` home page provides information on each of the latest releases of the language. It also provides information on future releases, the features planned for those releases, and the planned release dates. In addition, other related PHP information can be found, including links and information to major PHP conferences.

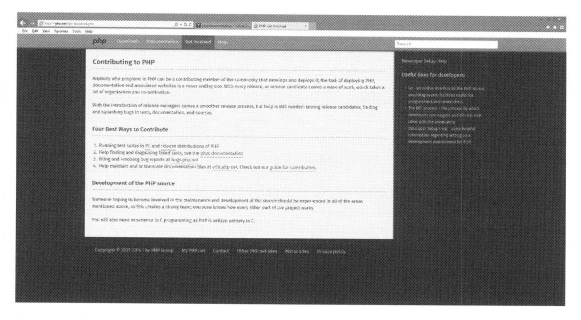

**Figure 1-2.** *Get involved (09/24/15)*

As mentioned, this site provides the ability for users to help with the future development of the language. Users can get involved with testing beta versions and reporting errors or program bugs. Visitors can also view documentation related to the development of possible future versions. This is a good way of discovering future enhancements or security fixes before major announcements have been made to the public.

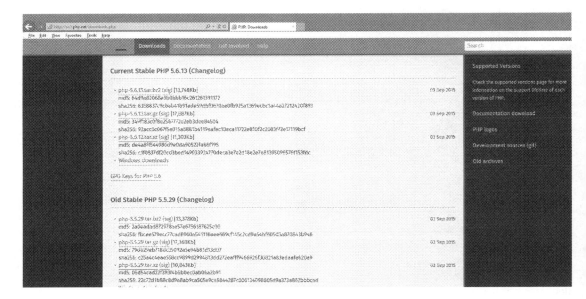

*Figure 1-3.* *Download page (09/24/15)*

The download page, as you might have guessed, provides the ability to gain easy access to the latest versions of the language. However, as you will note, only the language itself is provided. It is more common, and recommended, that the beginning user use a **WAMP** (Windows, Apache, MySQL, PHP); **LAMP** (Linux, Apache, MySQL, PHP); or **MAMP** (Mac, Apache, MySQL, PHP) package for initial installation. These packages (which we will look at later) allow for easy installation of multiple products at the same time. Otherwise, you have to run many separate installations, which can become complicated and error-prone if incompatible versions are installed.

> *WAMP/LAMP/MAMP—Open source (free) combinations, including Apache Web Server, MySQL, and PHP for a specific operating system (Windows, Linux, and Mac). These packages are open source. The combination of software is used for creating dynamic web sites and web applications.*

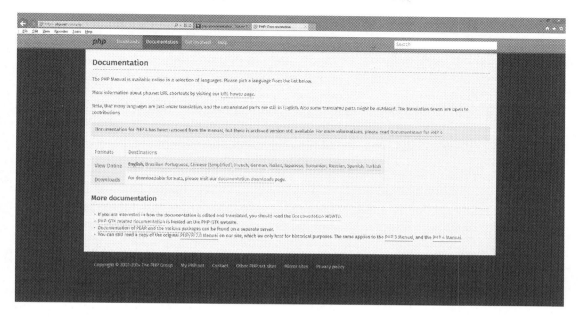

**Figure 1-4.** *Documentation pages (09/24/15)*

One of the more important pages of the PHP web site is the documentation page. This page allows users to search for descriptions and functionality of the language itself. You can also download the complete documentation. However, since this is a "live" site, with possible changes occurring, the most current information is best obtained by directly accessing it from the web site.

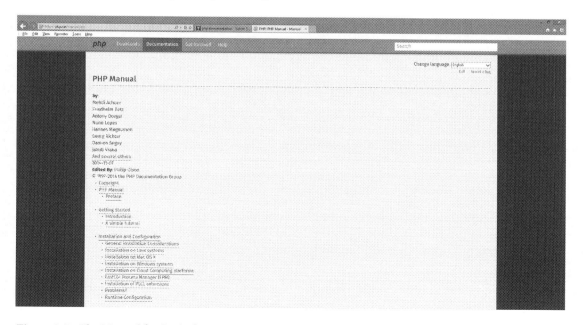

**Figure 1-5.** *The Manual (11/11/14)*

You can use the manual as if it were a textbook by clicking through each link from the beginning. The limited amount of explanation provided with each section of the manual might cause a beginner to want to give up on programming and change interests to something ghastly like networking! The manual does provide a great guide for experienced programmers, as the syntax of the language is similar to other languages such as JavaScript, Perl, and Java.

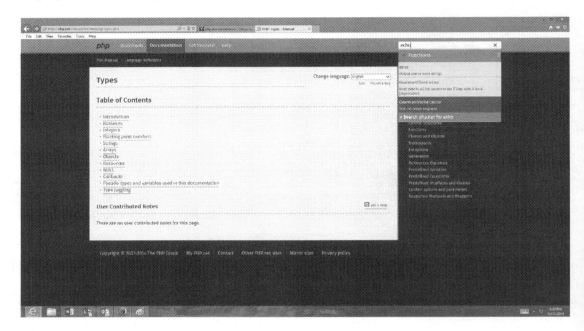

***Figure 1-6.*** *Search (11/11/14)*

On any page of the web site, the user can enter a term, an expression, or even a function name to find more information. As the information is entered in search box, the web page will provide the user with one or more options below the box for the user to select.

*Figure 1-7.* Echo (11/11/14)

Once the user has selected an option (such as echo shown in Figure 1-7), the results of the search provide the user with a general description of the item requested, any inputs or outputs for a function (parameters), and example code.

*Figure 1-8.* Echo code (11/11/14)

The example code provides explanations of the use of the function within the code itself by using comments (indicated by the // and gold color in Figure 1-8). The comments are not executable code. The executable code is color-coded to highlight strings (red), variables (blue), keywords (green), and the PHP opening and closing tags (blue). Color-coding helps make the code more readable. It also can make it easier to find syntax errors when creating programs. Many PHP editors provide similar color schemes.

# PHP 5.6+ and PHP 7+

With the release of the PHP 7 environment, great improvements have taken place. PHP 5.5+ has dramatically improved security. In this book, we will use the newest PHP encryption tool "password hash" instead of MD5 which many current books use. Over the last several years, MD5 has proven to be vulnerable to hacking.

> *"PHP 7 is based on the PHPNG project (PHP Next-Gen), that was led by Zend to speed up PHP applications. The performance gains realized from PHP 7 are huge! They vary between 25% and 70% on real-world apps, and all of that just from upgrading PHP, without having to change a single line of code!"* —www.zend.com

PHP 7 also replaces fatal errors, which previously would crash a program, with exceptions that can be handled within the program itself.

If you are migrating from a previous version of PHP to PHP 7, please review the following link:

http://php.net/manual/en/migration70.php

The code used in the examples in this book is compatible with PHP 7. Most examples are also compatible with PHP 5.5 and PHP 5.6.

# Do It

1. Go to www.php.net. Search for information on the print and printf functions. How are these functions similar? How are they different?

2. How do you "join the team" and help with the creation of the next version of PHP? Hint: Go to the "Get Involved" section of www.php.net, select "Guide for Contributors," and then find the "Join the team" link. Of course, the web site changes, so you may need to find a different route to the information.

3. Which ways can the www.php.net web site be useful for a beginning PHP programmer?

4. What language is used to create PHP? Hint: The answer is somewhere on the www.php.net web site.

5. Go to www.php.net. Search for the list of improvements and changes with PHP 7. List those improvements and changes. Which of these do you think will affect a beginning level programmer?

# PHP, JavaScript, CSS, HTML, and Apache Web Server

PHP is a scripting language. A **scripting language** is different than an actual programming language. **Programming languages** (such as Java) are written by the programmer in an English-like syntax. The program is compiled, which means it's converted from the English syntax into machine code (0s and 1s). This code is then executed (run) within a compatible operating system and hardware. Scripting languages do not use a compiler. The first time the code is accessed it is interpreted line by line as the program is executed.

You may wonder if this causes the code to be slower than compiled code. The answer is no. Once the code has been executed once, the interpreted code stays in the memory of the computer, or server, for other executions. If the programmer changes this code, a new version will replace the previous version in memory.

**JavaScript** is also a scripting language. As you may be aware, JavaScript code can be seen within a **web browser** by viewing the source, as shown in Figure 1-9.

***Figure 1-9.*** *JavaScript, HTML, and CSS code from yahoo.com (11/11/14)*

The **source code** displayed in Figure 1-9 is from `www.yahoo.com` and it shows a combination of several languages, including **HTML**, **CSS**, and JavaScript. The JavaScript code (displayed in black) is located between **script tags** (`<script type="text/JavaScript">` and `</script>`). This JavaScript code will attempt to create a cookie on your machine, if your browser allows cookies.

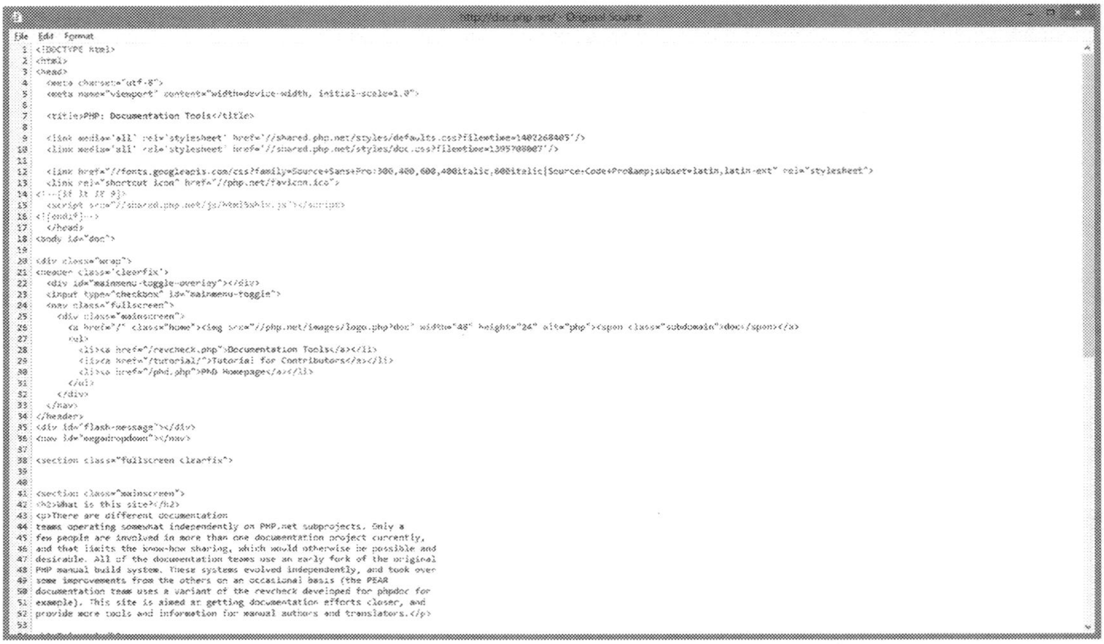

***Figure 1-10.*** *The* www.php.net *source code (11/11/14)*

However, when we look at the `www.php.net` source code (in Figure 1-10), we cannot see any PHP script code. There are links to some PHP files present, but no actual PHP code is displayed. Why?

JavaScript code resides on the user's computer. It is interpreted and executed within the browser. PHP code resides on a **web server**. The code is also interpreted and executed, but by the web server, not by the browser. The results of executing the PHP code are returned to the browser, not to the actual code itself.

```
<?php
Print "Hello";
?>
```

---

▓ **Note**  You may notice other formats for using PHP (such as: `<%`, `<%=`, `%>`, or `<script language="php">`); with PHP 7 these styles are no longer valid. There were actually depreciated previously, but still usuable.

---

You might guess that this code will display Hello. While this is correct, the question is, what processes happen to produce this result?

If this code is placed in a file (such as hello.php) on a web server, we would use our web browser to request this file by entering its name and location in the URL (address) box (such as http://servera.com/hello.php). The address entered instructs the browser to send an HTTP Get request to the web server (servera.com) to return the web page (hello.php).

*Figure 1-11.* Requesting an HTML/JavaScript web page

The web server receiving the request will determine that PHP code must first be interpreted and executed. It determines this simply by looking at the file extension (.php) of the file requested. Any PHP code within the file is then sent to the PHP processor for interpretation and execution. The results of the execution of the code is returned to the web server, which in turn sends it (and any other HTML and/or JavaScript code) back to the browser. In this example, Hello would be returned and displayed by the browser. If we then viewed the source code, as mentioned, we would only see the actual word Hello. We would not see any HTML or PHP. Why? Because we did not send any HTML back to the browser.

*Figure 1-12.* Requesting a web page with PHP code

You may be wondering if you can use this process to send back actual HTML (and/or JavaScript) code to create a dynamic web page. The answer is yes. The PHP print function will return any HTML (or JavaScript) code that has been placed between the "". The browser will interpret any code returned by the web server.

> *Print function. The print function is not actually a function. It is a language construct. Functions require that strings be included in quotes when passed. Language constructs do not require quotes around strings. However, it is still recommended. Print will pass whatever has been passed into it to the browser. It will attempt to convert any item that is not a string to string (text) format since all items displayed within a web page are in text format.*
>
> *For more information,* visit:
>
> *http://php.net/manual/en/function.print.php.*
>
> *For a more in-depth explanation of the print command, visit the free "The New Boston" (thenewboston.com) video(s) at:*
>
> *https://www.thenewboston.com/videos.php?cat=11&video=16996.*

---

▒ **Note**     All links provided in this book can be accessed from `http://www.littleoceanwaves.com/securephp`.

---

```php
<?php
Print "<h1>Hello</h1>";
?>
```

If we change our code to the listing above, the browser will display `Hello` as an HTML header (`h1`). The disadvantage of using the `print` function is that the program will have no control over where the statement is displayed on the web page. The statement will actually be displayed as the first line of code, even before any other existing HTML tags. This might be okay if we are just returning a statement to the user, such as "Your process has been completed". However, this might not be acceptable if your goal is to format output at an exact location on the page. There are other techniques and functions that we could choose to eliminate this problem. However, it is beyond our current discussion.

Now that we know we must interpret and execute PHP code with the help of a web server, what server should we use?

The Apache web server is the server that is most commonly used to host and handle PHP web page requests. Like other web servers, Apache can also accept and return requests for other types of files, including HTML, JavaScript, PERL, images, and RSS feeds. Apache, as mentioned, determines what processes need to be completed from HTTP requests by first looking at the file extensions of the requested files.

***Figure 1-13.*** *Apache.org web site (09/24/15)*

Apache, like PHP, is an open source product. All changes to the Apache web server are coordinated by the Apache Software Foundation. ASP maintains the `apache.org` web site to provide users and developers the ability to discover projects currently under development and the ability to download the latest versions of Apache. However, as mentioned, downloading separate versions of PHP, Apache, and MySQL can cause issues with incompatible versions. Unless you know what you are doing, it's much wiser to download a complete WAMP, LAMP, or MAMP version.

**Figure 1-14.** *Apache's Get Involved (09/24/15)*

The Apache Software Foundation also encourages all users of their products to keep up to date and to get involved in the development of future products. Users are encouraged to join discussion and mailing groups, test out new releases, and even help fix bugs or add new features to their products.

# Do It

1. What are the differences in executing PHP code compared to executing Java code?

2. What is the difference between a scripting language and a programming language? What type of language is PHP?

3. How does the Apache web server handle requests for a PHP web page?

4. Why can we see JavaScript code within a web browser but we can't see PHP code?

5. Go to www.apache.org. What are some of the ways that you can become involved with the development of Apache projects, even though you have limited experience?

# PHP, Apache, and MySQL

What happens when a web page requests information from a database?

Commonly databases are stored on servers that are separate from the web server itself.

Does the request for data come from the web server or from the PHP processor?

Since the SQL statements are contained within the PHP code itself, the PHP processor sends the SQL statements to the Database Management System (MySQL) to be processed.

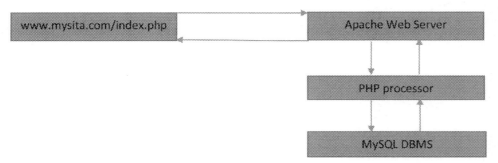

*Figure 1-15.* *Requesting a PHP web page that retrieves information from a MySQL database*

> *SQL—Structured Query Language is a special language used to update, insert, or delete data from a DBMS (Database Management System). A DBMS is an application that interacts with a program language and a database to update, insert, or delete data. The DBMS uses SQL to interpret the required changes to the data within the database. For more information on SQL, visit http://en.wikipedia.org/wiki/SQL. For more information on DBMS, visit http://en.wikipedia.org/wiki/Database.*

The Apache server will first discover that PHP code must be interpreted. The PHP code will then be sent to the PHP processor. The PHP processor interprets the code (line by line). While doing so, it will discover that SQL statements must be executed against a database. The SQL statements are then transferred to the appropriate Database Management System (DBMS) for processing. The DBMS will return the results of the execution of the SQL statements to the PHP processor. The PHP processor will then use those results to format output to be given to the Apache server. The Apache server will then combine the results of what is returned by the PHP processor with any other HTML (and/or JavaScript) code that might reside on the original page requested and return all output to the browser on the user's machine. The browser will then interpret the HTML and JavaScript to display the results of the page requested.

Did you catch all of that?

Let's look at a "real-world" example, shown in Figure 1-16.

*Figure 1-16.* *Google.com search for "green cats" (11/12/14)*

For some very strange reason we have decided to look up "green cats" on the Internet. As we enter the string into our favorite search engine (Google in this example) and then click the Search button, the information is passed to a Google server farm somewhere. Where?

Who knows; it could be anywhere on the planet. But the power of the Internet is that we don't care as long as we get our results back quickly.

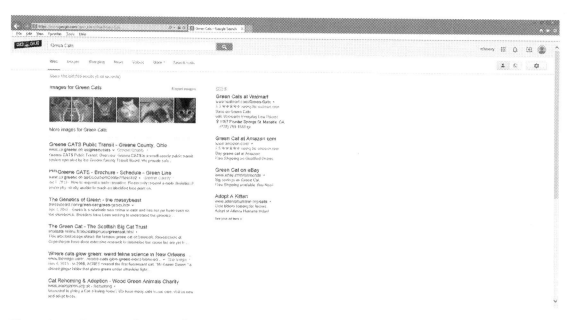

***Figure 1-17.*** *Green cats (11/12/14)*

Okay, I must say I am amazed that there are 104 million possible links to green cats. Wow. Maybe we should have filtered that down some. The point, however, is that Google returns a web page with a listing of links and descriptions of those links (plus ads).

Did Google return a *static* page that already existed?

No. The servers created a *dynamic* page from the request of the user. The Google algorithms (software) searched the massive Google database farms. The request was first sent to a Google web server from the user's browser. The web server then sent a request to the Google databases (actually using a Google Query Language similar to SQL) to return information about "green cats". The software on the web server then compiled the results, added HTML and JavaScript (also some Google Script Language code) for formatting the results web page, and returned the information to the user.

> *Static vs. dynamic web pages—A static web page does not change in relation to user requests or input. The page is created by a web developer and resides on the web server. When the user requests the page via a browser, a copy of the page is sent to the browser for display. A dynamic page does not exist within a web server. The page is created using input from the user. A program residing on the web server will create and format the page. The page that is created by the program is then downloaded to the user's browser. A copy of the page is not (usually) maintained on the web server. For more information on static web pages visit* http://en.wikipedia.org/wiki/Static_web_page. *For more information on dynamic web pages visit:* http://en.wikipedia.org/wiki/Dynamic_web_page.

Did every page get downloaded to the user's web browser?

No, just the first page. The page links at the bottom of the first results page return information to the web server requesting the next set of information (to dynamically create the second page, or another requested page). As you might now be starting to figure out, the same process we have just discussed related to processing PHP files on the Internet is a very common process for creating dynamic pages.

Your might have noticed something interesting about the results page URL address that was displayed. The address is now https://www.google.com/?gws_rd=ssl#q=Green+Cats, not www.google.com. Google algorithms use the *GET HTTP Request* when sending search requests to their servers.

> *HTTP—Hypertext Transfer Protocol is the protocol (standard) for transferring messages (text and web pages) between nodes (computers and servers) on the Internet. It is a request-response protocol. For example, a user "requests" a web page though a browser. The web server "responds" to the request and returns the page to the browser. The browser changes the request into an HTTP Get Request (such as GET /pages/mypage.html HTTP/1.1) that is sent to the web server. The web server responds with the information requested and a status code (such as HTTP/1.1 200 OK). For more information on HTTP, visit http://en.wikipedia.org/wiki/Hypertext_Transfer_Protocol#Request_methods.*

```
<form name="orders" method="get" id="orders" action="searchprocess.php">
Name: <input type="text" name="customername" id="customername"><br />
<input type="submit" value="Submit your name">
</form>
```

Let's look at a simpler example above to discover what occurs. Assume the code above is saved in an index.html file on your localhost web site under the projects folder.

***Figure 1-18.*** *Index.html example*

If the user enters Fred in the textbox displayed in the browser, the results page (created by interpreting and executing the searchprocess.php file on the web server and sending the results back to the browser) will display the URL line : http://127.0.0.1/projects/searchprocess.php?customername=Fred.

***Figure 1-19.*** *Execution of searchprocess.php*

The name of the textbox (`customername`) and the value entered in the textbox (Fred) are now visible on the URL line. Actually, `customername` is now a parameter and `Fred` is now the value the parameter holds. This is the result of using the GET process.

When we click the Google Search button or the Search button in our simple example, the requested information is send via the GET HTTP process. All information (and variables) needed for the receiving program are sent on the actual URL line to be received by the program on the web server that will process the initial request.

Why does the Google search engine send information via GET instead of POST (which would have hidden the information)?

The main reason is to save server memory. Just think of the millions of requests that Google has for information. If all of these requests resided in memory, the servers would soon crash. Also, since the user is doing a "public" search for information, there is no reason to hide the information. In later chapters, we will discover how to read both GET and POST parameters within PHP programs.

However, for now let's get back to our discussion of Apache, PHP, and DBMS.

PHP can access information from many types of DBMS systems, including Oracle and SQL Server. However, the most popular combination (as mentioned already) is to pair PHP with MySQL. I bet at this point you can guess why? Yes, it's open source and free. MySQL is also one of the easier DBMS systems to use.

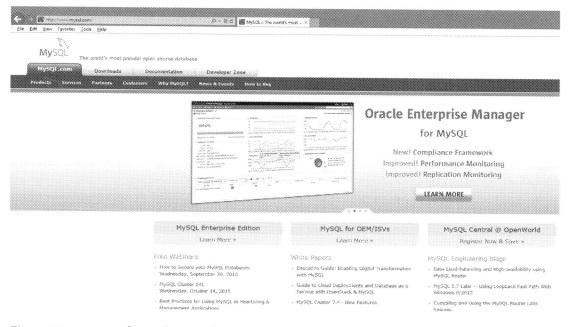

*Figure 1-20.* www.mysql.com *(09/24/15)*

Just like all the open source products we have discussed, the user can go to the official web site (www.mysql.com) to download the latest versions. Also, as you can probably guess, you can join in on the fun of helping to develop new versions of MySQL and related products. Documentation of current and several previous versions are available for download. The documentation is pretty intense and not for the weak of mind or the beginner. Also, as you probably are tired of reading it is not recommended that you download a new version of MySQL individually until you have more experience. Stick with the WAMP, LAMP, and MAMP packages, at least for now.

## Do It

1. Why does the PHP processor send SQL to the DBMS instead of the Apache web server sending it directly to the DBMS?

2. What might Apache do with the information received from the DBMS before sending it back to the user's browser?

3. Go to www.mysql.com. What is the latest version of MySQL? Which versions of Apache and PHP are compatible?

4. Why do search engines pass information via GET HTTP requests instead of POST HTTP requests? When would you use a POST request?

# Putting it All Together—PHP, Apache, and MySQL

As you have hopefully discovered by this point, PHP, Apache, and MySQL need to run seamlessly together to successfully create dynamic web pages. There are numerous development packages available that provide a combination of these products, along with other tools such as PhpMyAdmin (which is a great help in setting up your web server and databases). By installing one of these products, you will greatly reduce your frustration level and maybe even manage to keep most of your hair. We will briefly look at two of the most popular; EasyPHP and XAMPP. We will not dive in-depth or provide step-by-step install directions for two reasons. As soon as this book is published the directions probably will change, and it's fine to use the default settings. Accepting what the developers suggest works most of the time.

## EasyPHP

*Figure 1-21. www.easyphp.org (09/24/15)*

You can download the developer's version of EasyPHP from the following link. It is not necessary to download the host version unless you are planning on hosting "live" web pages directly from your computer onto the Internet.

```
http://www.easyphp.org/easyphp-devserver.php
```

The developer's version of EasyPHP is a WAMP (Windows, Apache, MySQL, PHP) package that's used in the Microsoft Windows environment. There are additional tools that you can choose to also install to assist in development. However, for our purposes you need only the basic install. After installation, the files will be located in your program files directory under the EasyPHP directory.

---

▓ **Warning**   Pay attention to which buttons you click on the web site during download. You might download extra items you are not interested in if you don't read what you are downloading before you click the button(s).

---

After downloading the installer by clicking the download arrow on the web site, follow the directions provided with the software. On your first attempt, leave all the default settings. Hopefully, everything will install correctly. If not, read the next section entitled, "Common Installation Problems".

# Common Installation Problems
## Missing C# Library

PHP 7 (and earlier versions of PHP) require the Microsoft Visual Studio C# library. If you have Windows 8 or later, this library is probably already installed. Also, if you have a recent version of Microsoft Visual Studio, it is also probably already installed. If you receive an error indicating that C# is missing or the wrong version, paste the message into a search engine on the Internet. Search for a response from Microsoft for directions to fix the error. The response should include a link to download the missing files and installation instructions.

## Port Conflicts

If you already have a service using port 80, the default port for HTML traffic between your PC and the outside world, you will receive an error message from Apache when it attempts to run. You can fix this problem in multiple ways.

> *Wikipedia defines a port as:*
>
> *In computer networking, a port is an application-specific or process-specific software construct serving as a communications endpoint in a computer's host operating system. The purpose of ports is to uniquely identify different applications or processes running on a single computer and thereby enable them to share a single physical connection to a packet-switched network like the Internet. In the context of the Internet Protocol, a port is associated with an IP address of the host, as well as the type of protocol used for communication.*
>
> *For more information on ports, visit:*
>
> `http://en.wikipedia.org/wiki/Port_(computer_networking)`.

A. If you don't mind shutting down other services using the port while you are developing, you can follow the directions below. Once you are done using Apache and PHP, you can turn the services back on or just reboot your PC and the services will turn back on.

1. Go to the Microsoft Windows 7/8/10 Task Manager (press Ctrl+Alt+Delete at the same time).

2. Select the Services tab.

3. Look for any of the following services in Windows 7/8/10. If you find one running, right-click it and turn it off. Then try restarting Apache again. If that does not work, turn that one back on and try another one. (The names may be slightly different depending on the version of Windows.)

   SQL Server Reporter, Web Deployment Agent, BranchCache, Sync Share Service, WAS (IIS Administrator), and W3SVC

B. If you need your other services running or you do not have the administrative privileges to turn off services on port 80, you can change the default listening port location for Apache.

Go to your system tray (bottom-right corner of your screen). Find the EasyPHP icon by scrolling over the icons. A description of each should appear. If you don't see the icon, click the up arrow in the system tray to see more icons. Right-click the EasyPHP icon. Select Configuration and then select Apache. This will open the Apache configuration file (`httpd.conf`) into Notepad (or your default text editor). First save a copy of this file somewhere in case you make an error. This will allow you to recover from any major mistakes that occur. Then search for `Listen 127.0.0.1:80` within the file. Change the occurrence of 80 to 8080 or to 81; on that line only. This will allow the Apache server to listen to one of the ports that are not commonly used. Resave the file (make sure you are resaving the original file to the original location).

---

▓ **Note**    Make sure when you're using Notepad or any other text editor that you use Save As, and then select All Files for the file type. Also make sure to include the `.conf` file extension. If you do not change the file type to all files, your file will be saved as `httpd.conf.txt`. If that happens, the server will not see the file. You can easily fix the problem by reopening the file and saving it in the proper method.

---

You can then restart Apache by going back to your system tray to find the EasyPHP icon. Double-click the icon; a message box will appear that will give you the status Apache and MySQL. You will probably see red for the Apache status. Click the Apache button. Within a few moments, it should turn green. This will indicate that the server is now running. Do the same for MySQL.

## Missing Files

If you receive an error message related to this, somehow your files have become corrupted before installation. Return to the EasyPHP web site and download the files again. Also, if you somehow mess up the Apache configuration file, go back and reinstall the product again.

## Can't Install Files In Program Files Directory

This indicates that you or something else has a high security restriction on that directory. Rerun the installation and change the location of your installation to another directory. Just remember, when we reference the program files directory later in this book, that you should instead look at the directory in which your files were installed.

## Apache Delays and Hang-ups

In Windows 8/10 you may experience problems with Apache working slowly or hanging-up. To correct this problem go to your system tray (bottom-right corner of your screen). Find the EasyPHP icon by scrolling over the icons. A description of each should appear. If you don't see the icon, click the up arrow in the system tray to see more icons. Right-click the EasyPHP icon. Select Configuration and then select Apache. This will open the Apache configuration file (httpd.conf) into Notepad (or your default text editor). First save a copy of this file somewhere in case you make an error. This will allow you to recover from any major mistakes that occur.

Then add the following two lines to the bottom of the file.

```
AcceptFilter http none
AcceptFilter https none
```

Resave the file (make sure you are resaving the original file to the original location).

## Other Errors

For errors that have not been discussed here, copy and paste the error into a search engine. Locate an answer column or blog that provides suggestions to fix your error. There are many free resources on the Internet. Do not pay for a web site (or someone else) to fix your problem.

# Configurations

You need to determine when you want Apache to run. Apache can be set to run when you boot your PC, when an application needs it, or manually. To change settings, you can right-click the EasyPHP Icon in the system tray (bottom-right corner of your screen), then select Configuration and then select EasyPHP. If you don't see the icon, click the up arrow in the system tray. A small screen should appear that will allow you to check (or uncheck) two options—Start on Session Startup and Launch Servers When the Application Starts.

There are many optional libraries that you can link or unlink to PHP as needed. In many cases the libraries are already loaded and just need to be linked. You can add these libraries by going to the PHP configuration file (php.ini) and removing the comment (;) character at the beginning of the line. The PHP configuration file can easily be found by right-clicking the EasyPHP icon in the system tray. Then select Configuration and PHP. It is not necessary to make any changes at this point. It is also suggested that you make these changes only when needed. Other libraries can be added using Curl and other methods discussed in later chapters of this book.

For a more in-depth explanation of the php.ini file, view the free "The New Boston" (thenewboston. com) video at https://www.thenewboston.com/videos.php?cat=11&video=16993.

## XAMPP

*Figure 1-22.* *XAMPP at* www.apachefriends.org *(09/24/15)*

Although **XAMPP** is similar to EasyPHP, XAMPP is more popular because it has free Windows, Linux, and OS X versions. It also includes a lot of add-ons, including some of the most popular content management systems—Drupal, Joomla, and WordPress. The latest downloads can be accessed directly at the official XAMPP web site or at many other download locations.

```
https://www.apachefriends.org/
```

---

■ **Warning**   Pay attention to what buttons you click on the web site. You might download extra items you are not interested in if you don't read what you are downloading before you click the button(s).

---

During your first attempt at installing, use the default settings that the developers have suggested in the installation software. You will greatly reduce the possibility of problems or headaches. If you do have errors, read the next section entitled "Common Installation Problems" for assistance.

## Common Installation Problems

### Port Conflicts

If you already have a service using port 80, the default port for HTML traffic between your PC and the outside world, you will receive an error message from Apache when it attempts to run. You can fix this problem in multiple ways.

A. If you don't mind shutting down other services using the port while you are developing, you can follow the directions on the video link. Once you are done using Apache and PHP you can turn the services back on or just reboot your PC and the services will turn back on.

1. Go to the Windows 7/8/10 Task Manager (press Ctrl+Alt+Delete at the same time).

2. Select the Services tab.

3. Look for any of the following services in Windows 7/8/10. If you find one running, right-click it and turn it off. Then try restarting Apache again. If that does not work, turn that one back on and try another one. (The names may be slightly different depending on the version of Windows.)

   SQL Server Reporter, Web Deployment Agent, BranchCache, Sync Share Service, WAS (IIS Administrator), and W3SVC

B. If you need your other services running or you do not have the administrative privileges to turn off services on port 80, you can change the default listening port location for Apache.

Go to your system tray (in Microsoft Windows it's at the bottom-right corner of your screen). Find the XAMPP icon by scrolling your mouse over the icons. A description of each should appear. If you don't see the icon, click the up arrow in the system tray to see more icons. Double-click the icon. The Control Panel should appear. You should see start up error messages in red on the console. If it is a port conflict, click the Config button to the right of Apache. Select `httpd.conf` from the list provided. This will open the Apache configuration file (`httpd.conf`) into Notepad (or your default text editor). First save a copy of this file somewhere in case you make a mistake. This will allow you to recover the original file. Search for Listen 80 within the file. Change the occurrence of 80 to 8080 or to 81. This will allow the Apache server to listen to one of these ports that are not commonly used. Resave the file (make sure you are resaving the original file to the original location).

---

■ **Note** Make sure when using Notepad or any other text editor that you use Save As, then select All Files for the file type. Also make sure to include the `.conf` file extension. If you do not change the file type to All Files, your file will be saved as `httpd.conf.txt`. If that happens, the server will not see the file. You can easily fix the problem by reopening the file and saving it in the proper method.

---

You can then restart Apache by clicking the Start button next to Apache in the XAMPP console. If you get a green status for Apache, you will also want to start MySQL by clicking the Start button to the right of MySQL.

## Missing Files

If you receive an error message related to this, somehow your files have become corrupted before installation. Return to the XAMPP web site and download the files again. If you somehow have messed up the Apache configuration file, you also will need to download the files again.

## Can't Install Files in Program Files Directory

This would indicate that you or something else has a high security restriction on that directory. Rerun the installation and change the location of your installation to another directory. Just remember, when you reference the program files directory later in this book, that you should instead look at the directory in which your files were installed.

## Apache Delays and Hang-ups

In Windows 8/10 you may experience problems with Apache working slowly or hanging-up. To correct this problem go to your system tray (bottom-right corner of your screen). Find the XAMPP icon by scrolling over the icons. A description of each should appear. If you don't see the icon, click the up arrow in the system tray to see more icons. Right-click the XAMPP icon. Select Configuration and then select Apache. This will open the Apache configuration file (httpd.conf) into Notepad (or your default text editor). First save a copy of this file somewhere in case you make an error. This will allow you to recover from any major mistakes that occur.
     Then add the following two lines to the bottom of the file.

```
AcceptFilter http none
AcceptFilter https none
```

Resave the file (make sure you are resaving the original file to the original location).

## Other Errors

For errors that have not been discussed here, copy and paste the error into a search engine. Locate an answer column or blog that provides suggestions to fix your error. There are many free resources on the Internet. Do not pay for a web site (or someone else) to fix you problem.

# Configurations

You can change configurations for XAMPP by going to the Control Panel (double-click the XAMPP on the system tray at the bottom-right of your screen). Then click on the config button at the upper-right of your screen (not the config buttons to the right of the applications). You can then check (or uncheck) those applications that you want to have automatically start the next time the Control Panel starts. You should check Apache and MySQL for the lessons in this book. Of course, you can always start them from the Control Panel when needed.
     There are many optional libraries that you can link or unlink to PHP as needed. In many cases, the libraries are already loaded and just need to be linked. You can add these libraries by going to the PHP configuration file (php.ini) and remove the comment (;) character at the beginning of the line. The PHP configuration file can easily be found by double-clicking the XAMPP icon in the system tray. Then click the Config button to the right of Apache. A list will display; select php.ini. It is not necessary to make any changes at this point. It is also suggested that you make these changes only when needed. Other libraries can be added using Curl and other methods discussed in later chapters of this book.

# Microsoft Internet Information Server

Alternatively, if you are unable to get Apache to perform properly in Windows (especially Windows 8 or Windows 10), or you like Microsoft's IIS Server, you can install PHP to use Microsoft IIS (Internet Information Server) instead of Apache. For more information, visit:

```
http://www.microsoft.com/web/platform/phponwindows.aspx
```

# Do It

1. Use a search engine to answer this question: You receive the following error either while installing or as soon as you try to start XAMMP or EasyPHP. How can you find the solution to your problem? What might be causing this error?

   ```
   Internal Server Error
   The server encountered an internal error or misconfiguration and was
   unable to complete your request.
   Please contact the server administrator, you@example.com and inform
   them of the time the error occurred, and anything you might have
   done that may have caused the error.
   More information about this error may be available in the server
   error log.
   ```

2. Use a search engine to answer this question: What is XAMPP error #1130? How can you fix this error?

3. Use a search engine to answer this question: When trying to run a PHP program using EasyPHP (and Apache) you receive the error below. What is causing this error? How can you fix it?

   ```
   Cannot load mcrypt extension. Please check your PHP configuration.
   ```

4. If you have not already attempted to do so, install either EasyPHP or XAMPP on your personal machine. Did you have any problems with your installation? If so, what problems did you have? How did you solve those problems?

# Testing Your Environment

You have green lights now, right? Everything is working correctly?

Well, hopefully. However, you need to make sure. The best way to do this is to test your environment.

## Testing Your Administration Environment

First we need to test the server and see if our administration pages will display. In EasyPHP, you can do either of the following:

1. Right-click on the EasyPHP icon and select Administration.

or

2. Open your favorite browser and enter the following:

   ```
   http://127.0.0.1/home/
   ```

If you had to change your port due to conflicts, you may need to enter the port number, such as:

```
http://127.0.0.1:8080/home/
```

You should see a screen similar to the one shown in Figure 1-23.

***Figure 1-23.*** *EasyPHP administration screen (PHP 5.6)*

For XAMPP, open your favorite browser and enter this address:

```
http://127.0.0.1/dashboard/
```

If you had to change your port due to conflicts, then you must also include this port:

```
http://127.0.0.1:8080/dashboard/
```

If XAMPP is installed properly, you should see a screen similar to the one shown in Figure 1-24.

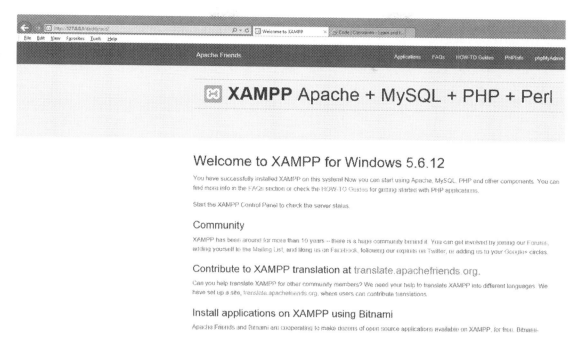

*Figure 1-24.* *XAMPP dashboard screen (09/24/15)*

If at this point you are not seeing this page (or some page with XAMPP displayed), something is wrong. Check the following:

Is EasyPHP or XAMPP running (started)? Do you see the green light or green shaded color for Apache either in the XAMPP Control Panel or in EasyPHP? If not, try clicking the start buttons or links.

If Apache will not start, are you seeing an error message? If not, check the error log file. For EasyPHP, right-click the icon on the system tray and select the error log file for Apache. For XAMPP, click the Log button on the Control Panel next to Apache and select Error Log.

If you see green and the pages seem to be locked up, try stopping and restarting Apache. If might take a couple of attempts to wake it up. If it continues to hang, check your computer settings. Are you maxing out on CPU usage?

Can you determine the problem? If you have an error message, paste it in your favorite search engine and see what the experts say about the problem.

# Do It

1. If you have not already done so, test your environment using the directions above. Did you have any problems? If so, what problems occurred? How did you fix those problems?

# Testing Your PHP Environment

Hopefully everything is good at this point. Either you have been flying through with great luck, or you managed to fix all the problems you have encountered. However, you still need to see if you can actually run your own PHP program in Apache.

Open a text editor (not Word, but Notepad or Notepad++ are good), and enter the following code exactly as it has been shown.

```
<?php
print "Hello World";
?>
```

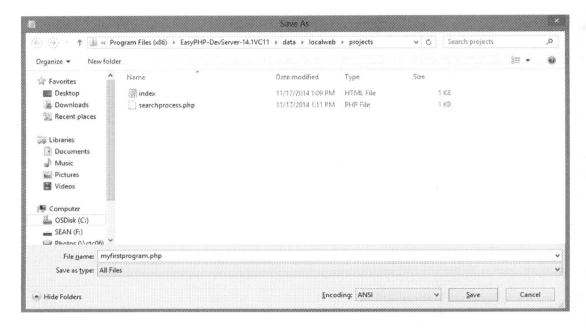

***Figure 1-25.*** *Using Save As with All Files to save PHP programs*

Using the Save As selection on the File menu, change the File Type to All Files or to php. Enter the file name myfirstprogram.php and save it in one of the locations below.

If you are using EasyPHP, save it to:

```
C:\Program Files (x86)\EasyPHP-DevServer-14.1VC11\data\localweb\projects
```

Of course, you should change the version name (or Program File name) to the correct version (location) that you are using on your machine. If you have a version of EasyPHP that does not have the localweb\ projects folders, find the location of the www folder under the EasyPHP folder and create a folder called projects. Then save the file under that folder.

If you are using XAMPP, first go to C:\xampp\htdocs and create a folder called projects. Then go back to your text editor, choose Save As (don't forget to change the file type to All Files or php), name the file myfirstprogram.php and save it to the location below.

```
C:\xampp\htdocs\projects
```

If you saved your files correctly in the EasyPHP or XAMPP locations, you can attempt to run your program by entering the following in your browser URL box.

```
http://127.0.0.1/projects/myfirstprogram.php
```

If you changed the port, then change the first part to http://127.0.0.1:8080/ (enter the correct port you are using in place of 8080).

Your program should display the message shown in Figure 1-26.

**Figure 1-26.** *Hello World*

## Common Problems

Nothing is displayed, error 404:

1.  Make sure you typed the address exactly as shown.

2.  Your server might be hung up. Stop and restart it.

3.  Make sure you placed your file in the correct location.

4.  Make sure you saved your file as a .php file and not as .txt. Try Save As again and renaming the file (make sure file type is either All Files or php).

5.  Check for typos in your actual program code. Did you remember the semicolon (;)? Fix any and resave. You might need to stop and start the server if it does not see the changes for some reason. You can go to the log files and look at the PHP log files to see any errors that might exist in your code.

6.  Go to the Apache log files (see directions in previous common problems) to look for errors. If you cannot correct them, copy the errors and paste them in a search engine to see what others have found as solutions.

The actual program code is displayed not the results of executing the code:

1.  Make sure you saved your file as a .php file and not as .txt. Try Save As again and renaming the file (make sure file type is either All Files or php).

2.  Your Apache server or PHP might not be started or is hung. Stop and start Apache again.

3.  Did you forget or have a typo in the <?php or ?> lines?

4.  Go to the Apache log files (see directions in previous common problems) to find the errors. If you cannot correct them, copy the errors and paste them in a search engine to see what others have found as solutions.

For any other errors, copy and paste them into a web search engine to see what others have discovered as a solution.

## EasyPHP's Code Classroom

If you are still having problems getting a version of LAMP, MAMP, or WAMP to work on your computer, all is not lost.

EasyPHP (`www.easyphp.org`) now has an online coding environment for students and teachers. This environment (see Figure 1-27) allows you to enter code (black window below), click a Submit button (red button), and see your results on the right (white window).

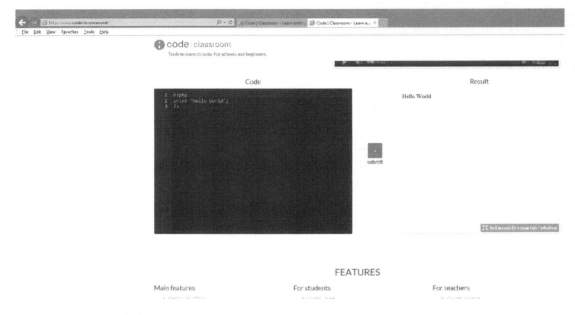

*Figure 1-27.* `www.codeclassroom.net`

## Do It

1.  If you have not already tested your environment, do so. Did the test work? What problems, if any, did you have? How did you solve those problems?

# Alias Directories

It is common practice in the real world to create *alias* directories in web servers. Alias directories are "fake" locations of files that trick the user of your web site into believing a file is in one location when it is in another.

Why would you use an alias directory? As web sites grow, the locations of files on servers may have to change. By using an alias the user of your web site will not know that the actual location of the file has changed. The alias gives you the ability to store your files in any location on your computer (server). If you are not using an alias all your files must be stored in the default location. The default locations are:

```
EasyPHP: C:\Program Files (x86)\EasyPHP-DevServer-14.1VC11\data\localweb\
XAMPP: C:\xampp\htdocs\
```

You might want to consider creating an alias directory, especially if you want to locate your files on a jump drive. In this book, we assume that files are located under the default locations in a `projects` folder.

```
EasyPHP: C:\Program Files (x86)\EasyPHP-DevServer-14.1VC11\data\localweb\projects
XAMPP: C:\xampp\htdocs\projects
```

This will allow us to test programs using the same URL whether we are using EasyPHP or XAMPP.

```
http://127.0.0.1/projects/myfirstprogram.php
```

If you do create an alias directory, just remember to replace `projects` with whatever alias name you are using.

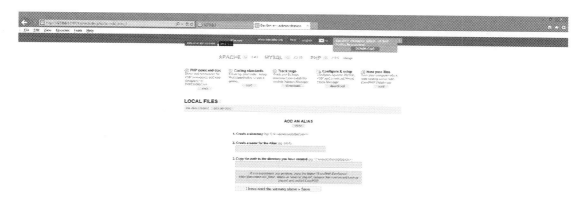

***Figure 1-28.*** *EasyPHP alias screen*

In EasyPHP, alias directories can be created from the Administration screen. Go to the system tray (bottom-right of your screen), right-click the EasyPHP icon, and select Administration. In the middle of the screen, locate Local Files, and then locate the Add an Alias button to the right. Click and follow the directions. Before adding your alias, the folder must already exist.

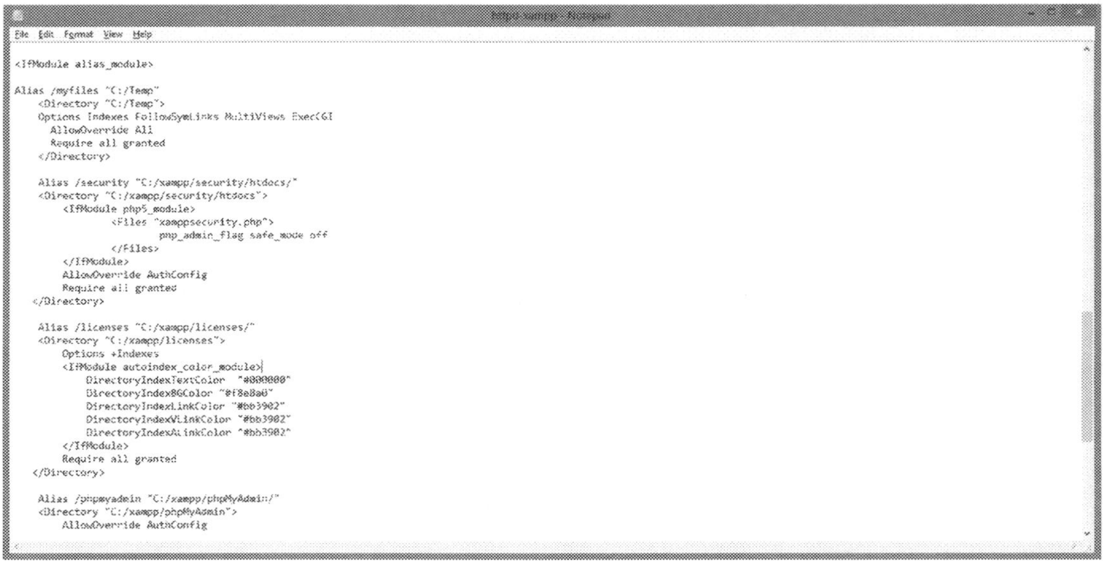

```
<IfModule alias_module>

Alias /myfiles "C:/Temp"
    <Directory "C:/Temp">
    Options Indexes FollowSymLinks MultiViews ExecCGI
      AllowOverride All
      Require all granted
    </Directory>

    Alias /security "C:/xampp/security/htdocs/"
    <Directory "C:/xampp/security/htdocs">
        <IfModule php5_module>
            <Files "xamppsecurity.php">
                php_admin_flag safe_mode off
            </Files>
        </IfModule>
        AllowOverride AuthConfig
        Require all granted
    </Directory>

    Alias /licenses "C:/xampp/licenses/"
    <Directory "C:/xampp/licenses">
        Options +Indexes
        <IfModule autoindex_color_module>
            DirectoryIndexTextColor  "#000000"
            DirectoryIndexBGColor "#f8e8a0"
            DirectoryIndexLinkColor "#bb3902"
            DirectoryIndexVLinkColor "#bb3902"
            DirectoryIndexALinkColor "#bb3902"
        </IfModule>
        Require all granted
    </Directory>

    Alias /phpmyadmin "C:/xampp/phpMyAdmin/"
    <Directory "C:/xampp/phpMyAdmin">
        AllowOverride AuthConfig
```

***Figure 1-29.*** *The httpd-xampp file*

In XAMPP, it takes a little more work. Open the system panel by double-clicking the XAMPP icon. Then click the Config button to the right of Apache. Select the `httpd-xampp` configuration file from the list. Choose Edit. Find from your text editor menu. Search for the string `'<IfModule alias_module>'`. Do not change anything that is already listed in this section. However, you can add locations (using the following code) for your executable files. Once you have entered the required lines, stop and start Apache to help it find the new changes.

```
Alias /myfiles "C:/Temp"
<Directory "C:/Temp">
Options Indexes FollowSymLinks MultiViews ExecCGI
  AllowOverride All
  Require all granted
</Directory>
```

For more information on creating alias directories, visit:

`https://www.youtube.com/watch?v=XX6t3zJRXF8.`

---

▒ **Note** This directory setting allows complete read and write capability to the directory. We will discuss options to secure the directory for "live" sites in a later chapter.

---

***Figure 1-30.*** *Hello World running from the alias directory called myfiles as an index.php file*

This listing would allow any files in the `C:/Temp` directory to execute in Apache when the user enters `myfiles` as a directory name in the URL line. The directory settings provided don't provide much security. However, this is just for testing on a test machine. If you are in a live environment, you would need to tighten the security settings under the `directory` tag. To execute the files within this directory, you would enter the URL `http://127.0.0.1/myfiles` in a browser. If you do not include a file name, Apache will try to find an `index.html` or `index.php` file. If neither exists, Apache will list the files in the directory, with the current settings. This allows easy access to files for testing. However, it is not a good idea in a live environment. You can request a file that is not the index file by adding the file name (`http://127.0.0.1/ myfiles/myfirstprogram.php`). Remember to include the port number if you had to change it (`http://127.0.0.1:8080/myfiles/myfirstprogram.php`). Of course, the directory must exist and the files must be in the directory before you test the URL in a browser.

## Do It

1. Create an alias folder called `myfiles` that points to an existing location on your hard drive or jump drive. Place the `hello world` program that you used to test your environment in the folder. Try to run the program from the folder using the previous instructions. Were you successful? If not, what problems did you have? How did you fix those problems?

# Notepad++, Editors, and Code Testers

When creating PHP code, you do not need to use a specific editor or purchase an editor. You can create all code within a text editor (even in Notepad). However, it does help to have an editor that highlights (colors) your code to make it easier to discover coding (syntax) errors.

# Notepad++

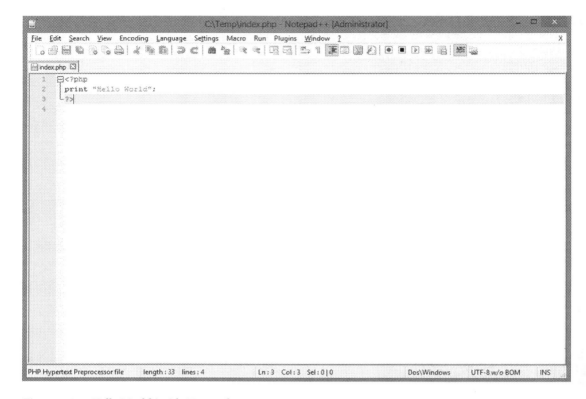

***Figure 1-31.*** *Hello World inside Notepad++*

Notepad++ is available for download at `www.notepad-plus-plus.org`. This editor is basic and easy to use. It can create files in over 20 different forms (including PHP). Most of the coding examples provided in this book are created with Notepad++. When you're creating a new PHP program in Notepad++, you must tell the application the file type. You can do this by choosing the Language menu item and then choosing PHP. This will allow the application to help you with color-coding and other features.

# Other Editors

There are hundreds of other editors available. I suggest you pick one that you are most comfortable using; `www.download.com` is a good site to find PHP free editors. Pick one that has lots of users and a strong rating.

As mentioned previously, you may want to also try EasyPHP's code classroom at:
`www.codeclassroom.net`

## Do It

1. Decide on a text editor that you will use to complete your coding while using this book. Download the editor to your PC. Retype your `hello world` program in the editor and save the program. Run the program from your browser. Why did you choose the editor that you downloaded? What do you like about the editor? What do you not like about the editor?

# Chapter Terms

| | |
|---|---|
| PHP | Procedural Language |
| Object-Oriented Language | `www.php.net` |
| WAMP | LAMP |
| MAMP | Scripting Language |
| Programming Language | JavaScript |
| Web Browser | Source Code |
| HTML | CSS |
| Script Tags | Web Server |
| `print` Function | Apache |
| Apache Software Foundation | SQL |
| Database Management System | Static Page |
| Dynamic Page | GET HTTP Request |
| MySQL | EasyPHP (Developer's Version) |
| Port 80 | `httpd.conf` |
| `php.ini` | XAMPP |
| XAMPP Control Panel | Alias Directories |
| Open Source | Notepad++ |

# Chapter Questions and Projects

**Multiple Choice**

1. MAMP stands for

    a. Mobile Application Motor Processor

    b. My Awesome Mobile Program

    c. Apache-MySQL-PHP

    d. Modern Application Modular Programing

    e. None of these

2. The goals of the Apache Software Foundation (ASP) include

   a. Coordination of all changes to the Apache web server

   b. Overseeing the selling of all Apache software

   c. Licensing all web servers

   d. Maintaining membership to open source programming through the Apache web server

3. What scripting languages can be viewed within a web browser?

   a. Java

   b. XML

   c. JavaScript

   d. PHP

4. Select the statements that are true about static web pages:

   a. They are sometimes called flat page/stationary pages

   b. They are generated by a web application

   c. Static web pages display the same information for all users

   d. All of the above

   e. A and C

5. _____ is an object-oriented computer programming language commonly used to create interactive effects within web browsers.

   a. HTML

   b. XML

   c. JavaScript

   d. PHP

6. What is the correct way to end a PHP statement?

   a. ;

   b. New line

   c. <!php>

   d. .

7. The configurations button on the XAMPP Control Panel allow the user to do what?

    a. Install XAMPP

    b. Select applications to automatically start

    c. Manage add-ons

    d. Configure MYSQL

8. php.net provides all of the following except

    a. Information of each latest release

    b. PHP language documentation

    c. LAMP, MAMP, and WAMP downloads

    d. Contributions to the PHP documentation

9. Which of the following best describes a scripting language?

    a. The language is compiled.

    b. The program must be compatible with operating system and hardware.

    c. The first time the code is accessed is when the program is first executed.

    d. The code is slower than compiled code

**True/False**

1. The alias directory allows you to save your web page files in a directory (folder) of your choice rather than a www directory. It allows a URL address to point directly to that folder.

2. A static page is a page added to the dryer when drying clothes to prevent static cling.

3. A client browser submits a GET HTTP request to the server, then the server returns a response to the client browser.

4. The (Developer's Version) of EasyPHP can be purchased only for one year at a time.

5. A dynamic web page never changes but a static web page is always changing.

6. WAMP stands for Windows, Apache, MySQL, and PHP.

7. Apache is an example of a web server.

8. HTML stands for Hypertext Markup Language.

9. PHP originally stood for Personal Home Page.

10. A procedural language is a programming language that uses classes and objects.

11. While viewing a web site in a browser, you may view the source code, which can show you HTML, JavaScript, and CSS. However, PHP code will not be visible.

12. Java is a procedural programming language.

**Short Answer/Essay**

1. Explain the process that occurs when a browser requests a static web page.

2. Explain the process that occurs when a browser requests a dynamic web page.

3. Explain the difference between a procedural language and a scripting language.

4. How do you add access to PHP library code to your program?

5. Why should you use WAMP, MAMP, or LAMP instead of installing each application individually?

**Projects**

1. Create a PHP program to display a summary of your work history and educational history.

2. Create a PHP program to display your major and the courses required to complete your major.

3. Create a PHP program to display the goals and/or objectives of your college/university.

**Term Project**

1. Your supervisor has requested that you design a secure application that will keep track of inventory in the warehouse of the ABC Computer Parts Corporation. This application will be accessible both within the warehouse itself and outside (via the Internet and/or smart phones). What data fields are necessary to keep track of this information? What size and data types (string, integer, floating point) should define these fields? What other restrictions on input (no negative values for item number) should be defined for these fields?

   For example, if a Social Security Number (SSN) was a required field:

   SSN: SIZE: Min: 9 characters (string) Max: 9 characters (string) Restrictions: Valid SSN format

   Notice that it uses characters, not integers, because no calculations will be done on the SSN number.

# CHAPTER 2

▓ ▓ ▓

# Interfaces, Platforms, Containers, and Three-Tier Programming

*"As of January 2013, PHP was installed on more than 240 million web sites (39% of those sampled) and 2.1 million web servers."*

—Ide, Andy (2013-01-31). "PHP Just Grows & Grows"

## Chapter Objectives/Student Learning Outcomes

After completing this chapter, the student will be able to:

- Give examples of platforms or containers that can host PHP programs
- Create a simple dynamic web application using PHP
- Explain three-tier design and determine what is contained in each tier
- Design a three-tier application
- Explain each step of the program development lifecycle (PDLC)
- Define and explain MVC and Dependency Injection

## PHP Platforms and Containers

PHP is a powerful language because it can be adapted for use on almost any hardware or software platform. The ease at which it interfaces with HTML and JavaScript provides the ability for PHP applications to run on any system that can host a browser. More and more applications are now being created using browsers as the main interface tool for the application. This allows the application to run on PCs, the Internet, and even in smart phones without the requirement of installing the actual application (or other software) on the device. It also allows users to experience the same "feel" for the application when they switch between devices.

In the following sections, we will take a brief look at some of the platforms and containers that can host PHP applications. We will use the words *platform* and *container* interchangeably. In this discussion we consider a platform or container a software tool that "hosts" the PHP program and any output returned by executing the program.

---

**Electronic supplementary material**  The online version of this chapter (doi:10.1007/978-1-4842-1730-6_2) contains supplementary material, which is available to authorized users.

© Steve Prettyman 2015
S. Prettyman. *Learn PHP 7*. DOI 10.1007/978-1-4842-1730-6_2

# PHP PC Applications

PHP programs can be developed to run as PC applications hosted within an operating system. However, the skills needed to create these applications require an in-depth understanding of communication between operating systems and event-driven PHP programs. These advanced skills are beyond the concepts shown in this introductory book. However, some might also argue that the skills needed to accomplish this are unnecessary since a PHP program can run within any browser residing in any operating system.

PHP PC applications do have the ability to "create once" and "run anywhere," as with other languages (such as Java). PHP PC applications can be created to require no (or little) code changes between PC operating systems and hardware platforms.

The **GTK SDK** (Software Development Kit) is one of several tools that can be used for PC application development. If you visit the web site (`http://gtk.php.net/`), you can find information on the latest version and future development.

> *If you are curious about PHP PC application development, try the link below or search in your browser for "PHP GTK Tutorial".*
>
> `http://www.developertutorials.com/building-desktop-applications-in-php-8-02-01/`

# PHP Smart Phone Applications

PHP can also be used to create smart phone apps. Usually this occurs as an attempt to retrofit a current web application to the smart phone environment. Smart phone application development requires advanced skills in developing communication links between your program and the smart phone operating system.

Smart phone apps may be necessary to use some of the features built into the smart phone operating system (such as GPS). All smart phone operating systems provide **API** (Application Program Interface) calls that allow applications residing on the phone to use these features. Although web applications (discussed later in this chapter) can run in a browser on a smart phone, they cannot make API calls to the smart phone operating system (since they are not hosted within the phone itself). If the application requires the ability to interface with the smart phones operating system, it must reside on the smart phone.

Developing smart phone applications require advanced programming skills and an in-depth knowledge of the smart phone operating systems. Some of this hassle can be reduced by using one of the free smart phone SDKs (Software Development Kits) available today. Some SDKs now provide the ability to convert applications for use on multiple operating systems.

You should have good basic PHP skills before attempting to create smart phone applications.

# PHP Facebook and Other Social Applications

PHP can be used to create applications (and games) that are hosted in the Facebook Canvas Platform and other social applications (such as Twitter). The techniques used in these applications are similar. We will take a brief look at the Facebook Canvas as an example.

Applications can uses tools in Facebook itself (such as the Facebook Login) using API (Application Program Interface) calls. For example, an application can use Facebook tools to monitor the use of the application. When a user signs in to an application (or game) using the Facebook sign-in, the user must acknowledge and accept the security levels necessary to run the program. By accepting these settings, the user is giving the application permission to make API calls to retrieve information (and may be change information) from the user's Facebook environment.

You can create PHP applications that are merely hosted by Facebook that do not require the knowledge of API programming. Many advertisements that include click-through ability for more information are hosted in the Canvas but actually reside on a web server located somewhere else on the Internet. The Facebook

Canvas does have the ability to interpret HTML and JavaScript code. This enables the developer to create an application that could both be displayed in the Canvas and externally in a browser.

Let's take a brief look at how you could host an application in the Facebook Canvas.

You will keep the development in "developer's" mode. This simply means that when you have completed the demo, everyone in Facebook will not be able to access the application. There are additional steps you must go through to make your application 'live' (see developers.facebook.com for details).

---

▒ **Warning**    Facebook constantly changes its security settings and API (Application Programmer Interface). Some of the following steps might slightly change over time. If you find these steps do not work, search the Internet for "A Simple PHP Facebook App" and check the creation date of the tutorial or videos to ensure that you have the most up-to-date information.

---

# Do It

Complete the following:

1. For this example, you need to use your browser to search for an existing secure web page (one that uses https instead of http). Facebook no longer allows non-secured web pages to be hosted in the Canvas. Since this is a PHP book, it would be preferable to find a web application that includes PHP code (one that has a file ending of php instead of html). However, you can use an HTML site for this example. Remember, this is just for demonstration and educational purposes. You should always request permission to host a web site in another site (such as Facebook Canvas). All web sites are assumed to be protected by copyright laws (even when there is no indication on the site that they are copyrighted).

   Note: Some sites are secured to not allow their site to be hosted in another site. If you follow these directions and the site does not display, that may be the cause. If that happens, search for another secured web page.

   You could elect to use your own web page (such as the hello world example). However, the web page will need a hosting environment (besides your PC). Facebook cannot interface with your localhost development environment. There are many low-price hosting sites now available; some for as little as $1 a month. Most hosting companies enable you to have secured sites (using https). However, there is usually an additional fee for this service.

   When picking a host site, make sure to read the fine print to determine if it will host PHP applications. It is a good idea to have a hosting site for you to upload your test programs. Programs should be tested in multiple environments. Sometimes programs react differently in different environments.

   If you have your own secure URL, or one that your school allows you to use, upload your Hello World program onto the host. Then test it to make sure it still works in the host and make sure that you know the actual URL address that will run the program.

2. Sign in to Facebook (www.facebook.com). If you do not have a Facebook user ID/password, you can create one for free. This demo does not require you to completely build a Facebook page. If you have an existing account, you might consider creating an extra account (with a different e-mail address) just for your development needs.

3. Once you are signed in to Facebook, go to the developer's page (developers.facebook.com). Find the Menu on the page. Select Apps, and then select Add New App. A screen similar to the one shown in Figure 2-1 will appear. Locate and select the Facebook Canvas option.

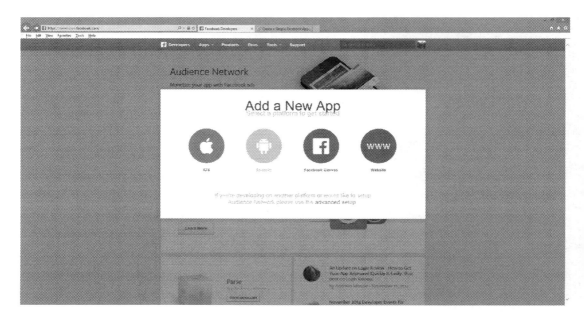

***Figure 2-1.*** *Selecting Canvas from Facebook developer's page (11/17/14)*

(Remember that Facebook does change their screens. However, the sign-in process should be similar to this demo.)

The next screen requires you to enter a name for your application. Any unique name is fine since this application will not become live. You might also be prompted with some other questions related to whether this app is part of another app (no) and you may be requested to select a category (Apps for Pages would be fine). Once you have filled (and selected) the required information click the Create App ID button.

4. You should now see a Quick Start page similar to Figure 2-2. Ignore the code at the top of the Quick Start page (it's beyond what we want to accomplish). Scroll down the page to find the textbox that says, "Where Is Your App Hosted?". You may see a textbox (not required) that requests you to enter a unique URL for your app. If you do not enter one, Facebook will generate one. For our demo, we will leave it blank.

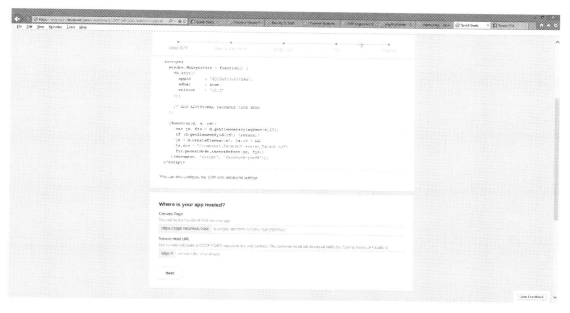

***Figure 2-2.*** *The Facebook Quick Start page*

Another textbox requires you to enter a secure URL to link your app into Facebook. This is the actual location of your application on the Internet. Enter the complete address of the secure web page you have discovered or enter the location of your "Hello World" program if it is hosted on a secure site (https).

Note: Facebook requires (at least) an ending slash for your link, something similar to:

`www.mysita.com/projects/myfirstprogram.php/`

Click the Next button.

5. The next page displayed will show more example code. This code can be used to log in to your application using the Facebook login and has the ability to request Facebook permissions for your application. However, our demo does not need login ability or any Facebook permissions. Just click the Next button at the bottom of the page.

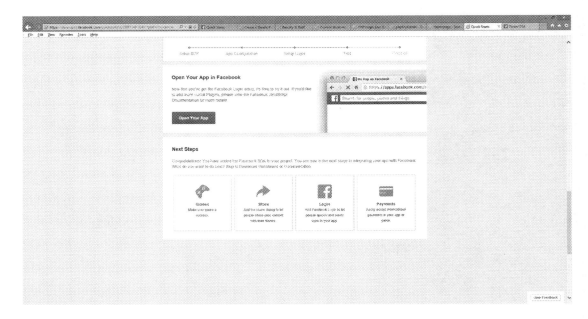

***Figure 2-3.*** *The Facebook Open App page*

6. Click the Open Your App button. Once you click the button, Facebook will try to load your page in the Canvas.

However, if you have picked an existing secure web page and see a message similar to Figure 2-4, the page you selected might not allow hosting in another site. If this happens, go to Steps 7-10. If you were successful, skip to Step 11. However, copy and paste the URL (from the browser) that Facebook uses to display your page, so you can test it again, if needed.

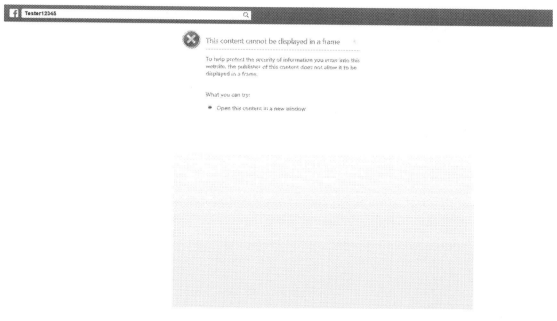

*Figure 2-4. Facebook open app failure*

7.  If your page did not display, do the following. After you have copied the URL, close the test page. You now want to find the "Dashboard" for your app. If it is not visible on your Developers Facebook page, go to the menu at the top of the page and select Apps. A drop-down list should display showing the name of your app(s). Select your app.

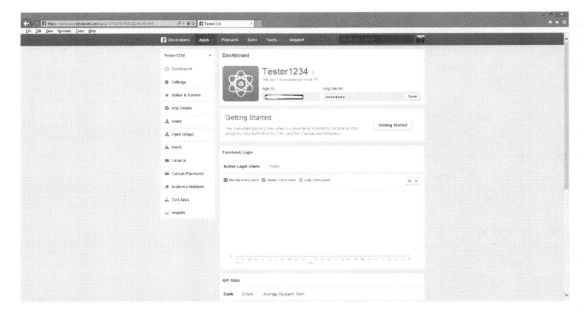

***Figure 2-5.*** *The Facebook dashboard*

8. Once you have displayed your dashboard, select Settings on the left menu.

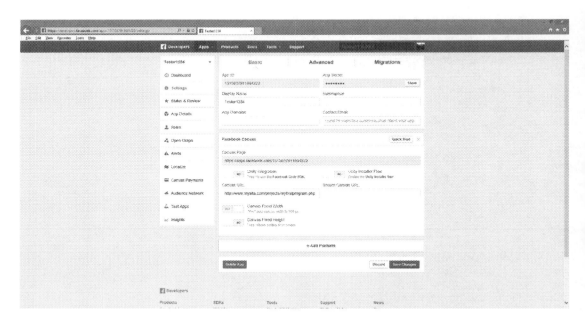

***Figure 2-6.*** *The Facebook Settings page*

9.  Scroll down to the bottom of the page. Locate Secured Canvas URL and erase the address that resides in this textbox. Type the location of another secured web page (https) in the box.

    Remember, this must be a URL on the web, not your localhost. Click the Save Changes button.

10. Now paste the URL of your app (if you lost the URL address, it is under Canvas Page on the Settings Page) in your browser.

***Figure 2-7.*** *Facebook working app*

11. You should now see your app display on the canvas within your Facebook page.

12. Were you successful? What problems did you encounter following this example? How did you solve those problems?

Congratulations, you have created your first Facebook app (although it is not live). If you would like some of your friends to see your app, you can go back to the dashboard and select Rolls from the menu. You can then use your friends (yes, they have to be Facebook Friends) and give them a "role" in the development of your app (such as "Developers" or "Testers"). They then will have access to your app without it going live.

You are on your way to making lots of money as a Facebook game developer! Well, maybe not just yet. We left out a lot of coding to react with Facebook's API. But hopefully you get the idea that Facebook can easily be used as a container for your PHP applications.

# PHP, AJAX, and CSS—Web Applications

PHP and AJAX (Asynchronous JavaScript and XML) work well together. AJAX provides the ability to dynamically change portions of a web page without reloading the complete page. Most web pages have static areas (menus, headers, and footers) that do not change relative to user interaction. It is not necessary for these areas of the web page to change when the user interacts (clicks a button) with the page. AJAX can enable you to develop a container (in the following example, the container is located between the div tags) to display output from a program hosted on a web server; without disturbing the complete web page. Users can then view content on a web page (menu, header, and footer) when the results of the user's interaction (clicking a button) is still being processed. If for some reason the program is slow, hung, or missing, the rest of the page still functions. You may have experienced this when you have displayed a page that hangs because a lot of information (a lot of ads) is trying to load at once and the page will not function because it must be completely loaded before it is usable.

AJAX also allows you to change the content of your PHP application on the web server without disturbing the web page. You can then update the code in your application without the user's knowledge (as long as you keep the name of the application the same).

Let's look at an example.

47

▓ **Note**   Code example files are included on the book's web site. You can copy and use these example without any changes. Every attempt has been made to ensure that code shown in this book is correct. Printing errors might affect the code shown (such as uppercase and lowercase being adjusted and parentheses being replaced with angled parentheses). All code available on the web site is functional.

***Example 2-1.*** AJAX_Example_JavaScript.js

```
function getXMLHttp()
{
  var xmlHttp;
  try
  {
    xmlHttp = new XMLHttpRequest();
  }
  catch(e)
  {
    //Internet Explorer is different than the others
    try
    {
      xmlHttp = new ActiveXObject("Msxml2.XMLHTTP");
    }
    catch(e)
    {
      try
      {
        xmlHttp = new ActiveXObject("Microsoft.XMLHTTP");
      }
      catch(e)
      {
        alert("Old browser? Upgrade today so you can use AJAX!")
        return false;
      }
    }
  }
  return xmlHttp;
}
function AjaxRequest()
{
  var xmlHttp = getXMLHttp();
  xmlHttp.onreadystatechange = function()
  {
    if(xmlHttp.readyState == 4)
    {
      HandleResponse(xmlHttp.responseText);
    }
  }
  xmlHttp.open("GET", "myfirstprogram.php", true);
```

```
xmlHttp.send(null);
}
function HandleResponse(response)
{
  document.getElementById('AjaxResponse').innerHTML = response;
}
```

*JavaScript—A scripting language that provides the ability for a web page to be interactive. With JavaScript, a web page can react to the user entering information into a textbox and/ or clicking a button. If you need to brush up on JavaScript or need additional examples, review the free "The New Boston" (thenewboston.com) videos at:*

*https://www.youtube.com/watch?v=yQaAGmHNn9s&list=PL46F0A159EC02DF82*

*For a more in-depth review of AJAX, review the free "The New Boston" (thenewboston.com) videos at:*

*https://www.youtube.com/playlist?list=PL6gx4Cwl9DGDiJSXfsJTASx9eMq_HlenQ.*

If you don't know JavaScript, don't get too hung up on the details of this program. Let's just look at a few key points. AJAX uses HTTP GET to request a program, similar to a browser requesting a page. In this example, an instance of the class XMLHttpRequest (which exists in the JavaScript libraries) is named XmlHttp. This object is then used to open the request for the myfirstprogram.php (like opening a pipe). Then the send method of the object sends the request (pushes the water down the pipe). If the file is returned back properly, the output of the file is placed on the HTML web page between div tags with an ID of AjaxResponse. If the browser can't handle AJAX communication, an alert box will display suggesting the user upgrade the browser. Although it is unlikely that anyone is using a browser that cannot interpret AJAX code, you still should handle all possibilities.

***Example 2-2.*** ajaxdemo.html

```
<head> <title>PHP Ajax Demo</title>
<meta charset="utf-8">
<link href="ajaxdemo.css" rel="stylesheet">
<script type='text/javascript' src='Ajax_Example_JavaScript.js'></script></head>
<body>
<div id="wrapper">
  <div id="header"> <h1>PHP Ajax Demo</h1>  </div>
  <div id="content">   <h2>"Watch it!!"</h2>
    <p>The words below will be replaced by "Hello World" which is pulled from the
    'myfirstprogram.php' file via AJAX.</p>
<h2>AJAX DEMO</h2>
    <input type='button' onclick='AjaxRequest();' value='Find Hello World!'/><br /><br />
    <div id='AjaxResponse'>
      Pay attention… Notice when you click the button that only this section changes.
    </div>   </div> <!-- end of content -->
  <div id="footer">Copyright &copy; 2015 Little Ocean Waves - Steve Prettyman
 </div><!-- end of footer -->
  </div> <!-- end of wrapper -->
</body></html>
```

For you to use this script, change the `xmlHttp.open` statement to select the file you wish to execute (instead of `myfirstprogram.php`). Change the `document.getElementById` line to include the ID of the `div` tag you want to use to host the output (instead of `AjaxResponse`) in your HTML file (see the HTML code in the next example).

> *HTML—Hypertext markup language is a markup language used to format the layout of a web page. HTML is interpreted by a browser, which then displays the results to the user.*
>
> *For a more in-depth review of HTML, visit the free "The New Boston" (thenewboston.com) videos at:*
>
> *https://www.youtube.com/playlist?list=PL081AC329706B2953.*

If you don't know a lot about HTML, don't worry. You only need to look at a few lines in this example. First, near the top of the code, a link tag pulls in the `ajaxdemo.css` file. This CSS file allows you to see a page with some graphic details. It allows you to demo that the page updates without the graphics from the CSS file repasting or blinking. Right below this line the script type tag loads in the JavaScript file from Example 2-1. If you named your file something else, this is the line you need to adjust with the new file name. If your files are not all in the same folder, you should include the folder name along with the file name.

In the middle of the HTML body section, the input type tag creates a button that will call the `AjaxRequest` function (contained in the JavaScript file) when clicked. This causes all the JavaScript code in Example 2-1 to execute. The last line we need to pay attention to is the `<div id='AjaxResponse'>` tag. The value in id (`AjaxResponse`) must match the object name used in the JavaScript `getElementById` code exactly. Assuming that they match correctly, once the button is clicked, the JavaScript code will request the `myfirstprogram.php` file and display the results between the `div` tags with the `AjaxResponse` ID.

***Example 2-3.*** ajaxdemo.css

```
body { background-color: #000000;
                   font-family: Arial, Verdana, sans-serif; }
#wrapper { margin: 0 auto;
                     width: 85%;
                     min-width: 800px;
                     background-color: #cc0000;
                     color: #000066; }
#header { background-color: #ff0000;
                     color: #00005D; }

h1 { margin-bottom: 10px; }
#content { background-color: #ffffff;
                   color: #000000;
                   padding: 10px 20px;
                   overflow: auto; }
#footer { font-size: 80%;
                   text-align: center;
                   padding: 5px;
   background-color: #0000FF;
                   color: #ffffff;
                   clear: both;}
h2 { color: #000000;
               font-family: Arial, sans-serif; }
#floatright { float: right;
               margin: 10px; }
```

Just to be complete, the **CSS** file is shown here. Don't worry if you don't know CSS. This file only makes the web site look nice for the demo. If you are going to use this file, make sure to save it in a file with the .css file extension. Also, if you are going to change the name of the file, make sure to also change the file name in the link tag (in the HTML file) to exactly match. Make sure to include any folder names, if necessary.

*CSS—Cascading Style Sheets (CSS) work with HTML to display graphics on a web page. CSS describes the layout of the page, colors, text fonts, background images, and other characteristics of the web page. For a more in-depth review of CSS, visit the free "The New Boston" (thenewboston.com) videos at:*

`https://www.thenewboston.com/videos.php?cat=40&video=18754.`

Double-check all three files (.js, .css, and .html) to make sure the names of the files match (exactly) the links that call them. If all the files are properly linked, the ajaxdemo.html file will first display, as shown in Figure 2-8.

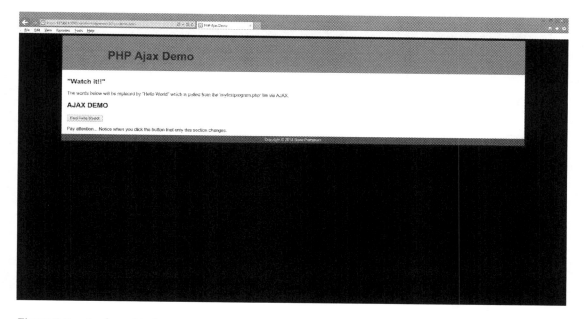

*Figure 2-8. ajaxdemo.html*

If your code does not work, double-check the file names (make sure they do not have a .txt ending). If you see a blank page, there is something wrong. Look for typos in your code. Did you forget ;, {, (, or other coding? If you get an error message, paste it in your browser to discover possible solutions. If you do not see an error message, go to the logs (see Chapter 1) for Apache and PHP to determine other possible problems.

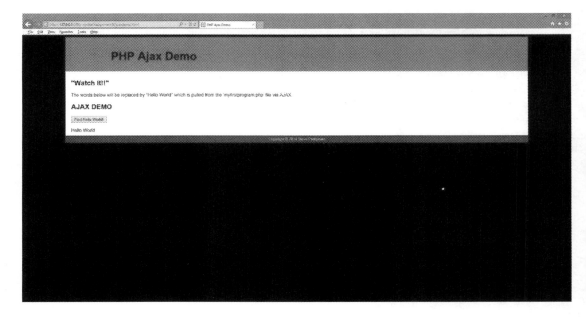

***Figure 2-9.*** *The ajaxdemo.html file after the AJAX request*

If there are no syntax errors (or incorrect file names or locations), when the user clicks the button, the page will request the `myfirstprogram.php` file using AJAX and will display the result of the execution of the program between the `div` tags. In this example, `Hello World` will be displayed.

## Do It

1. Copy the three files shown previously from the book's web site into your projects folder (the location that you are running your projects in Apache). Run the HTML program. Was your test successful? If not, why not?

2. Change the file name of your `.js` file and change the link tag in your HTML file to reflect the new file name. Test your HTML program. Was your test successful? If not, why not?

3. Change the name of your PHP program. Make changes to the `.js` file to reflect the new name of your PHP program. Test your HTML program. Was your testing successful? If not, why not?

## PHP, AJAX, and CSS—Smart Phone Web Applications

At this point, you should be beginning to discover the flexibility and power of creating PHP applications. You might be a little disappointed that we did not cover app development for smart phones in any detail. As mentioned, apps on smart phones usually do API calls to the operating system to request the use of applications residing on the phone (such as GPS). That level of coding is beyond entry-level. Thus, beyond what is covered in this book. However, there are times when we want to provide smart phones with the ability to access a web application from the browser on the phone. We can provide this ability with just a few changes to the previous demo. This provides you with an application that works with any size device that includes a browser.

You will make this change without adjusting the HTML (except for adding a link), JavaScript, or PHP code. You can adjust the ajaxdemo web page to format properly in smart phones or other mobile devices using CSS. In this example, you only need to change the HTML file to discover the size of the display (interface). Then CSS can be used to change the graphics to fit the proper screen size.

If the PHP file includes a lot of HTML (and/or other CSS code), we might need to also adjust the PHP file. However, we should always consider having CSS format the overall output (instead of the PHP file). This will allow you to use the same code in multiple containers (hosts) as you have seen demonstrated in this chapter.

You can add the following lines just below the link to the original CSS file in the ajaxdemo.html file.

```
<link href="ajaxdemomobile.css" rel="stylesheet" media="only screen and
(max-device-width:480px)">
<meta name="viewport" content="width=device-width, initial-scale=1.0">
```

■ **Note** The new complete HTML file is located on the book's web site.

These two lines will attempt to determine the size of the display screen and use the new CSS file for any screens that are 480px or less. The demo program, as is, will fit on most mobile devices. However, let's adjust it to remove some of the spacing, padding, and margins.

■ **Note** You can also use the CSS3 Flexbox Attribute for multiple device sizes. Since its use requires a little more understanding of CSS, we will stick with the "old style" method. You can find more information on CSS3 Flexbox at the following w3schools link.

```
http://www.w3schools.com/css/css3_flexbox.asp
```

*Example 2-4.* The ajaxdemomobile.css file

```
body { background-color: #000000;
            font-family: Arial, Verdana, sans-serif;
      margin: 0;         }
#wrapper { margin: 0 auto;
                    width: 100%;
                    margin: 0;
                    min-width: 0px;
                    background-color: #cc0000;
                    color: #000066; }
#header { background-color: #ff0000;
                    color: #00005D;
                    font-size: 100%;
                    padding: 0.5px 0.5px 0.5px 0.5px; }
h1 { margin: 0px; }
#content { background-color: #ffffff;
                    color: #000000;
                    padding: 0.5px 0.5px;
                    overflow: auto; }
#footer { font-size: 80%;
                    text-align: left;
                    padding: 0px;
                    background-color: #0000FF;
                    color: #ffffff;
                    clear: both;}
```

53

```
h2 { color: #000000;
          font-family: Arial, sans-serif;
          margin: 0px;              }
#floatright { float: none;
                         margin: 0px; }
```

Compare Example 2-4 to Example 2-3. The code in Example 2-4 is not perfect, but it does give you an idea of what can be adjusted in the original CSS file for display in mobile devices. This example reduces margins and padding to zero, or almost zero. This greatly reduces the wasted space on the display of a smaller mobile device.

## Do It

1. Locate the new HTML file and CSS file on the book's web site. If you have a web host provider, upload these files (and the .js file) to the host. Try to access the HTML page from your smart phone. You can also try to display the page by using the URL location of the file on the book's web site. Was your test successful? If not, why not? Did the page format properly on your phone? If not, what do you think needs to be adjusted?

---

░ **Note** If you don't have a host web site on the Internet, you can also test this CSS file by downloading one of the free mobile emulators available on the web (try www.download.com). You can also change the link tag in the HTML file to point to the ajaxdemomobile.css file instead of the ajaxdemo.css file. Then try reducing the size of your browser to simulate a smart phone screen.

---

## PHP, HTML, JavaScript, CSS, and Dynamic Web Pages

As a last example of containers (hosts) for PHP programs, let's consider the browser. As you have seen in this chapter, you can use an HTML file to call our PHP program (clicking the button in the previous demonstration). This, as detailed in Chapter 1, will cause the PHP program to execute and the results to be returned to the browser. You could also have your PHP program return HTML code.

***Example 2-5.*** Dynamic HTML page created by a PHP program

```
<?php
print "<html>";
print "<head><title>My Program</title></head>";
print "<body>";
print "<h1>Hello World</h1>";
print "</body>";
print "</html>";
?>
```

You could return a complete HTML page (even with JavaScript and links) back to the device (browser) that requested the PHP program to execute. Example 2-5 would create a complete dynamic HTML page from within PHP code. The output created can even contain links to CSS files and embedded CSS tags for formatting. However, I urge caution on embedding CSS tags that depend on the container being a certain size. As the developer, you do not know what type of device will display the result (PC, smart phone, tablet, or pad). It would be better to provide multiple CSS files (as shown previously) to format the output for different devices.

In the previous examples, we have separated the initial interface (HTML and JavaScript) from the PHP program. You could actually place the HTML (to display the initial web page) and PHP code in the same file.

You can create a PHP file that will determine whether the user has ever requested the page before. If they have not, or the browser has timed them out, then the PHP program could display an initial HTML page for the user to interact (such as clicking a button). The same program could then call itself again to determine if the button has been clicked and return a response.

Let's look at a different version of the Hello World program to do just that.

***Example 2-6.*** The callmyself.php file

```php
<?php
if (isset($_POST['submitbutton']))
{
print "<h1> Hello World </h1>";
}
else
{
print "<html><head><title>PHP Example</title></head>";
print "<form method='post' action='callmyself.php'>";
print "<input type='submit' id='submitbutton' name='submitbutton' value='Find Hello World!'/>";
print "</form>";
print "</body></html>";
}
?>
```

> *For a more in-depth demonstration of PHP If statements, visit the following free videos from "The New Boston" (thenewboston) at:*
>
> *https://www.thenewboston.com/videos.php?cat=11&video=17004.*

This program includes a simple if conditional statement to determine if the user has clicked the submit button.

The format of the if statement is as follows:

```
if (conditional statement)
{
// code to execute if the conditional statement is true
}
else
{
// code to execute if the conditional statement is false
}
```

A conditional statement usually compares two values to determine if they are the same or different or calls a method which returns a true or false value. We will look at functions returning values in a moment. Let's look at a quick example of the first type.

Conditional statements use a comparison operator (==, <, >, <=, and >=) to determine if the statement is true or false.

```
If ( a > b)
{
print "it's A!";
}
else
{
print "it's B!";
}
```

In this example, the values in properties a and b are compared. If a is greater than b, then "it's A!" is displayed. Otherwise, "it's B!" is displayed. PHP does some type conversion when it determines that it might be necessary. For example, assume a = "5", and b = 6. PHP would convert the value in a from a string 5 to a number 5 so it can do the comparison. Many languages do not do this and will display an error if you try to compare strings and numbers. If you don't want this conversion to occur, you can use some special comparison operators. For example, you can use three = signs to see if values are exactly the same (a === b) instead of two.

> *Security and performance—Whenever possible use === instead of ==. This will assure that you get exactly what you expect.*

In Example 2-6, the if statement calls a method (isset). $_GET tries to retrieve the property ('submitbutton') and its value ("Find Hello World!") from the HTML form, which used HTTP GET to pass the information (you could have used $_POST and HTTP POST). isset will return a false or true back to the if statement, depending on whether or not $_GET could retrieve the property (and its contents). The true or false will cause the if statement to determine which block of code to execute.

As mentioned in Chapter 1, an object (such as a button) within an HTML form will produce a property and value combination based on the object's name and whatever is contained in the value statement of that object. This is even true for submit buttons that have been given a name (id) and value (as in Example 2-6).

The first time the program is called from the browser, the button has not been clicked. So there is no submitbutton variable created. A false is returned by the isset method. The code jumps to the else section and executes the print statements that display the HTML form and submit button (as in Figure 2-10).

***Figure 2-10.*** *callmyself.php before the button is clicked*

When the user clicks the button, the program calls itself (look at the action parameter of the form tag). This time, since the user has clicked the button, there is a submitbutton property and a value ('Find Hello World!') for that variable. The program determines that the variable is "set" (has a value in it) and returns a true. The if statement then executes the one line of code between the if and else statements. Hello World is then displayed. The PHP program handled all the functionality of the application without using any existing static HTML page.

***Figure 2-11.*** *callmyself.php after the button is clicked*

The advantage of this technique is that all code can be contained in one file. Thus, all changes occur in one place. The disadvantage of this technique is that all code is in one file. The more complicate the code, the "messier" it can become. One way to clean up the code would be to move the code into functions contained within other PHP libraries (we will look at this later). The additional disadvantage is that the file name cannot be changed without affecting the users. If you changed the file name to `mynewprogram.php`, you would need to inform all your users of the new name (and maybe location). The previous examples using AJAX allowed you to change the file name within the HTML code page, but did not require you to change the actual name of the HTML page that the user would request.

## Do It

1.  Find the `callmyself.php` file on the book's web site. Download the file to your Apache `projects` folder. Change and add `print` statements to display your complete name, the term, and your major. Test your program. Did your program run successfully? If not, why not?

# PHP Three-Tier Architecture

Most of this chapter has been discovering the different platforms (or containers) that can "host" PHP applications. We have found that PHP can display its output in almost any container (PC, Facebook, smart phone/mobile device, or browser). The ease at which PHP can interact with JavaScript, HTML, and CSS has provided this flexibility. Today, almost any platform has the ability to interact with the Internet (and those that don't will sometime in the future). Any platform that can interact with the Internet can also interact with a PHP application.

This independence (or flexibility) of the interface demonstrates a logical separation of the platform or host of the interface from other "tiers" (parts) of the application. This leads into a discussion of the three-tier architecture and the logical design of PHP applications. The larger the application, the more likely the application will need to be broken into modules. Also, it's more likely that these modules could reside on different servers (or web servers). Larger applications likely will require multiple programmers writing code at the same time. These programmers may even use different languages to create the program modules.

Building a large application is not much different than assembling a car. The individual components of the car (body, wheels, electronics, and engine) are assembled individually first. Each completed component is then placed inside the chassis of the car. The components are then connected (hoses, wires, and belts) to other components. When completed, all components of the car work together. If a component breaks, it can be replaced without causing replacement or changes to any other component in the car.

The idea of modular (or component) programming is based on the methodology of blocks of code that can be created individually to be assembled with other modules to produce a working application. The modules can be modified or replaced without requiring changes to other modules. This methodology has been around for a while. Even today, many programs are not modular because smaller programs can work efficiently without being broken into modules. However, as these applications expand into larger applications they become more difficult to update or maintain. A change requires updating the complete application rather than just a module. At some point, an expanding application that has not be created with modules has to be redesigned from the ground up into modules for better maintenance and reliability.

As discussed in Chapter 1, a search engine can display a web page interface in a browser on the user's PC. Once the user enters the search request, the information can be transmitted across the Internet to a remote server (we don't know where), which executes a search application (we don't know what program language was used to create it). The application then searches a database (we don't know what DBMS or where it is located) for the requested information. The results are sent back to the application, which in turn, sends the information back to the browser (via the web server) on the user's PC.

***Figure 2-12.*** *Three-tier modular application design*

The flow of information in this process causes the design of this type of web application to naturally fall into (at least) three tiers (modules); interface tier, business rules tier, and data tier. One advantage of breaking code into different tiers is the ability to reuse tiers with multiple applications. For example, our search engine could use the same business rules tier and data tier for multiple devices while using a different interface (PC app or smart phone app). Distinct tiers can also be updated without affecting other tiers. The smart phone app interface could be updated to use the latest features of the newest operating system without changes to the business rules or data tiers. Code within the business rules tier could be updated to fix logical bugs without requiring changes to the interface or data tiers. Let's take a look at what typically occurs in each tier.

> *Modular Three-Tier Applications, Design, Programming—Three-tier design provides the ability to create programs that can be separated into an interface tier, business rules tier, and data tier. The interface tier contains all graphics and program code related to displaying information to the user. The business rules tier does not contain an interface. However, it processes any information submitted from the interface tier and can then submit information to the data tier to be stored. The data tier is the primary storage location for the application, which may include the use of a database. Each tier can be independently changed and built (compiled) without affecting the other tiers.*

## Do It

1. What are the name of the three tiers of modular design?
2. How is modular design similar to designing a building?
3. How does modular programming make coding more efficient?

# Interface Tier

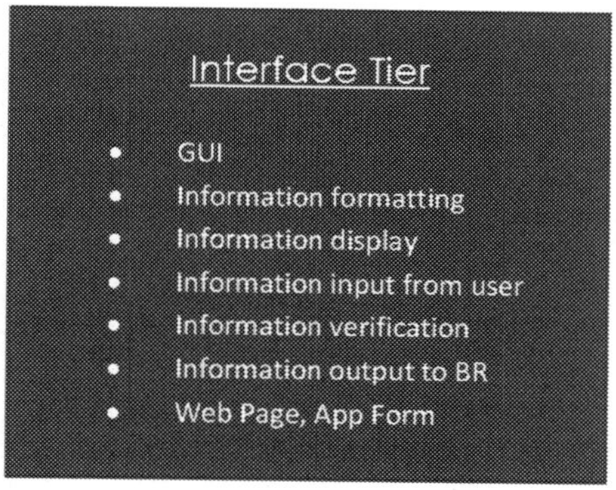

**Figure 2-13.** *Interface tier*

The interface tier (IT) displays information and provides the user the ability to interact with the application. Most interfaces provide a Graphical User Interface (GUI), which allows the user an attractive way to view information and interaction with the application. GUI interfaces provide common **objects**, including textboxes and buttons, which help the user to quickly adapt to new applications. In addition, pictures, images, icons, video, and sound can often be included to keep the user's interest. Menus and other navigation objects are also commonly included to help the user move through the application successfully.

> *Objects—Objects are blocks of code that have already been compiled for use within an application. Objects can be placed into a program by making an instance of the object. Objects contain methods and properties. Methods (or functions) are blocks of code that accomplish a task (such as placing items in a list box). Properties (or variables) are characteristics of an object that can be changed (such as a background color). Objects are usually well tested and error free. By reusing existing objects, the programmer can quickly create more reliable programs.*

This tier will display information using objects (such as labels and picture boxes) or scripting code (such as the ajaxdemo.html example in this chapter). The tier will also accept information from the user through interactive objects (such as textboxes and buttons). Static information can be provided from within the tier (via menus, logos, or footers). Dynamic information is usually provided to the tier from the business rules tier (such as the output from myfirstprogram.php shown in this chapter).

Some coding (shown in later chapters), which prepares information to be send to other tiers may be present in the interface tier. For example, JavaScript code that verifies that the user has entered all the required information or the proper information (numeric characters in an age textbox) is acceptable. Additional code may also prepare information received from the business rules tier to be displayed (such as converting numbers to text format) in the interface.

> *Verification/Verification Code—Verification code validates information. The code compares the information received to an expected standard format. For example, the code can verify that an e-mail address has both a @ and a . (period). If the information has both symbols, it could be considered "valid" (although we still are not sure that the e-mail address actually exists). If it does not have both symbols, the code is not valid. Information that is not valid usually will cause the program to display an error message to the user requesting valid information be reentered.*

59

The interface must provide code with the ability to react to user interactions (clicking the Submit button), commonly called *user events*. Code may also be provided that prepares information provided by the user for use by other tiers (such as converting text entered by the user into number format for a calculation in the business rules tier).

> *Event—Event-driven languages (such as PHP) can execute blocks of code when an event occurs. Events can be something that the user has done (such as clicking a button). Events can also be fired by the operating system. Programs provide listener code that "hears" an event. When an event occurs, the code provides an event method, which then executes. A program chooses which events to listen for by the presence, or lack of, listener code.*

The interface tier should not directly interact with a database management system or a database itself. By doing so, this would lock the tier into the database location and actual design of the database. The tier should not manipulate data (except for display purposes). Any accounting, mathematical calculations, or processing of data related to the application itself should be accomplished in the business rules tier.

> *Database Management System (DBMS)—A Database Management System is software that allows a user or an application to create and define a database. It also provides the ability to insert, update, or delete information in the database.*

| Do | Don't |
| --- | --- |
| Format data for display | Access data from database |
| Verify correct information from user | Calculate results |
| Respond to user events | Process information |
| Handle the unexpected (exceptions) | Verify user IDs and passwords |
| Format data for business rules tier | |

# Do It

1. Give three examples of items that would be included in the interface tier.

2. Give three examples of items that would not be included in the interface tier.

3. Can some program code exist in the interface tier? If so, what tasks does this code provide?

# Business Rules Tier

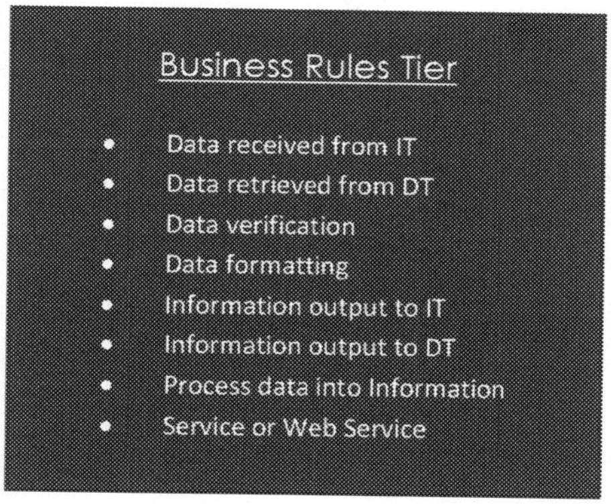

**Figure 2-14.** *Business rules tier*

The business rules tier processes all information and data received from the interface tier and the data tier. This tier will also return information requested by the interface tier (such as returning "Hello World") and submit information to the data tier for storage. Most of the actual programming code is contained in this tier.

The business rule tier code usually makes an application truly unique from another application. If an application is copyrighted, the uniquely creative algorithms are probably hidden in this tier. For example, many of the differences in web search engines and how the information will ultimately be displayed are embedded in the business rules tier.

Unlike the interface tier, which may contain code in the browser, all coding in the business tier is completed using a program(s) (such as PHP) on a server. Scripting and programming code residing on a server is secured by the server itself and cannot be accessed by the user. Business tier code can also reside on an application server (as a service) or on a web server (as a web service). Servers ensure that code in this tier is secure by not allowing direct access by the user.

> *Server/Application Server/Web Server—A server is connect to a network to provide services to any node (machine) on the network (or the Internet). A server can provide more than one service (communication, security, and/or storage) or can provide a specific service. Application servers house applications that are accessible to users on the network (or Internet). Web servers host web pages and web applications. They are usually exposed to access outside a corporation.*

> *Service—Services are applications that reside in the memory of a computer or server that respond to requests from other applications. Services can be automatically loaded into memory when the computer or server is booted or they can manually be started and stopped when required. Services do not have GUI interfaces. The business rules tier can reside as a service(s) on a computer or server.*

If information passed between the tiers of the application can be subject to possible manipulation by hackers, this tier may contain code, similar to the interface tier, to verify the validly and proper format of the data received.

Information passed from this tier to other tiers can be format for easy acceptance. For example, a *dataset* (similar to a table or spreadsheet) can be returned to the interface tier for display in a table or list box existing on a web page. A dataset could also be sent to the data tier to be inserted into a database.

> *Dataset—A dataset is a structure that can hold multiple data tables. A data table is similar to a table in a database (with rows, columns, and data) or a spreadsheet. Datasets are commonly used to pass information between tiers and between methods.*

The business rules tier returns values to the tiers that request it. The tier does not provide any GUI interfaces or forms of any kind. Interfaces are not needed because the tier has no direct contact with the user at any time. All communication to the business rules tier is handled either through the interface tier or the data tier. Like the interface tier, the business rules tier does not directly update stored information in databases. All storage updates occur in the data tier.

| Do | Don't |
|---|---|
| Manipulate data | Display information |
| Format data | Save data on secondary device |
| Store data in memory | Display error messages |
| Raise exceptions | |
| Verify data | |

# Do It

1.  What tasks can business rule tier code accomplish that is similar to a task accomplished by code in the interface tier? Why is this code possibility duplicated in both tiers?

2.  How does the business rules tier pass and receive data (information)?

3.  Why must the business rules tier talk indirectly through the interface tier to provide information to the users?

# Data Tier

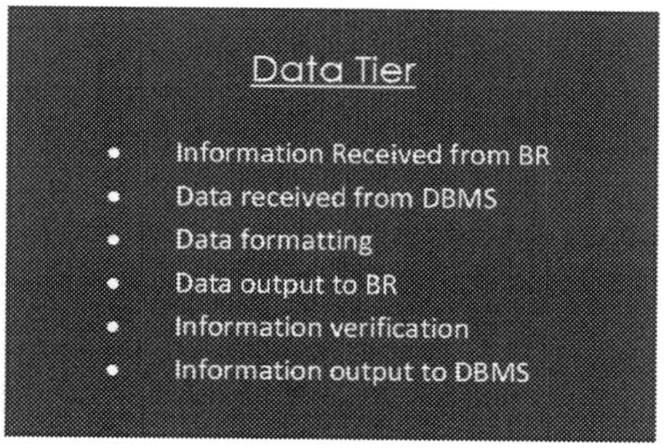

**Figure 2-15.** *Data tier*

The data tier's main function is to store information on a secondary device or to return data to the business rules tier. Data can (and usually is) be stored in a database using a Database Management System (like MySQL). The tier interfaces with the business rules tier, since data may be manipulated before being displayed, as in the creation of a report. Data is returned from the tier in a format that the business rules tier (and program languages) can accept. Common formats include JSON, XML, SOAP, and datasets.

*JSON—JavaScript Object Notation is a format, similar to XML, to store and exchange data. JSON can be viewed within an editor or browser. It is most commonly used to pass data between tiers.*

*XML—Extensible Markup Language is a markup language, similar to HTML, to store and describe data. XML can also be used to transmit data between tiers. We will provide an example of XML in Chapter 3.*

*SOAP—Simple Object Access Protocol is used to exchange data with a web service. It works with HTTP (Hypertext Transfer Protocol) and SMTP (Simple Mail Transfer Protocol) to provide communication between an application and a web service.*

*Web Service—An application, without an interface, that can be called to process information. A web service can provide the functionality of the business tier and/or data tier remotely on a web server. The Web Services Description Language (WSDL) is used to describe calls to the web service and the format of information accept and returned by the web service. WSDL is similar to XML.*

Validation with the data tier is done in the Database Management System and/or via program code. Validation in this tier is the last chance to make sure data is reliable and accurate before the database is updated. It is much easier to catch validation problems before they are stored than after invalid information has been recorded.

Data storage can be local and/or remote. Mobile devices can restrict storage to local databases (smart phones), but can also use **WSDL** (web services) to store and retrieve information remotely on a server or within a cloud (such as Microsoft Azure). Additionally, many applications save small amounts of information locally with cookies, or larger amounts of information in remote databases.

*Microsoft Azure—Microsoft Azure is a cloud platform that provides data services, app services, and network services. Visual Studio Applications can be uploaded and secured in the Microsoft Azure cloud.*

The data tier uses **SQL** statements (INSERT, DELETE, UPDATE, and SELECT) to retrieve and update information in a database. However, the actual request for the information to be changed comes from within the business rules tier. For example, a user requesting an address change in a web application would have to enter the requested change in the interface tier, format the update request in the business rules tier, and change the information in the database in the data tier.

| Do | Don't |
|---|---|
| Save data on secondary device | Manipulate data |
| Update data on secondary device | Display error messages |
| Raise exceptions | Display information |
| Verify data | |

# Do It

1. Why must the data tier validate information again, before it is placed in a database?

2. What type of code, if any, can exist in the data tier?

3. What is SQL used for?

# Putting It All Together

The Program Development Life Cycle (PDLC) leads us through the overall design and creation process for application development. The key to application development success is to properly plan the layout of your system before beginning the coding and development. By doing so, you reduce the amount of errors and problems that can occur. Many projects can run into a "corner" that the developer cannot get around because of poor planning up front. Different authors and instructors will vary on their estimates on the time to spend in the planning process because it is based on the individual. A more skilled, or more experienced individual may do less planning than someone who is not as confident. However, everyone plans out, at least, the required modules and the type of data flowing between the modules; even if it is done just on scratch paper. The key, also, is to revise your plan as you work through the coding and development process. As you start coding, you will discover "I did not think of that" scenarios. Go back, right then, and adjust your plan. The more you do so, the less likely that you will hit a "corner" that you cannot find a way to get around.

Always involve the user in your PDLC process, along with as strong a team of experts. Remember you are developing this project to make your customer happy. You may believe you have the ultimate design and solution. However, that does not matter if your user does not agree with you. Sometimes you do have to adjust your thinking to be more in line with the customer. Working in the industry I remember a major change-management system that was being created within my work group (I was so happy to not be involved in the project). The designers and coders created a very fancy and expensive, system that, once it was implemented in the data centers, was hardly used. Why? The data center personnel did not want a fancy system; they wanted a simple system that could quickly complete the tasks needed. Even though the original project took six months to complete, a data center employee spent a few weekends of his own time creating another system that accomplished what they wanted. That system was implemented and used for many years afterward.

Commonly the PDLC is defined with five steps; Planning and Information Gathering, Analysis, Design, Implementation, and Evaluation. In the planning and information gathering step, all requirements for the project and the project team are assembled. Initial documents are also created answering the questions "What are we trying to accomplish?", "How are we going to accomplish it?", and "What team are we going to use?" In the analysis step, a determination is made as to the feasibility of the project. Documents answer the questions "Can we accomplish the project with the team and resources available?", "What additional resources need to be gathered?", and "Can the project be accomplished in the timeframe and budget allocated?" If the project makes it past the analysis step (many projects don't), then the actual design begins. In the design phase, a top-down approach begins by first looking at the overall required modules, and the data flow between the modules. More details are gradually added as the methods required are determined, a platform is decided on, communication tools come together, and information storage is designed.

After a detailed design has been created, and approved, the project goes into development and testing. Both unit testing (individual modules) and complete application testing will occur. After successful testing, the project is ready for the Implementation Step. During implementation decisions have to be made on how to install the project and when to install it. After implementation, the application is "live". But still continuous evaluation should occur to determine efficiently needs, security problems, logical problems, and possible overall enhancements to the project. Eventually, most projects will then revert back to the first step of the process for the development of a new version.

This section assumes that the planning and information gathering and analysis steps have been completed successfully, which would move you into the design step. We will look, in general, at the process of determining what type of activities should occur in which tiers of an application. We will also look at the type of data or information that may flow between the tiers. In later chapters we will refine this analysis by determining the types of methods that would be required and the information and data that must flow into and out of these methods. We will also look at the actual activities and code that would be created for these methods.

The best way to learn is by doing, so let's look at a case problem and go from there.

## Case Study

*Company*: Atomic Fish Hatchery, Inc.

*Project*: Field Sales Ordering and Commission Application

*Scope*: This application will be accessible from multiple devices (mobile and PC) to allow field sales agents, managers, and payroll personnel easy access to necessary information. The system will accept information from the sales agent that will be used to determine purchase costs to the customer, sales volume for the sales manager, and commissions for the payroll department. Phase one of the project is the development of the application to accept information from the sales agents, display purchase cost, determination of commissions, and storage of the information into a MySQL database. After successful testing the platform, it will be moved and secured in the company's cloud platform.

*Inputs (from Sales Agent)*: Sales Agent Number, Customer Number, Order Number, Item Number, Quantity, and Special Needs

*Outputs*: (Additional information may be determined for future phases)

*To database*: In addition to the input from the sales agent: commission, sales total

The goal is to determine the types of information and processes that will occur in each tier and the data flow between the tiers. Once determined, this information could be used to develop a general empty structure of tiers that would eventually hold the completed project.

## Interface Tier

The company has requested access from multiple devices. Thus, we must keep in mind that mobile devices (tablets and smart phones) will be used to input and output information in addition to laptops and PCs. We may decide to create multiple interfaces for each type of device. With three-tier design, you could design a system that shares the business rules tier and data tier contents while allowing this flexibility.

As a designer and/or programmer, you must determine the type of information that will be entered; several fields (Sales Agent Number, Customer Number, Order Number, Item Number, and Quantity) all indicate that numbers will be entered. You need to determine the size of these fields and verify that only numeric information is entered. The Amount field is the only field that possibly could be used in a future calculation. Therefore, all other fields can remain in text format. The Amount field would need to be converted to integer format before passing the information to the business rules tier. The Special Needs field would be a larger field that can accept alphanumeric characters. The database does not currently exist, so you would determine field sizes from company policy and/or current paper forms used. Once reviewed, it has been determined that the customer and sales agent numbers are eight characters. The order number and item numbers are currently six characters.

After gathering this information, you can now design the top view of the interface tier, as shown in Figure 2-16.

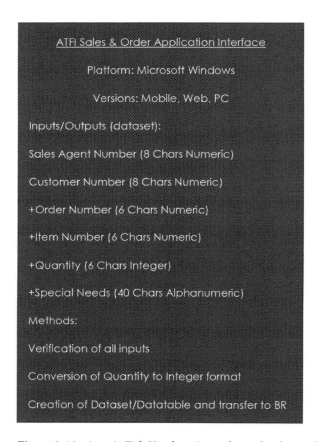

**Figure 2-16.** *Atomic Fish Hatchery Inc. sales and order application interface*

Fields with + may be used more than once to enter in all information by the sales agent. When the actual datasets and data tables are created, multiple columns must be available for these entries.

An additional form (not pictured) would also exist to display the results of the order. This form would display a summary of the items purchased and the total cost. All information could be entered by the sales agent, submitted, and held in the interface tier (a cookie?), until the sales agent indicated that the order is complete. Then the information could be transferred to the business rules tier for processing. The business rules tier could then return the information to be displayed in the second form. The second form could include an "approved" (or cancel) button. Once "approved," the information could then be passed to the data tier for storage.

## Business Rules Tier

The business rules tier would include two processes. One process would accept the complete order (dataset/data table) and determine the total sales cost after the sales agent clicked a "competed order" button. It would then return a summary of this information to the second form. The other process would execute when the agent clicks an "approved" button. The process would then determine the commission and create a dataset (there are now additional fields) to be passed to the data tier. The information would then be passed for storage.

Additionally, to make sure order data is valid, methods would be needed to validate the fields received from the interface. The top view of the Business Rules Tier would the following shown in Figure 2-17.

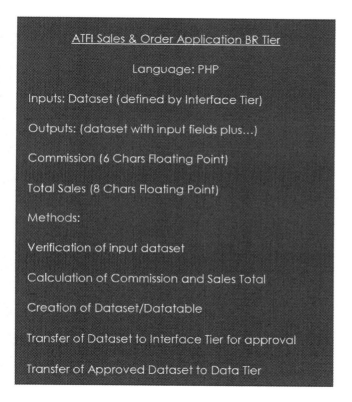

ATFi Sales & Order Application BR Tier

Language: PHP

Inputs: Dataset (defined by Interface Tier)

Outputs: (dataset with input fields plus...)

Commission (6 Chars Floating Point)

Total Sales (8 Chars Floating Point)

Methods:

Verification of input dataset

Calculation of Commission and Sales Total

Creation of Dataset/Datatable

Transfer of Dataset to Interface Tier for approval

Transfer of Approved Dataset to Data Tier

*Figure 2-17. Atomic sales and order application business rules tier*

## Data Tier

In this case, the data tier is only used to store the information provided by the business rules tier. The tier would verify the information received and store it into the database, as shown in Figure 2-18.

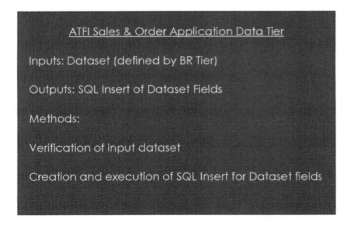

**Figure 2-18.** *Atomic sales and order application data tier*

There are many tools available to help in the design process. The important factor is that the designer include all the important information in the process. As an alternative to the example, you could remove the description of the datasets from the tiers and place them in the data flow between the tiers, as shown in Figure 2-19.

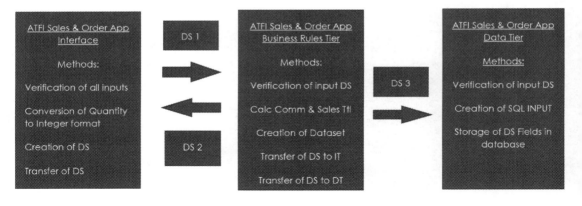

**Figure 2-19.** *Alternate three-tier model*

Dataset 1 (DS 1):

Sales Agent Number (8 Chars Numeric)

Customer Number (8 Chars Numeric)

+Order Number (6 Chars Numeric)

+Item Number (6 Chars Numeric)

+Quantity (6 Chars Integer)

+Special Needs (40 Chars Alphanumeric)

Dataset 2 (DS 2):

Sales Agent Number (8 Chars Numeric)

Customer Number (8 Chars Numeric)

+Order Number (6 Chars Numeric)

+Item Number (6 Chars Numeric)

+Quantity (6 Chars Integer)

+Special Needs (40 Chars Alphanumeric)

Commission (6 Chars Floating Point)

Total Sales (8 Chars Floating Point)

Dataset 3 (DS 3):

Sales Agent Number (8 Chars Numeric)

Customer Number (8 Chars Numeric)

+Order Number (6 Chars Numeric)

+Item Number (6 Chars Numeric)

+Quantity (6 Chars Integer)

+Special Needs (40 Chars Alphanumeric)

Commission (6 Chars Floating Point)

Total Sales (8 Chars Floating Point)

*Figure 2-20.* *Atomic Sales and Order Application Three-Tier Model*

## Do It

1. When must you convert numbers to numeric form (such as Integer) for storage within a database?

2. Why use datasets to pass information between tiers?

3. What items have been missed or ignored in the case example?

# MVC and Dependency Injection

MVC (Model-View-Controller) is a design pattern used by software engineers (including PHP application designers) to communicate between the view and model using a controller. The *controller* is software that transfers any user input to the model. MVC design can be considered circular because the model, controller, and view have the ability to communicate with each other. The standard three-tier model is linear; for the Interface to receive or pass information to the data tier, it must pass the information through the business rules tier. There are many tools on the market (such as Ruby on Rails) that can assist software engineers in designing MVC applications.

> *Visit thenewboston.com for a generic example of an MVC application:*
>
> `https://www.thenewboston.com/videos.php?cat=88`

MVC and Component Based Design can use **Dependency Injection**. Dependency Injection allows the program (client) that will use a block of code (such as a class) while not know the actual implementation of the block of code. This allows for independent development, updating, testing, and reusability of modules. This is similar to the ability of the ignition of a car communicating with the starter. The ignition has little knowledge of the starter component and how it operates. It does not even know the brand of starter. The ignition merely knows to send a signal (electricity) to the starter to tell it to operate. If the starter is replaced, the ignition is unaware and unaffected by the change, as long as the starter still operates when it receives the signal. While MVC and dependency injection are advanced topics, we will explore on example of dependency injection in Chapter 4.

# Chapter Terms

| | |
|---|---|
| Platform or Container | GTK SDK |
| Smart Phone API | Facebook Canvas Platform |
| Facebook API | Facebook Developer's Page |
| AJAX | HTTP GET |
| XMLHttpRequest | document.getElementById |
| CSS | Conditional Statement |
| If Statement | Three-Tier Architecture |
| Interface Tier | Business Rules Tier |
| Data Tier | Graphical User Interface (GUI) |
| Objects | Verification Code |
| Events | Database Management System |
| Servers | Application Servers |
| Web Servers | Service |
| Dataset | JSON |
| XML | SOAP |
| WSDL | SQL |

(*continued*)

| | |
|---|---|
| Microsoft Azure | PDLC |
| Planning and Information Gathering | Analysis Step |
| Design Step | Implementation Step |
| Evaluation Step | MVC (Model-View-Controller) |
| Dependency Injection | |

# Chapter Questions and Projects

**Multiple Choice**

1. The interface tier

   a. Is the primary storage location for the application, which may include the use of a database

   b. Provides common objects, including textboxes and buttons, that help the user quickly adapt to new applications

   c. Should be used for any accounting, mathematical calculations, or processing of data related to the application

   d. Displays information and provides the user the ability to interact with the application

2. A *service* is an application that

   a. Can be manually started and stopped when required

   b. Does not have an interface

   c. Resides in the memory of a computer

   d. All of the above

3. SOAP stands for

   a. Security Object Access Protocol

   b. Simple Object Access Process

   c. Simple Object Access Protocol

   d. None of the above

4. The five steps of PDLC are

   a. Planning and Information Storing, Analysis, Design, Implementation, and Evaluation

   b. Planning and Information Gathering, Analysis, Design, Implementation, and Evaluation

   c. Planning and Information Gathering, Analysis, Data, Implementation, and Evaluation

   d. Planning and Information Gathering, Analysis, Design, Observing, and Evaluation

5.  The Web Service Description Language is used to

    a.  Describe calls to the web server and the format of information sent and returned by the web service

    b.  Describe calls to the web service and the format of information accepted by the web service

    c.  Describe the code being used in HTML documents

    d.  Describe calls to the web service and discard the information received

6.  CSS stands for

    a.  Cascading Static Styles

    b.  Cascading Style Sheets

    c.  Cascading Script Sheets

    d.  Cache Style Scripts

7.  What type of code belongs between the `<script>`……`</script>` tags?

    a.  Java

    b.  HTML

    c.  Servlets

    d.  Javascript

8.  What is the three-tier architecture composed of?

    a.  GUI/tags/validation

    b.  interface/business/data access

    c.  Objects/variables/SQL

    d.  JSPs/servlets/sockets

9.  The best description for the Model View Controller (MVC) is

    a.  An architectural pattern that divides a given software application into three interconnected parts.

    b.  A programming language used to validate and secure information in any browser.

    c.  A type of validator mainly used to check if the user entered the information on the correct format

    d.  A type of method that is used to convert a harmful code so it cannot be executed by the compiler.

10. What is performed in the Analysis step?

    a.  Determination of the feasibility of the project

    b.  Creation the code and error correction

    c.  Determination of the logical data flow of the project

    d.  Re-evaluation of the implemented application for possible improvements

11.     Why must you validate your code?

    a.     To determine the capabilities of the browser you are using

    b.     To make sure your information is correct and secure

    c.     To make sure that you have only JavaScript and HTML5 code

    d.     To check if your browser can run your code

12.     What is the correct HTML syntax for referring to an external cascading style sheet?

    a.     `<stylesheet>my_style_sheet.css</stylesheet>`

    b.     `<link rel="stylesheet" type="text/css" href="my_style_sheet.css">`

    c.     `<style src="my_style_sheet.css">`

    d.     None of these

13.     Which tier is used to store and retrieve data?

    a.     Presentation tier

    b.     Data tier

    c.     Application tier

    d.     None of these

14.     What does SQL stand for?

    a.     Structured Question Language

    b.     Structured Query Language

    c.     Strong Question Language

15.     Which is true about smart phone APIs?

    a.     The smart phone APIs allow procedural (method) calls to be made to the phones operating system.

    b.     The smart phone APIs will allow web applications to make procedural (method) calls to the phone's operating system.

    c.     The smart phone APIs re not needed for applications that use GPS.

    d.     Not all smart phones come equipped with an API.

16.     A dataset is similar to

    a.     A paragraph of data

    b.     Sets of two words together

    c.     A table or spreadsheet

    d.     None of these

**True/False**

1. Facebook Canvas Platform can accept apps written in any code, not just in PHP.

2. WSDL stands for Web Service Definition Language.

3. AJAX is used to create more interactive applications.

4. AJAX provides the ability to dynamically change portions of a web page with reloading the complete page.

5. When using the HTTP GET function, the URL must be in quotation marks.

6. A service is a function provided by a web server.

7. The design step comes after the analysis steps have been completed successfully.

8. MVC (Model-View-Controller) is a design pattern used by software engineers (including PHP application designers) to communicate between the view and model using a controller.

9. Planning and information gathering is part of the PDLC.

10. Dependency Injection allows the program client to enter a block of code to know the implementation of the block of code it will be using.

11. Objects are blocks of code that have already been compiled for use within an application.

12. HTML stands for Hypertext Markup Language.

13. Method signature includes the method name, and the number, types, and order of its parameter.

14. Datasets are not one of the many formats used when sending data between tiers in a three-tier architecture.

**Short Answer/Essay**

1. In your own words, briefly describe each of the steps in the PDLC.

2. Why do you think development of PC applications using PHP has decreased?

3. Why do you think some web sites do not allow themselves to be inserted inside other sites (such as the Facebook Canvas)?

4. What are the advantages of creating web pages that use AJAX?

**Projects**

1. Using the steps of the PDLC demonstrated in this chapter, design the logic for a smart phone and mobile device application that allows your water meter reader to enter the full address and meter readings. The application should validate the information and send valid information to a MySQL database. If the information is not valid, a message should be displayed back to the user indicating the problem.

2.  Adjust the AJAX example in this chapter (the code is available on the book's web site) to display a mini version of your resume.

3.  Adjust the Hello World (Example 2-6, callmyself.php) program to display your college/university name, address, and main phone number.

**Term Project**

1.  Using the information you have determined from the Chapter 1 Term Project assignment and the design techniques shown in this chapter, develop a logical design of the ABC Computer Parts Inventory application. This design should include all possible programs, interfaces, and data storage. The application design must be three-tier (interface, business rules, and data). Your final design should look similar to the examples shown in this chapter.

# CHAPTER 3

# Modular Programming

*"Yes, I am a terrible coder, but I am probably still better than you :)"*

—Rasmus Lerdorf

## Chapter Objectives/Student Learning Outcomes

After completing this chapter, the student will be able to:

- Create an error-free simple objected-oriented (OO) modular PHP program
- Create a PHP class and make an instance of the class (object)
- Create an OO PHP encapsulated program, including GET and SET methods
- Create PHP methods (functions) that accept parameters and return information
- Create PHP public and private properties (variables)
- Import existing PHP code from another file or library into a program
- Validate information received using ternary (conditional) operators

## PHP Libraries, Extensions, Classes, and Objects

One of the strengths of PHP is the ability to easily store modules of code in libraries. Once code has been installed in a library it can easily be reused in other programs. The reuse of code that has already been well tested and used in "live" environments greatly reduces program errors and increases productivity because you don't have to reinvent the wheel. There is no need to recreate code that is already successfully working. It's a waste of time and energy and likely to cause unnecessary program errors. The programmer actually may not know what actual code exists in a module of code (class). However, the programmer knows what parameters (such as numbers) can be passed into the "black box" and what is returned (sum of the numbers) from the black box.

It may concern you that the programmer blindly passes information into the black box and blindly receives information back. However, this is an advantage, not a disadvantage. This allows the creator of the module to update the code without affecting the way the module is used. As long as the module accepts the same input and returns the same output, the programmer who is using the module notices no changes. Updates can occur to the module for better efficiently, better security, or to correct any program code problems without causing the users to change how they handle the module in their code.

**Electronic supplementary material**  The online version of this chapter (doi:10.1007/978-1-4842-1730-6_3) contains supplementary material, which is available to authorized users.

# PHP Extensions

***Example 3-1.*** Extensions in the php.ini file

```
extension=php_bz2.dll
extension=php_curl.dll
;extension=php_fileinfo.dll
extension=php_gd2.dll
;extension=php_gettext.dll
;extension=php_gmp.dll
;extension=php_intl.dll
;extension=php_imap.dll
;extension=php_interbase.dll
;extension=php_ldap.dll
extension=php_mbstring.dll
;extension=php_exif.dll
extension=php_mysql.dll
extension=php_mysqli.dll
;extension=php_oci8.dll
```

> *For a complete list and explanation of PHP extensions, visit:*
>
> *http://php.net/manual/en/extensions.alphabetical.php.*

PHP has a large amount of libraries available with thousands of lines of well tested code. Example 3-1 is a partial copy of the php.ini file showing several **extensions** (libraries) that are available to be activated in PHP. Each of these libraries is C code with a PHP wrapper (for better communication with PHP programs). The code is already compiled (notice the .dll extensions). A library that exists in the PHP environment can be activated by removing the comment symbol (;) in front of the extension statement in the php.ini file. Once the INI file has been saved, PHP and Apache must be reloaded (see Chapter 1 for examples on the location of the php.ini file and reloading PHP and Apache). This ease of adding libraries is one of the reasons PHP has become so popular. Additional libraries can be "installed" into PHP using several methods. One of the more popular methods, *Pear* (PHP Extension and Application Repository), handles code distribution and maintenance of third-party libraries.

> *The use of Pear and other third-party library installation methods is beyond the scope of this book. However, you can find additional information at the link below.*
>
> *http://pear.php.net/manual/en/about.pear.php.*

In addition, programmers can "install" their own libraries of code (that are not already compiled) directly into an application via the require or require_once statement. It is common practice in corporations to include code that may be reused many times (such as accessing a database). By providing this (well tested) code in a local library, any changes (such as the movement of the database to another server) can be handled in one location (the local library file), instead of requiring multiple files to be changed. This also reduces code redundancy and increases its reliability.

While local libraries can contain just methods (functions) of code, it is more common that modules (classes) exist in these libraries. This allows programmers to code with the "black box" concept previously mentioned. The three-tier architecture (explained in Chapter 2) is based on this premise. The code classes can be accessed from the library by referencing the library containing the code (via the require or require_once statement). Once a reference is made, an instance of the class (object) is then created. Once an instance has been created, the program code has access to all the functionality of the object.

## Classes and Objects

A class is similar to a blueprint of a house. The blueprint contains a description (characteristics) of all the elements needed to construct the house. However, the blueprint is not the actual house itself. It describes what is possible if we hire a crew and construct the house. The blueprint is not considered to exist (as a house would exist). However, it describes the items needed to build the house (nails, drywall, and wood) and the process to build the house.

A *class* describes the characteristics (properties) of the module of code and the *actions* (methods or functions) that can occur in that code. However, it does not physically exist (within memory) until an instance of the class (called an object) is created. Once an instance is created, the characteristics and methods can be accessed. Classes and objects (when created properly) protect the characteristics (properties) from direct access. This provides the object the opportunity to verify that any request to change a value in a property is valid before the change occurs. This is commonly called *encapsulation.* To protect properties from direct access to the outside world, they should be declared using the private access type. Private access will only allow methods within the class the ability to change the values in the properties. Set **methods** (discussed later in this chapter) are used to change properties. Get **methods** (also discussed later in this chapter) are normally used to retrieve property values.

# Creating a PHP Class

Let's begin by creating a basic structure for a class. You will create a dog class which will allow you to set some characters of the dog (size, breed, color, and name) and you will provide the ability for the dog to speak and to display the values saved in each property. You will create the dog class in a separate file (library) that can be loaded into the program (or any other program) when needed.

To create a PHP class, you use the class keyword and encapsulate all code within the class in { }.

*Example 3-2.* Basic class structure in the dog.php file

```php
<?php
class Dog
{
// all code is placed here
}
?>
```

As seen in Example 3-2, the class keyword is lowercase. However, the name of the class, Dog, begins with an uppercase letter. PHP will allow you to create a class with a lowercase first letter. However, it is common practice to easily identify classes by the use of the uppercase first letter. The actual file name containing your class (dog.php) should also match the class name (Dog).

> For more information on classes, methods, and properties visit php.net at:
>
> http://php.net/manual/en/classobj.examples.php.
>
> For videos, visit "the new boston" at:
>
> https://www.thenewboston.com/videos.php?cat=11&video=17175.

Class names cannot include spaces. You should also avoid using special characters. However, the _ is permitted and commonly used to connect two words together (set_name). You many notice that some class names include two underscores (__) before the actual class name (__Myclass). However, this is not a recommended technique due to the existence of "magical" classes (we will look at two of these classes later in this chapter) that use this format.

As mentioned previously, a class contains properties. *Properties* are also called *variables*. Properties include characteristics of the class. When an instance of a class is created, the properties are unique for that object. The operating system reserves a space in memory to hold the properties. The operating system handles memory management for us, including cleaning up properties that are no longer needed. In PHP, anytime a closing bracket (}) is reached, properties that have been created are scheduled for removal by the garbage collector of the operating system. The program can no longer access the property at that point.

Properties can hold many different types of data. In most languages, when a property is created you must also include a data type to describe the kind of data being stored (such as string). However, PHP does not require the defining of a data type. PHP determines the type of data to be stored in a property the first time data is placed in the property. Properties are created with an initial $ and the name of the property. Property names can include alphabetic characters, numbers, and the _. The _ can be used at the beginning of the property (after the $) or between words. No spaces are allowed. Properties are commonly created with lowercase letters. However, PHP does allow uppercase letters. PHP is case-sensitive and will consider a lowercase property (speak) and an uppercase property (Speak) two different properties.

***Example 3-3.*** Basic class structure with properties in dog.php file

```php
<?php
class Dog
{
private $dog_size = 0;
private $dog_breed = "no breed";
private $dog_color = "no color";
private $dog_name = "no name";
}
?>
```

> *Program design recommendation—Properties are created on the fly in PHP. Properties are created the first time you use them. This can both be a help and a pain. If you misspell a property name, PHP will not produce an error. Instead it will create a new property with the misspelled name. It is recommended (when possible) that properties be created with initial values at the top of your program (or method, or class) to more easily determine what your property name is and whether it has been created.*

As seen in Example 3-3, each of the properties (except $dog_size) for the Dog class has been declared private and initially set with a string (text). The $dog_size property has been set to the number zero (we know it is a number and not a string because there are no "" around the zero). The operating system will store the strings values in the properties ($dog_breed, $dog_color, and $dog_name) in ASCII format (combinations of zeros and ones to represent each character) and will store the value in the $dog_size property in a numerical format in memory. The operating system creates memory tables to look up the actual memory address of the value in a variable when it is used in a program.

---

▓ **Note**    The format of the code must also include a semicolon at the end of the code statements (all code lines that are executed must include semicolons).

---

As you may note, at this point the example is not very useful. Even if you were to create an instance of the class, you could not access anything in the class or display the values in the properties. Let's add a method to the class to allow you to display what is contained in the class. To do so, you need to create a method to display the values using the print statement. You can also take this opportunity to build one single string of output using *string concatenation*.

String concatenation can be done in several ways in PHP. In many languages, building strings with properties require continuously opening and closing a string (using "").

```
print "Dog_weight is " . $this->dog_weight  . ". Dog breed is " . $this->dog_breed . "Dog
color is " . $this->dog_color;
```

The print code line above is valid in PHP. However, as you can see, you have a lot of quotes and many periods. It can be difficult to get everything matched up correctly. The period is a string concatenation character in PHP and would be required, if you choose to use this technique (you would have to use a similar madness in many languages). However, PHP is much friendlier than this.

*This pointer—The $this pointer is used to gain access to properties contained in an object. this indicates that the code wants to retrieve the value contained in a property that exists in the particular object (instance of the class). Soon we will be creating an instance of the class named $lab. When the code that will exist in the $lab instance is executed, the $this pointer will tell the operating system that it wants the value in the property (such as dog_weight) that exists in the $lab instance only. Note that the format of the statement includes a $ sign for the $this pointer but not for the variable ($this->dog_weight).*

*You might ask, why do we need the $this pointer? The simple answer is that you can create a property that exists for every instance of the class (called a static property). If this type of property changed, it would change for all the instances of the class. Our private properties only change for the particular instance ($lab) of the class in which it was referenced.*

```
print "Dog weight is $this->dog_weight. Dog breed is $this->dog_breed. Dog color is
$this->dog_color.";
```

PHP allows you to place properties within strings (quotes). This allows you to use fewer periods and quotes (and maybe reduce pulling too many hairs from your head).

*For examples of the $this pointer, visit:*

*http://php.net/manual/en/language.oop5.basic.php*

*For videos of the $this pointer, visit:*

*https://www.thenewboston.com/videos.php?cat=11&video=17177*

Now that you have the code needed to produce an output, you need to add a method in the class to execute the print line. All "actions" that take place in a class must be included in a method. Methods are created in a similar style as classes (except they are actually contained within the classes). Methods are declared using the keyword function followed by a method name and (). It is common practice for method names to be lowercase, although PHP will accept uppercase characters. The _ can also be included at the beginning or within the method name. All code with a method is contained within {}.

***Example 3-4.*** Basic class structure with properties and a method in dog.php file

```php
<?php
class Dog
{
        private $dog_weight = 0;
        private $dog_breed = "no breed";
        private $dog_color = "no color";
        private $dog_name = "no name";
```

```
    function display_properties()
    {
        print "Dog weight is $this->dog_weight. Dog breed is $this->dog_breed. Dog color is
        $this->dog_color.";
    }
}
?>
```

*Program design recommendation—As seen in Example 3-4, it becomes much more important to be aware of the proper use of the opening and closing brackets ({ and }). For every open bracket, there must be a closing bracket. It can become difficult to determine if you are missing something. Editors (discussed in Chapter 1) can help color code everything to make it easier to see. Also, indenting (as seen in Example 3-4) can help visually line up the brackets. The PHP engine ignores extra spacing (called whitespace). So the programmer can make the code more visually pleasing and easier to debug.*

This class now has the ability to perform an action (via the `display_properties` method). So you can finally test its functionality. In order to do so, the code from Example 3-4 must be placed in the `dog.php` file (same as the class name) in the same location as the program that will use it.

We now need to create a program that will pull in this library (via the `require_once` statement). The program will then need to make an instance of the class (Dog). Finally, the program will need to call the method (`display_properties`) to display the contents of the properties.

*Program design recommendation—PHP will allow the `include`, `include_once`, `require`, and `require_once` statements to be used anywhere in your program code. This could cause potential issues if it's used in the incorrect location or used more than once. It is strongly recommended that these statements be include together as close to the top of your code as possible for easy review to determine if libraries have already been installed.*

*Security and reliability—PHP has several methods available to pull libraries into PHP programs. The `include` method will attempt to pull in a library. However, if the library does not exist, the program will continue to run (or crash). The `include` method also does not concern itself with possibility that the library might already have been attached to the code. It is possible that a large program might accidentally try to pull in the same library more than once (which would crash the program due to duplicate method and/or class names). The `include_once` method eliminates the possibility of attempting to pull in a library more than once. If the library has already been included, the statement will not execute. The `require` method does not allow the program to continue running if the library cannot be found. However, like the `include` method, it could attempt to pull in the same library more than once. The `require_once` method solves these potential problems by shutting the program down if the library cannot be found and by only installing the library if it has not already been installed.*

The format of the `require_once` statement is simple. The keyword `require_once` is followed with the library name (`dog.php`). The statement should be included near the top of your code and before you make an actual instance of the class (Dog).

```
require_once("dog.php");
```

*You can include path names within a* `require_once` *statement. However, it is recommended that you do not include absolute paths. For more information visit:*

`http://php.net/manual/en/function.require-once.php`

*For Examples visit:*

`https://www.thenewboston.com/videos.php?cat=11&video=17028`

*For videos visit:*

`https://www.thenewboston.com/videos.php?cat=11&video=17029.`

To create an instance of a class, a property is created that "points" to the instance of the class in memory. The new keyword is included to inform the operating system that an instance of the class should be created in memory (and the constructor method should execute, as mentioned later). The actual class name is included to determine which class is to be built into an object.

```
$lab = new Dog;
```

This code would create an instance of the Dog class and refer to it with the $lab property (pointer). Actual individual copies of each of the properties ($dog_size, $dog_breed, $dog_color, and $dog_name) are created for each instance of a class. This allows you to change what is in the properties for that instance ($lab) without changing the properties for other.

```
$lab->display_properties();
```

Once the instance is created, you can then access any methods by using the object name ($lab) and the method name (display_properties).

***Example 3-5.*** Basic program structure including a library, object, and method call in lab.php

```
<?php
require_once('dog.php');
$lab = new Dog;
$lab->display_properties();
?>
```

Figure 3-1 shows the successful output of the lab.php program, which includes the Dog class contained in the dog.php file.

***Figure 3-1.*** *Output of lab.php*

*For more examples on creating an object (instance of a class), visit:*

*Examples:* `http://php.net/manual/en/language.oop5.basic.php`

*Videos:* `https://www.thenewboston.com/videos.php?cat=11&video=17181.`

# Do It

1.  Add a speak method to the Dog class to give each instance the ability to "bark". Hint: Include a print (or echo) statement in your method. Add a call to your speak method after the call to the display_properties method in the lab.php file.

2.  Create a second object from the Dog class in the lab.php file called $chow. Call the speak method (#1) to make him "bark".

3.  Create a new library file that contains a class of another animal of your choice. Within that class, create four properties that provide characteristics of that animal. Include a method that will print each of these characteristics. Also include a method that will cause the animal to speak. Create another file that will use this library file to create an instance of the class. The program should also call the method to display the properties and the method to cause the animal to speak.

*Program errors—If you encountered errors when trying this example, check the following:*

1.  *Did you name the class (Dog) and the file name (dog.php) the same? Make sure the file ending is .php and not .txt for both the dog.php and lab.php files.*

2.  *In the require_once statement in the lab.php file, is the file name exactly the same as the dog.php file?*

3.  *Are the dog.php and lab.php files in the same folder?*

4.  *Did you include the same amount of opening ({) and closing (}) brackets in both programs?*

5.  *Did you forget any semicolons (;)?*

6.  *For each $this statement, make sure the $ is part of this and not of the property ($this->dog_weight).*

7.  *For any other errors, copy and paste your error into a search engine to find possible solutions. Remember, the error may be in either the Apache or PHP error logs (see Chapter 1 for details).*

# Return Method

In Chapter 2, the business rules tier was defined to contain modules of code that return information requested, but do not provide an interface or format for displaying the data returned. In the previous example, the Dog class violates this requirement. However, you can fix this problem with just a few code changes to the dog.php and lab.php files.

The print statement in the Dog class should be replaced. However, you want to pass multiple values (dog_weight, dog_color, dog_breed, and dog_name) back to the program that has called it. There are many ways that you can accomplish this task. However, since you are just starting programming, let's keep it simple. We can create a comma-delimitated string easily by reformatting the original string. You can replace the print statement with

```
Return "$this->dog_weight, $this->dog_breed, $this->dog_color.";
```

The new Dog class would now contain what's shown in Example 3-6.

***Example 3-6.*** Basic Dog class with return statement—dog.php

```php
<?php
class Dog
{
private $dog_weight = 0;
private $dog_breed = "no breed";
private $dog_color = "no color";
private $dog_name = "no name";

function get_properties()
{

return "$this->dog_weight,$this->dog_breed,$this->dog_color.";

}
}
?>
```

---

■ **Note**   In PHP 7, you can enable Scalar Type Hints. PHP 7 provides the developer the ability to declare the data type that is expected to be returned. The function in Example 3-6 could be coded as follows.

```php
declare(strict_types=1);
function get_properties() : string
{
return "$this->dog_weight,$this->dog_breed,$this->dog_color.";
}
```

If the `declare` statement is not included or `strict_types=0`, the data type will not be enforced. The current valid data types that can be used are `string`, `int`, `float`, and `bool`.

Since Scalar Type Hints are not backward compatable, they are not used in the examples in this book.

---

You now need to adjust the `lab.php` file to be able to accept what has been passed back from the `get_properties` method (`display_properties` is renamed `get_properties` to reflect that it no longer displays the properties; it now returns them). You can accomplish this by creating a property in the `lab.php` file to receive what has been passed back from the `get_properties` method.

```php
$dog_properties = $lab->get_properties();
```

If you were to use the `print` function to display `$dog_properties` at this point, you would display:

```
no weight, no breed, no color
```

However, we intended to produce a similar result as was shown previously. You can do this, but you need to be able to break the string into three pieces based on the "," delimiter. Luckily there are PHP methods available that can easily accomplish this task. The `explode` method will break a string based on a delimiter.

The substrings (pieces of the string) can then be dropped into individual properties using a list object. For our needs, you can split the $dog_properties string as follows.

```
list($dog_weight, $dog_breed, $dog_color) = explode(',', $dog_properties);
```

*For more information on the explode function, visit:*

```
http://php.net/manual/en/function.explode.php
```

This will drop no weight into $dog_weight, no breed into $dog_breed, and no color into $dog_color. These three properties are also being created inside the lab.php program in this same line of code. I happen to give them the same names as their counterparts in the Dog class. However, remember if you had not created the Dog class, you would not know the original variable names. It would not matter, because you can call them anything you want and accomplish the same task.

Now that you have the variables containing the information, you can recreate the original print statement in the lab.php program instead of in the dog.php library.

```
print "Dog weight is $dog_weight. Dog breed is $dog_breed. Dog color is $dog_color.";
```

Notice that you did *not* include the $this pointer. You are not executing this statement within a class. You don't create instances of the lab.php program. There is only one instance of the program (because it is not a class and cannot have multiple instances). So the $this pointer is unnecessary.

The new lab.php program would now look like Example 3-7.

**Example 3-7.** The lab.php program with print statement

```
<?php
require_once("dog.php");
$lab = new Dog;
$dog_properties = $lab->get_properties();
list($dog_weight, $dog_breed, $dog_color) = explode(',', $dog_properties);
print "Dog weight is $dog_weight. Dog breed is $dog_breed. Dog color is $dog_color.";
?>
```

Assuming there are no errors in your program, the output will be the same as Figure 3-1, unchanged from the previous version of the program. However, the Dog class now meets one of the standards of the business rules tier by returning information to the program that calls it without attempting to format the output. The lab.php program now handles formatting the output.

# Do It

1.  Adjust the speak method in the dog.php file to return the bark string but not print it. Also adjust the call to the method in the lab.php file to display the output of the string. You can accept the string from the method and print the string in one line of code using syntax similar to the following:

    ```
    print $lab->speak();
    ```

2.  Adjust the $chow object in the lab.php file to properly handle the return of the properties string and the speak string.

3.  Adjust the animal class to return any strings instead of printing them. Adjust the program that makes an instance of the animal class to accept and display the strings that are returned.

# Set Methods

This example is still very limited because you can't currently adjust the values in the properties to relate to the actual objects you created (such as $lab). In order to adjust these properties, you must have some ability to access the properties from the program that uses the object (lab.php). However, because of encapsulation and security concerns, you do not want to expose the properties to be directly manipulated by the calling program. Object-oriented programming standards require that you create your properties as "private" (as you have done already) and then use actual methods in the class to change any values.

> *Security and reliability—Creating set methods in classes provides the ability for the class to verify that the information that is to be placed in a property is valid before the property is updated. If this verification is not done before changing the value in a property corruption of data could take place. After the fact, it may be impossible or very difficult to correct invalid data that has been accepted. Set methods can reject invalid data and return error messages to the calling program.*

A set method allows values to be passed into the method. These values can then be verified before updating the properties in the object. Parameters (values) are passed into a method between the parentheses ( ) in the method call.

```
$dog_error_message = $lab->set_dog_name('Fred');
```

If the set_dog_name method exists within the Dog class and accepts a string representing the name of the dog, you could use a method call similar to the previous code. This call would pass the string "Fred" into the set_dog_name method. It also provides the ability for the set method to return a value into the property $dog_error_message to indicate if the property was updated properly. You can simply pass a 'TRUE' or 'FALSE' Boolean value back from the method to indicate the status of the update. The calling program then can determine how to handle the status of the update.

If you simply pass back a 'TRUE' or 'FALSE' you can use a simplified version of the PHP conditional statement, called the *ternary operator* to check $dog_error_message.

```
print $dog_error_message == TRUE ? 'Name update successful<br/>' : 'Name update not
successful<br/>';
```

> *For more information on the ternary conditional operator, visit*
>
> *http://php.net/manual/en/language.operators.comparison.php*

> *Security and performance—Use caution when display error messages to actual live users of your applications. You can provide too much information and expose your program code unnecessarily. Displaying a generic error message to the user may be a safer option. In live applications, log files should be created to record errors and access to the application itself.*

With this format, the calling program (lab.php) can easily determine the status of the update and display a corresponding message. The message between the ? and the : ("Name update successful") will display if the string in $dog_error_message is 'TRUE'. If the value in $dog_error_message is 'FALSE' the string between the : and the ; ("Name update not successful") will display.

***Example 3-8.*** The lab.php file with set methods and error checking

```php
<?php
require_once("dog.php");
$lab = new Dog;
// ------------------Set Properties--------------------------
$dog_error_message = $lab->set_dog_name('Fred');
print $dog_error_message == TRUE ? 'Name update successful<br/>' : 'Name update not
successful<br/>';

$dog_error_message = $lab->set_dog_weight(50);
print $dog_error_message == TRUE ? 'Weight update successful<br />' : 'Weight update not
successful<br />';

$dog_error_message = $lab->set_dog_breed('Lab');
print $dog_error_message == TRUE ? 'Breed update successful<br />' : 'Breed update not
successful<br />';

$dog_error_message = $lab->set_dog_color('Yellow');
print $dog_error_message == TRUE ? 'Color update successful<br />' : 'Color update not
successful<br />';
//---------------------------Get Properties--------------------------
$dog_properties = $lab->get_properties();
list($dog_weight, $dog_breed, $dog_color) = explode(',', $dog_properties);
print "Dog weight is $dog_weight. Dog breed is $dog_breed. Dog color is $dog_color.";
?>
```

In Example 3-8, lab.php now has the ability to pass information into the properties in the $lab object of the Dog class. It also determines if the update for each property was successful and responds accordingly. There are opportunities in this example to be more efficient with the amount of code that you have created. However, we will hold off on efficiency until you have gathered a few more skills.

The lab.php code now calls a set method for each property to be updated (set_dog_name, set_dog_breed, set_dog_weight, and set_dog_color) and passes information into each method. Notice that strings are passed into each method, except for the set_dog_weight method, which accepts an integer (whole number) value.

You now need to create set methods within the Dog class. Each method now accepts a parameter (string or integer) and returns a 'TRUE' or 'FALSE' value. The method is created in a style similar to the previous get_properties method that you created. Let's keep the validation process simple for now and you'll learn how to improve it in later chapters.

```php
function set_dog_name($value)
{
$error_message = TRUE;
(ctype_alpha($value) && strlen($value) < 21) ? $this->dog_name = $value : $error_message = FALSE;
return $error_message;
}
```

The set_dog_name method will accept a string into the $value property (parameter) defined in the function header (function set_dog_name($value)). Next, the method creates a property $error_message and provides an initial value of TRUE. This property (along with the $value property) will only exist while the method is executing. As soon as the execution hits the } closing bracket, these properties will no longer be available.

*Programming note—TRUE and FALSE are constants that are included as part of the PHP language. Constants cannot be changed and are in all caps. TRUE is actually represented internally as a 1 and FALSE is represented internally as a 0.*

---

▓ **Note**   In PHP 7, Scalar Type Hints can be used to enforce the data type being passed and returned.

```
declare(strict_types = 1);
function set_dog_name(string $value) : string
{
$error_message = TRUE;
(ctype_alpha($value) && strlen($value) < 21) ? $this->dog_name = $value : $error_message = FALSE;
return $error_message;
}
```

If the declare line is not included or strict_types = 0, the data type will not be enforced. To allow for backward compatability, the examples in this textbook will not show the use of Scalar Type Hints.

---

*Programming note—&& is an AND operator. In order for the (ctype_alpha($value) && strlen($value) < 21) statement to be TRUE, $value must include only alphabetic characters and must be fewer than 21 characters.*

A ternary operator looks at the two possible statuses of the $value property (which contains whatever was passed into the method).

1.   The ctype method is used to determine if the characters in $value are alphabetic (ctype_alpha($value)).

2.   The strlen method is used to determine if the length of the string in $value is less than 21 characters (strlen($value) < 21).

To learn about additional ctype functions, visit:

http://php.net/manual/en/book.ctype.php.

If the $value property contains alphabetic characters only and is less than 21 characters, the $dog_name property is updated with the value that has been passed. If there are non-alphabetic characters or the length of the string is more than 20 characters, the $error_message is updated with a FALSE value (indicating the update did not occur). Finally, the value in $error_message (either TRUE or FALSE) is returned to the calling program.

*Security and performance—This process may be a bit confusing now. However, it is important to create secure programs. Whenever an application or object accepts information from an outside source (such as another program or user) the information must be validated. This validation should include limitations on the size of the information accepted, along with other restrictions. Data that has been passed across the Internet (such as from the user's browser to a web server) can be intercepted and changed. It is vital that the information be verified within the application on the server before it is used. Validation may be done in the browser (via JavaScript) to ensure the user has entered correct information. However, as stated, packet stiffing programs can intercept that information and change it before it is received by an application on a web server.*

One final note before you look at the code changes. PHP provides several operations to compare two values. The following table provides a summary of these operators, including the new PHP 7 Spaceship Operator.

```
                    Operation                Result - returns TRUE if...
                    $a == $b                 $a and $b are equal ignoring cases
                    $a === $b                $a and $b equal if case is the same
                    $a != $b, $a <> $b       $a and $b are not equal ignoring cases
                    $a !== $b                $a and $b are not equal or not same case
                    $a < $b                  $a is less than $b
                    $a <= $b                 $a is less than or equal to $b
                    $a > $b                  $a is greater than $b
                    $a >= $b                 $a is greater than or equal to $b
                    ---------------------------------------------------------
(Available with PHP 7)  $a <=> $b            returns -1 if $a < b, returns 0   if $a equals $b
                                             returns 1 if $a > $b
```

In addition, the Null Coalesce Operator can be used to check if a value is 'set' (contains something) before it is used in a ternary operation.

```
$dog_name = $_POST['value'] ?? 'No Name';
```

In this example, if something exists in value, it is placed in $dog_name. If value is not set, No Name is placed in $dog_name. This operator is available in PHP 7. To allow for backward capability, the examples in this book will not demonstrate this operator.

Let's update the Dog class to include all the set methods needed.

```php
<?php
class Dog
{
// ----------------------------------- Properties ------------------------------------------
private $dog_weight = 0;
private $dog_breed = "no breed";
private $dog_color = "no color";
private $dog_name = "no name";

}
```

***Example 3-9.*** Dog class with set methods in dog.php

```php
// ----------------------------- Set Methods ---------------------------------------------------
function set_dog_name($value)
{
$error_message = TRUE;
(ctype_alpha($value) && strlen($value) <= 20) ? $this->dog_name = $value : $error_message = FALSE;
return $error_message;
}
function set_dog_weight($value)
{
$error_message = TRUE;
(ctype_digit($value) && ($value > 0 && $value <= 120)) ? $this->dog_weight = $value :
$error_message = FALSE;
return $error_message;
}
```

```
function set_dog_breed($value)
{
$error_message = TRUE;
(ctype_alpha($value) && strlen($value) <= 35) ? $this->dog_breed = $value : $error_message = FALSE;
return $error_message;
}
function set_dog_color($value)
{
$error_message = TRUE;
(ctype_alpha($value) && strlen($value) <= 15) ? $this->dog_color = $value : $error_message = FALSE;
return $error_message;
}
}
function get_properties()
{
return "$this->dog_weight,$this->dog_breed,$this->dog_color.";
}
}
?>
```

*Program design recommendation—When coding and testing your programs, code just one* set *method. Then test the method to correct errors. After you have one successful* set *method, copy and paste it in your code and make the necessary changes. Do not attempt to completely code a program before testing it. Program piece by piece, then test. Although you may think that this slows down your coding, actually this is not true. By catching errors with each small addition to your program it will be easier to find them. If you attempt to code a complete program you may have lots of errors and could spend a lot of time trying to hunt down each error. If you are having difficulty finding an error, comment out (using //) the new lines of code in your program and retest. If all is okay, then gradually (just a few lines at a time) remove the comment lines (//) from your code lines and retest. This process should help you to find the lines of code that might be causing problems.*

*Security and performance—In a live environment the programmer should not display details to the users as to what caused an update to be unsuccessful. Providing too much information can inform hackers on what can be changed to successfully update properties with invalid information. Pass the details of what caused the unsuccessful update to a secure log file on a server.*

The code is starting to get lengthy. However, each of the set functions is very similar. As you code the set functions, you will find that this is a common occurrence. It also allows you to quickly create set methods once you have a working error free example by copying and pasting working methods and making simple changes. In Example 3-9 different string lengths are determined depending on the type of information being updated. Also, the $set_dog_weight method checks for numeric values in the string passed, instead of alphabetic characters. Otherwise, the methods are almost identical.

Figure 3-2 demonstrates the output when valid information is passed into each property. The 'successful' messages display. Also note that the get_properties method displays the new updated values for each property. In a live environment you might consider not displaying the successful messages and only displaying the not successful messages.

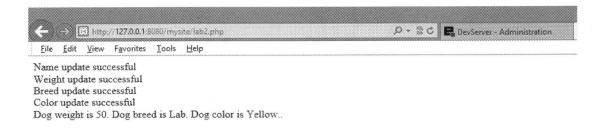

**Figure 3-2.** *Output of successful update via set methods in Dog class—dog.php and lab.php*

Figure 3-3 tests the output generated when invalid information has been passed to the set methods. Note that the default values are still in the properties that did not get updated. This stresses the need to include default values in case some properties do not get updated. In PHP, properties that are displayed and are NULL (have no value) do normally display a blank space for output. For example, if $dog_weight did not have a default value, the output would display "Dog weight is .".

**Figure 3-3.** *Output with invalid weight (1000) and invalid breed ('Lab12') in Dog class—dog.php and lab.php*

> *Program design recommendation—Although PHP is friendly and will attempt to change NULL values to spaces when displayed, it is not good programming to assume this will occur. Many program languages will not do this conversion for you and will display error messages when attempting to display properties with NULL values. Also, when using properties to do mathematical calculations, it is very important to set default values. PHP will, again, attempt to convert NULL values to zeros for calculations. However, in some cases this will not occur and an error message will display. In many program languages, error messages will occur when attempting to do a calculation with NULL values. Establishing programming habits that work for all languages will help you quickly develop skills for multiple languages.*

# Do It

1. Create an additional property ($dog_gender) in the Dog class. Create a set method (set_dog_gender). Determine if a valid value (Male, Female) has been passed into the set method. You can use the following code or develop your own version to check for valid information.

```
($value == 'Male' || $value == 'Female') ? $this->dog_gender =
$value : $error_message = FALSE;
```

2. Go to php.net and search for a method that will allow the checking of any case of "Male" or "Female" from #1. Update the conditional statement to allow any version (Male, MALE, male, Female, FEMALE, female, and so on). Hint: The characters in $value can be changed to all uppercase or all lowercase using the strtoupper or strtolower methods. Then check the string as all uppercase (MALE, FEMALE) or all lowercase (male, female) characters.

# Get Methods

In our previous examples, you created a get_properties method that returned multiple properties at the same time. This is a valid and useful method. However, it is common to have a get **method** to match each set method. This provides both write (set method) and read (get method) capabilities for the properties in a method. In some situations you may want to only provide a get method without a set method (making the property read-only). We could (although rarely done) provide a set method without a get method (making the property write-only).

Get methods are actually much easier to code than set methods. No verification of data is necessary because you are reading the data and not updating it.

```
function get_dog_name()
{
return $this->dog_name;
}
```

All that is necessary in the get method is the return statement, which returns the value in the property without the user of the object having direct access to the property.

*Example 3-10.* Dog class with set and get methods—dog.php

```php
<?php
class Dog
{
// ---------------------------------------- Properties ------------------------------------
private $dog_weight = 0;
private $dog_breed = "no breed";
private $dog_color = "no color";
private $dog_name = "no name";

}
```

```php
// ------------------------------- Set Methods -------------------------------------
function set_dog_name($value)
{
$error_message = TRUE;
(ctype_alpha($value) && strlen($value) <= 20) ? $this->dog_name = $value : $error_message = FALSE;
return $error_message;
}
function set_dog_weight($value)
{
$error_message = TRUE;
(ctype_digit($value) && ($value > 0 && $value <= 120)) ? $this->dog_weight = $value :
$error_message = FALSE;
return $error_message;
}
function set_dog_breed($value)
{
$error_message = TRUE;
(ctype_alpha($value) && strlen($value) <= 35) ? $this->dog_breed = $value : $error_message = FALSE;
return $error_message;
}
function set_dog_color($value)
{
$error_message = TRUE;
(ctype_alpha($value) && strlen($value) <= 15) ? $this->dog_color = $value : $error_message = FALSE;
return $error_message;
}
// ------------------------------------- Get Methods ------------------------------------
function get_dog_name()
{
return $this->dog_name;
}
function get_dog_weight()
{
return $this->dog_weight;
}
function get_dog_breed()
{
return $this->dog_breed;
}
function get_dog_color()
{
return $this->dog_color;
}
function get_properties()
{
return "$this->dog_weight,$this->dog_breed,$this->dog_color.";
}
}
?>
```

The code is lengthy. However, as pointed out previously, like the set methods, the get methods are very similar to each other. Once you have created one successful get method, you can copy and paste it to create the other methods. All that needs to change for each get method is the name of the method and the property being returned.

***Example 3-11.*** The lab.php program using set and get methods

```php
<?php
require_once("dog.php");
$lab = new Dog;
// ---------------------------Set Properties-------------------------
$dog_error_message = $lab->set_dog_name('Fred');
print $dog_error_message == TRUE ? 'Name update successful<br/>' : 'Name update not
successful<br/>';
$dog_error_message = $lab->set_dog_weight(50);
print $dog_error_message == TRUE ? 'Weight update successful<br />' : 'Weight update not
successful<br />';

$dog_error_message = $lab->set_dog_breed('Lab');
print $dog_error_message == TRUE ? 'Breed update successful<br />' : 'Breed update not
successful<br />';
$dog_error_message = $lab->set_dog_color('Yellow');
print $dog_error_message == TRUE ? 'Color update successful<br />' : 'Color update not
successful<br />';
// ---------------------------Get Properties-------------------------
print $lab->get_dog_name() . "<br/>";
print $lab->get_dog_weight() . "<br />";
print $lab->get_dog_breed() . "<br />";
print $lab->get_dog_color() . "<br />";
$dog_properties = $lab->get_properties();
list($dog_weight, $dog_breed, $dog_color) = explode(',', $dog_properties);
print "Dog weight is $dog_weight. Dog breed is $dog_breed. Dog color is $dog_color.";
?>
```

When viewing the code in Example 3-11, note that the print statements call the get methods (print $lab->get_dog_name() . "<br/>";). The order of operations, which will be discussed in more detail in a later chapter, causes the method (get_dog_name()) to be executed first, even though normally a line of code would execute from left to right. The method returns the value in dog_name (the string "Fred"). The string is placed in the same location in which the method call was located. After the get method executes, the code line is now

```php
print "Fred" . "<br/>";
```

Then the code line executes from left to right, producing the output

```
Fred <br/>
```

*Programming note—Unlike properties, methods must NOT be included in quotes ("" or ''). The string must be broken apart and concatenated using the '.', as shown in the example. If a method is included IN quotes, PHP will display an error message.*

95

As you can see from Figure 3-4, the get methods successfully display the updated values in the properties. If any properties were not updated, the get methods would display the default values.

> *Program design recommendation—While in coding and testing phase it is a good idea to display the values in your properties often to ensure that they are updated at the proper times. However, when you move a program from testing mode to production you should reduce the amount of display shown to the users. It probably is not necessary to show the users the update values in properties. It is usually best to just indicate to the users that the update was successful. You can simply comment out your unneeded print code lines before production. This then could help to quickly debug future upgrades to the application by simply removing comments from those lines.*

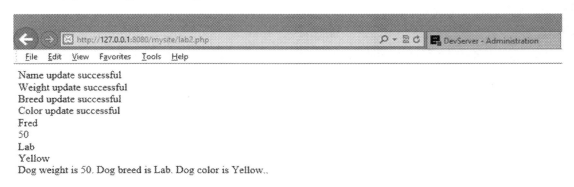

*Figure 3-4. Dog class output with set and get methods*

## Do It

1. In addition to creating an additional property ($dog_gender) and set method in the Dog class, create a get method to display the updated values. Also update the lab.php file to include a print statement (similar to the examples in this section) to call the get methods.

# Constructor Method

One difficulty with the previous examples is the amount of calls to set routines that would be required if you are initially creating an object and populating the properties of the object with values. The Dog class requires that you call four set methods (set_dog_name, set_dog_breed, set_dog_color, and set_dog_weight) in order to place values in all the properties. You can use a much more efficient way of updating all these properties at once. This could reduce the code in the lab.php file. You could then use the set routines in the Dog class to make any changes (maybe the dog gained some weight) after you have provided initial values. The initial values are not default values. You still need default values in case the initial values are invalid.

When an instance of a class (object) is created in memory, the operating system executes a constructor method that builds the object with any properties and methods. The system also builds tables in memory to keep track of the location of the object and the values that exist in the properties of the object. When the object is no longer needed, the operating system's garbage collector will call by the object's destructor method, which will remove it from memory.

You can also include a constructor method that will automatically be called when the object is placed in memory. When the code line that creates the object ($lab = new Dog;) is executed, it looks for a constructor method in the object. If it exists, the method is executed. You can pass all the initial values for the properties into this constructor method via same line that creates the object.

```
$lab = new Dog('Fred', 'Lab', 'Yellow', 50);
```

This becomes a much more efficient way of providing the initial values from within the lab.php program.

The constructor method is a generic format with a function name __construct (note there are two underscores before the word construct).

```php
<?php
class Dog
{
        function __construct($value1, $value2, $value3, $value4)
        {
        // code to update properties
        }
// other methods
}
?>
```

You can use the existing set methods in the constructor to update the properties. You will need to collect any messages (TRUE/FALSE) and return them to the calling program (lab.php). You can use a similar procedure as you initially coded with the handling of the get_properties method.

*Example 3-12.* Dog class with constructor—dog.php

```php
<?php
class Dog
{
// ---------------------------------------- Properties ----------------------------------------
private $dog_weight = 0;
private $dog_breed = "no breed";
private $dog_color = "no color";
private $dog_name = "no name";
private $error_message = "??";
// -------------------------------- Constructor --------------------------------------------
function __construct($value1, $value2, $value3, $value4)
{
$name_error = $this->set_dog_name($value1) == TRUE ? 'TRUE,' : 'FALSE,';
$breed_error = $this->set_dog_breed($value2) == TRUE ? 'TRUE,' : 'FALSE,';
$color_error = $this->set_dog_color($value3) == TRUE ? 'TRUE,' : 'FALSE,';
$weight_error= $this->set_dog_weight($value4) == TRUE ? 'TRUE' : 'FALSE';

$this->error_message = $name_error . $breed_error . $color_error . $weight_error;
}
//---------------------------------toString----------------------------------------
public function __toString()
{
        return $this->error_message;
}
//... There are no other code changes to dog.php below this line.
```

*For more information about the __construct method, visit:*

*Examples: http://php.net/manual/en/language.oop5.decon.php*

*Videos: https://www.thenewboston.com/videos.php?cat=11&video=17181*

First, let's discuss the use of the special method called __toString (note the two underscores) in Example 3-12. Constructor methods are not allowed to return information (by default). The return statement cannot be used within the constructor. In order to return error messages created in the constructor to the calling program (lab.php), you must trick the program. The __toString method allows the programmer to decide what will occur if an attempt is made to use the print (or echo) method with the object name (print $lab;). Normally an error message would occur claiming the object cannot be converted to a string (print and echo can only display strings). This can be overridden by including a __toString method with a statement that returns a string. You can overcome this problem of being able to return the error messages by allowing the value in the $error_message property to be returned if the print $lab; statement is executed.

*For more information on the __toString method and other magic methods visit http://php.net/manual/en/language.oop5.magic.php.*

The TRUE and FALSE constants that are returned by the set methods also cause a problem because they are constants and not strings. If you attempt to convert these constants to a string using a method (such as strval(TRUE);), the values that they represent (1 for TRUE, 0 for FALSE) would become a string instead of 'TRUE' or 'FALSE'. Therefore, they cannot be returned via the __toString method. To overcome this problem we create the following code in the constructor to do a conversion from TRUE to 'TRUE' or FALSE to 'FALSE'.

```
$name_error = $this->set_dog_name($value1) == TRUE ? 'TRUE,' : 'FALSE,';
```

The order of operations will cause the set_dog_name method to execute before any of part of this code. The set_dog_name method returns TRUE or FALSE (constants). Assuming that the method returns a TRUE after the execution, the code line would now be

```
$name_error = TRUE == TRUE ? 'TRUE,' : 'FALSE,';
```

The order of operations then requires that the comparison (TRUE == TRUE) be evaluated. Of course, this evaluates to TRUE. The statements between the ? and the : are used.

```
$name_error = 'TRUE,';
```

Thus $name_error is set to the string "TRUE,", which is now a string, not a constant.

Also note that a ',' has been added in preparation for the next 'TRUE' or 'FALSE' value. Each value passed (except the last value) must be separated by a ',' to allows the string to be separated later.

The other three similar lines are evaluated and also place a 'TRUE,' or 'FALSE,' in the error message properties (the weight error evaluation does not include a comma at the end of the string since it is the last one evaluated).

The last line of code in the constructor is evaluated.

```
$this->error_message = $name_error . $breed_error . $color_error . $weight_error;
```

This line places the values of each error property into the error_message property. If all the updates were successful, the $error_message property would contain

```
"TRUE,TRUE,TRUE,TRUE"
```

Notice that each item passed includes a "," for separation except the last item. This is necessary to break apart the results of the string.

***Example 3-13.*** The lab.php file calling a constructor

```php
<?php
require_once("dog.php");
$lab = new Dog('Fred','Lab','Yellow','100');
list($name_error, $breed_error, $color_error, $weight_error) = explode(',', $lab);
print $name_error == 'TRUE' ? 'Name update successful<br/>' : 'Name update not
successful<br/>';
print $breed_error == 'TRUE' ? 'Breed update successful<br/>' : 'Breed update not
successful<br/>';
print $color_error == 'TRUE' ? 'Color update successful<br/>' : 'Color update not
successful<br/>';
print $weight_error == 'TRUE' ? 'Weight update successful<br/>' : 'Weight update not
successful<br/>';
// ----------------------------Set Properties--------------------------
```

...There are no other changes to lab.php below this line.

There is a slight change to the creation of the object on the third line of Example 3-13.

```php
$lab = new Dog('Fred','Lab','Yellow','100');
```

You are now passing the initial values (Fred, Lab, Yellow,and 100) into the object via the constructor. Otherwise, you would have to make four calls to set methods (set_dog_name, set_dog_breed, set_dog_color, and set_dog_weight) to accomplish the same thing. This allows you to use the set methods for updates that are needed after you have initially set up the object ($lab).

In order to determine if the updates to the four properties were successful, you must retrieve your values (TRUE, TRUE, TRUE,TRUE) from the $error_message property in the object. The __toString method in the Dog class allows you to do this by treating $lab as if it were a string. This allows you to use the explode method in a similar process as the output to the get_properties method.

```php
list($name_error, $breed_error, $color_error, $weight_error) = explode(',', $lab);
```

This line of code will break the contents of $lab (TRUE, TRUE, TRUE,TRUE) by the commas and place each part into the properties $name_error, $breed_error, $color_error, and $weight_error. Each of these properties will now contain the string 'TRUE'. You can then evaluate your messages to see if the updates were successful in a very similar technique that evaluated the results of the set methods.

```php
print $name_error == 'TRUE' ? 'Name update successful<br/>' : 'Name update not
successful<br/>';
```

There are only a few minor differences between this format and the similar statements to evaluate the results of the set methods. Each of these code lines uses a different error message for evaluation ($name_error, $breed_error, $color_error, and $weight_error). Previously you used the same property ($error_message) for all the results from the set methods. You are now evaluating the string 'TRUE' instead of the constant TRUE (the only difference in the code is the actual quotes).

In Figure 3-5, the first four lines of output are produced from passing values into the constructor to provide initial settings for each property. The next four lines of output are produced when the set methods are used to change the values in the properties. The final four lines are produced from execution of the get methods (showing the contents of each property). The last line of output was produced by the get_properties method. Although the initial values (Fred, Lab, Yellow, and 100) are passed into the constructor successfully, the values in each property were the changed using the set methods (passing Sally, Labrador, Brown, and 5).

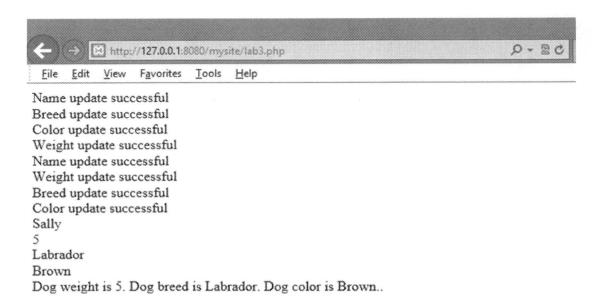

*Figure 3-5. Output from dog.php and lab.php with the constructor, set, and get methods*

> *Security and performance—Some would argue that it's overkill to check for errors every single time an update occurs. However, in the current environment with constant attempts to corrupt data, it is necessary to be as careful as possible when doing updates. No program is 100% protected from data corruption. Hopefully, you have noticed that once you develop a routine of checking data, your data checking code lines become very similar each time. Thus, by copying and pasting (with minor changes) code lines that successfully verify data, you can greatly increase your security without adding a lot of extra coding time.*

# Do It

1.  This chapter has covered a lot of PHP examples and terms. To help clarify any difficulties you might currently be experiencing in understanding the PHP language, visit this web site for additional tutorials:

    http://www.w3schools.com/php/default.asp

2.  Update the constructor in the Dog class to also allow the passing of the dog_gender value (Male or Female). Update the lab.php program to pass the gender through the constructor. Also update lab.php to explode the $lab string into five parts (one more for the dog_gender). Then evaluate the results ('TRUE' or 'FALSE') returned from the gender_error to display "Gender update successful" or "Gender update not successful".

# Chapter Terms

| | |
|---|---|
| PHP Extensions | Pear |
| require | require_once |
| Class | Properties |
| Variables | Methods |
| Functions | Object |
| Encapsulation | Private |
| set Method | get Method |
| $this Pointer | String Concatenation |
| Include | include_once |
| new Keyword | return |
| Comma-Delimitated String | explode Method |
| Substrings | set Method |
| Boolean Value | Conditional Statement |
| Ternary Operator | Integer |
| Parameter | Null Coalesce Operator |
| &&, And | ctype_alpha |
| strlen | ctype_digit |
| ||, Or | Spaceship Operator |
| NULL | Order of Operations |
| Constructor Method | Destructor method |
| __toString | List object |

# Chapter Questions and Projects

**Multiple Choice**

1.  PHP variables begin with which symbol?

    a.  ?

    b.  !

    c.  $

    d.  &

2.  A valid function name can start with which of the following?

    a.  A letter

    b.  An underscore

    c.  A number

    d.  Both A and B

3.  Which conditional statement syntax is valid for PHP?

    a.  `IF (condition) { execution };`

    b.  `IF (condition) { execution }`

    c.  `if (condition) { execution };`

    d.  `if (condition) {execution}`

4.  Which of the following includes properties and actions (methods or functions) that can occur in an application?

    a.  Class

    b.  `set` method

    c.  `get` method

    d.  `for` loop

5.  Which basic function does a constructor method perform?

    a.  Defines properties

    b.  Defines methods

    c.  Places an instance of a class into memory

    d.  A and B

6. The && symbol and/or the word AND

   a. Are relational operators, when used, and require all statements checked to be true for the complete if statement to be considered true

   b. Are conjunctions used in PHP to connect programs

   c. Are relational operators, when used, and require that only one statement checked to be true for the complete if statement to be considered true

   d. Are relational operators and conjunctions used in PHP to connect programs

7. An integer is which of the following?

   a. A string or text value

   b. A floating-point number

   c. A whole number

   d. A fraction

8. A ternary operator is which of the following?

   a. An alternative to setting a variable

   b. An alternative to using an if-else conditional statement

   c. An alternative to using an embedded if-else conditional statement

   d. B and C

9. How does one create an instance of the class fred and execute the constructor method in PHP?

   a. `$this->fred`

   b. `$variable = new fred`

   c. `$load_class = fred`

   d. `$fred`

10. What purpose does the method ctype_digit serve?

    a. Randomly generates an integer value

    b. Determines whether characters inputted are numeric

    c. Determines whether a class output is numeric

    d. Converts a string value to an integer

11. Pear is an acronym for

    a. PHP Extends and Applies Registry

    b. PHP Excellence in Applied Requirements

    c. PHP Extension and Application Repository

    d. Properties of Extension and Application Registry

12.   Creating set methods inside classes

   a.   Allows properties to be changed automatically

   b.   Should not be done as it corrupts data

   c.   Provides the ability for the class to verify information before the property is updated

   d.   Provides the ability for the class to verify information after the property is updated

13.   if statements

   a.   Are also called conditional statements

   b.   Can compare two values to determine if they are the same or different

   c.   Use comparison operators (==, <, >, <=, >=) to determine if the statement is true or false

   d.   All of the above

14.   $x && $y condition is TRUE if

   a.   Both $x and $y are true

   b.   $x or $y are true

   c.   Both $x and $y are false

   d.   $x or $y are false

15.   Select the statement about Boolean values that is false.

   a.   Boolean is a data type having two possible values—TRUE and FALSE

   b.   Boolean values represent the truth values of logic

   c.   Boolean values are only associated with conditional statements

   d.   In PHP Boolean literals, TRUE and FALSE are case-sensitive

16.   Which one of these numbers is an example of an integer?

   a.   1.01

   b.   2f

   c.   423

   d.   .002

17.   Protecting an object's data from code outside the class is called what?

   a.   Inheritance

   b.   Encapsulation

   c.   Classification

   d.   Blocking

18. Which kind of methods are easier to code than `set` methods and are known as read only methods since they do not change any property values?

    a. `explode` methods

    b. `get` methods

    c. `constructor` methods

    d. `match` methods

19. Why would you include objects in your program?

    a. To make notes in your code

    b. To make mini mobile programs

    c. To make your code more complex

    d. To protect your code from direct access

20. How do you call a function named `myFunction`?

    a. `call myFunction();`

    b. `myFunction();`

    c. `call function myFunction;`

    d. `call.myFunction();`

21. A class can contain all of the following except

    a. Properties

    b. Methods or functions

    c. Conditional statements

    d. Machine code

22. When working with a comma-delimited string, which character is used to separate the data in the string?

    a. Space

    b. Semicolon

    c. Asterisk

    d. Comma

**True/False**

1. Methods are functions that belong to a class.

2. You would use the symbol || or the word or when you want both conditions to be true.

3. When a function is private, it can only be used inside the class in which it exists.

4. The explode method can be used to separate a string at the specified delimiter.

5. The new keyword tells the operating system that an instance of that class should be created in memory.

6. The function Ctype_alpha will return true when a number is passed into it.

7. require_once will not execute if the file has already been attached to the program.

8. The ctype_digit function determines if the characters passed are alphabetic.

9. The ctype_alpha function determines if the characters passed are alphabetic.

10. A PHP constructor has the same name as the class.

11. A ternary operator is shorthand for a while loop.

12. If a file has already been included in a program, the require_once function will generate only a warning and allow the program to continue.

13. Destructor methods are called when there are no remaining references to an object or when that object has been explicitly destroyed.

14. Objects are blocks of code that have already been compiled for use in an application.

15. The else statement extends an if statement by allowing code to execute when the if statement evaluates to FALSE.

16. include or require statements can only be placed at the top of an PHP program.

17. Programmers can pull their own libraries of code into an application via the require or require_once statement.

**Short Answer/Essay**

1. Explain the meaning of encapsulation and how classes are encapsulated.

2. Why should a programmer use set and get methods?

3. Why should every entry on a web page from a user be validated?

**Projects**

1.  Create a PHP program with a class (Student) with the following properties: student_id, student_name, student_address, student_state, student_zip, and student_age. The program includes get and set methods for each property. Validate the proper type and size of data passed into each property. The program also includes the ability for each property to use the constructor to set values. Create an instance of the class passing properties through the constructor. Change two of the properties using set methods. Display the properties using get methods.

2.  Create a PHP program to keep track of inventory within a grocery store. Each item (class) includes an item number, description, size, self, isle, amount, and price. Each field must be verified for proper information before the entries are accepted. Item numbers range from 00000 to 99999. The store has 16 isles (00-15). No price in the store is greater than $1000. All entries are coded via a constructor or set methods. After all entries have correctly been accepted, the program will generate a report of the entries (using get methods).

**Term Project**

1.  Using the design from the Chapter 2 Term Project, create a PHP program that will provide the interface for entering in the ABC Computer Parts Corporation inventory items for the warehouse. The PHP class must verify the contents of the information passed from each field (via the set methods) to ensure that no corruption has taken place. Set and Get methods for each property must exist in the class. The constructor should use the set methods to populate the properties. Also create an interface program that will make an instance of the class and test the ability to populate the properties. The test program should generate a report of the item placed in inventory (similar to the output shown in this chapter). The files created should use logic similar to what was shown in the examples in this chapter.

# CHAPTER 4

# Secured User Interfaces

*"All great ideas look like bad ideas to people who are losers. It's always good to test a new idea with known losers to make sure they don't like it."* —Dilbert 11/18/97 *(http://dilbert.com/strips/comic/1997-11-18/)*

## Chapter Objectives/Student Learning Outcomes

After completing this chapter, the student will be able to:

- Explain why user input must be validated in the interface and business rules tiers
- Explain why user input must be filtered in the business rules tier
- Use HTML5 code to validate user input
- Use JavaScript code to validate user input
- Use PHP `if` statements (conditional statements) to validate and filter input
- Use the `foreach` loop to dynamically create an HTML select box from an XML file
- Use simple arrays for filtering and validation
- Pass simple arrays into methods (functions)
- Understand how to use dependency injection to control code version changes

**Electronic supplementary material** The online version of this chapter (doi:10.1007/978-1-4842-1730-6_4) contains supplementary material, which is available to authorized users.

# Secured User Interaction

In Chapter 2, the Hello World examples included user interaction (clicking a Submit button) to call a PHP program. This chapter will use the HTML web form to accept information from the user and then pass this information to a PHP program.

*Do not trust your users!* You must be prepared for any type of information your users will enter into a web form. You must also make sure that you validate and secure information every time before accepting it into your programs. You must remember that users may elect to not allow JavaScript to run in their browsers. Therefore, your program cannot be dependent on JavaScript code for verification of input. You must be able to handle these three scenarios:

1. If the user is using an HTML5 capable browser, you can verify all input using HTML5 before sending it to the PHP program on the web server.

2. If the user is using a browser that does not have HTML5 (or complete HTML5) capability, you can verify all (or some) input using JavaScript. Then you can send the validated information to the PHP program on the web server.

3. If the user is using a browser that does not have HTML5 capability and has JavaScript disabled, the user input can still be verified by the PHP program on the web server.

It is preferable to handle the initial verification using either of the first two methods. This would verify the correct information before sending it to the server. Method #3 will cause more server calls because the information must be sent to the server for verification, and then any error messages must be sent back to the browser for the user to correct.

Even if you verify the information using method #1 or #2, when the PHP programs receives the information on the web server, you will again evaluate that you have received valid information. Even though the user may have sent valid information, packet sniffing programs can change valid information into harmful information.

# HTML5 Form Validation

When building an HTML5 form, you can validate information entered into text boxes. However, browsers that have not implemented the HTML5 techniques (or all of HTML5) will treat the objects (such as text boxes) as if they were normal non-validation objects. The information in the boxes will be accepted without any verification. Therefore, you must also include a JavaScript routine to catch anything not validated by HTML5.

*Security and performance —Secure programming is just part of the complete process of protecting your information. The files, directories, servers, networks, and databases must also be properly secured. In addition, any highly important information (such as credit card numbers) must be sent across a secure channel (HTTPS) to additionally protect the information. User IDs and passwords should be encrypted to make it difficult for packet sniffing software.*

You will continue with the example from Chapter 3 by updating the Dog class example to accept information from the user for your properties. The Dog class already has security in place, so you will not need to make any additional security updates to the class.

***Example 4-1.*** The lab.html file with some validation

```html
<!DOCTYPE html>
<html lan="en">
<head>
<title>Dog Object</title>
<script src="validator.js"></script>
<style type="text/css">
#JS { display:none; }
</style>
<script>
function checkJS() {
document.getElementById('JS').style.display = "inline";
}
</script>
</head>
<body onload="checkJS();">
<h1>Dog Object Creater</h1>
<div id="JS">
<form method="post" action="lab.php" onSubmit="return validate_input(this)">
<h2>Please complete ALL fields. Please note the required format of information.</h2>
Your Dog's Name (max 20 characters, alphabetic) <input type="text" pattern="[a-zA-Z ]*"
title="Up to 20 Alphabetic Characters" maxlength="20" name="dog_name" id="dog_name" /><br />
Your Dog's Breed (max 35 characters, alphabetic) <input type="text" pattern="[a-zA-Z ]*"
title="Up to 35 Alphabetic Characters" maxlength="35" name="dog_breed" id="dog_breed" /><br />
Your Dog's Color (max 15 characters, alphabetic) <input type="text" pattern="[a-zA-Z]*"
title="Up to 15 Alphabetic Characters" maxlength="15" name="dog_color" id="dog_color" /><br />
Your Dog's Weight (numeric only) <input type="number" min="1" max="120" name="dog_weight"
id="dog_weight" /><br />
<input type="submit" value="Click to create your dog" />
</form>
</div>
<noscript>
<div id="noJS">
<form method="post" action="lab.php">
<h2>Please complete ALL fields. Please note the required format of information.</h2>
Your Dog's Name (max 20 characters, alphabetic) <input type="text" pattern="[a-zA-Z ]*"
title="Up to 20 Alphabetic Characters" maxlength="20" name="dog_name" id="dog_name" /><br />
Your Dog's Breed (max 35 characters, alphabetic) <input type="text" pattern="[a-zA-Z ]*"
title="Up to 35 Alphabetic Characters" maxlength="35" name="dog_breed" id="dog_breed" /><br />
Your Dog's Color (max 15 characters, alphabetic) <input type="text" pattern="[a-zA-Z]*"
title="Up to 15 Alphabetic Characters" maxlength="15" name="dog_color" id="dog_color" /><br />
Your Dog's Weight (numeric only) <input type="number" min="1" max="120" name="dog_weight"
id="dog_weight" /><br />
<input type="submit" value="Click to create your dog" />
</form>
</div>
</noscript>
</body>
</html>
```

In the head section of Example 4-1, after the `validator.js` file has been inserted into the program, some CSS has been included that hides (`display:none`) a division (`div`) tag with an ID of JS. Just below the CSS code is a small amount of JavaScript code. This code switches the JS division to be visible (`$("#JS")`. `show()`) and hides the noJS division. There is only one slight difference between the forms in the JS and noJS divisions. You should notice that the noJS form does not call the `validate_input` JavaScript function.

Why is this?

The answer is simple. If the browser does not have JavaScript enabled, the short JavaScript routine to hide and show the divisions will not run. Thus, the JS division will not be displayed in the browser (because the CSS at the top of the code set its display to none). The noJS division will be visible instead. This allows a browser that does not have JavaScript to send the information entered by the user directly to the PHP program on the web server. Hopefully, the user has an HTML5 browser that will still validate the information before it is sent to the server (#1 in this scenario). However, even if they don't, the information will be validated on the server (#3 in this scenario, as you will see later in the chapter).

If JavaScript is enabled in the browser, the hide-show routine will "hide" the noJS division and show the JS division. The form that submits the information to the `validate_input` function will display in the browser. This will allow browsers that have JavaScript enabled to validate information entered by using the `validate_input` JavaScript function. If the user has an HTML5 browser (#1 in this scenario), this might be overkill, since HTML5 can validate the information. However, you must be prepared for users who have not upgraded their browsers (#2 in this scenario).

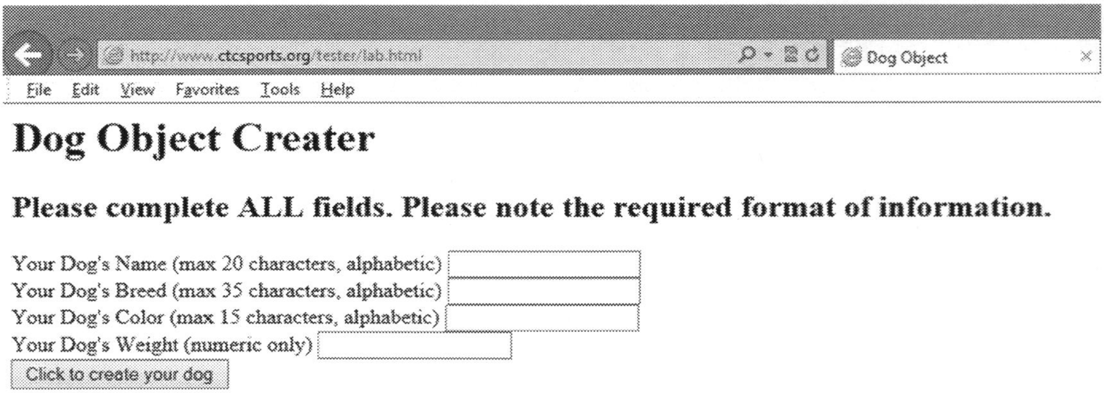

---

| ← → | @ http://www.ctcsports.org/tester/lab.html | 🔎 ▾ ☒ ♂ | @ Dog Object | × |

File   Edit   View   Favorites   Tools   Help

# Dog Object Creater

## Please complete ALL fields. Please note the required format of information.

Your Dog's Name (max 20 characters, alphabetic) [                    ]
Your Dog's Breed (max 35 characters, alphabetic) [                    ]
Your Dog's Color (max 15 characters, alphabetic) [                    ]
Your Dog's Weight (numeric only) [                    ]
[ Click to create your dog ]

***Figure 4-1.*** *The lab.html file*

In Example 4-1, the dog_name, dog_breed, and dog_color text boxes set field lengths to the same maximum values that were validated in the Dog class in Chapter 3. They also use the HTML5 `pattern` property (`[a-zA-Z]`) to only allow alphabetic characters. The `title` property is used to display an error to the user if incorrect information is entered. The dog_weight text box uses an input type of `number`, which automatically restricts the input. The `min` and `max` parameters are also set to restrict the dog's weight between 1 and 120 lbs. As mentioned, the browser might not interpret these restrictions if it has not fully implemented HTML5 standards. Therefore, you still must also validate the data using the JavaScript `validate_input` method to be sure that all validation has been completed.

HTML5 capable browsers will validate the information before it is sent to the `validate_input` function. Thus, if the browser is completely HTML5, all the information will also pass the validation from the JavaScript method. You could check the browser version to determine if the browser is 100% HTML5. However, that would take more JavaScript coding and is unnecessary since the application accomplishes its task without more code.

It is important that all validations are consistent throughout the process of accepting information from the user and passing that information to the application. HTML and JavaScript code are easily viewable by the user (you can "View Source" from within a browser to see the code). Validation of any highly secure format should be done from within a program language that is compiled and secured on a server.

> *Security and performance —You may be wondering why you should even bother to validate on the user side. Why not just pass all the information to the program on the server and let that program tell you if you need to fix anything? Some programmers actually do this. However, the goal is to have an efficient program. By attempting to validate the information in the user's browser, you reduce the number of calls to/from the server. This improves the application and web server performance and efficiency. In addition, as you will see, by validating in the browser, the contents in the text boxes will still be available to the user to adjust. If validation is done on the web server, information in the HTML form will be lost because the web page will be reloaded each time you send and receive information from the web server.*

The goal of validation in the browser is to make sure that the user provides information that meets the requirements of the program on the server. You may initially cringe that this example displays the format of required information to the user. However, the goal is not to secure the data; the goal is to make sure the data is valid. It is not a security breach to inform the user of the data format requested.

```
<form method="post" action="lab.php" onSubmit="return validate_input(this)">
```

The form uses the parameter `onSubmit` to pass all information that has been entered to the JavaScript method (`validate_input`). The `this` keyword indicates that all information from `this` object (which is the form itself and all the text boxes) is passed to the method. The `return` keyword indicates that the method will return a `TRUE` or `FALSE` status. The HTML code will submit the form to the PHP program (`lab.php`) on the server if a `TRUE` status has been returned from the `validate_input` method.

# Do It

1. Adjust Example 4-1 to include gender information from the Do It in Chapter 3. Use a text box to receive the information from the user. Try to use HTML5 to restrict the type of information the user can enter in the text box. Test your code.

# JavaScript Validation

Although this is not a JavaScript book, it will take a brief look at form validation used in the JavaScript method validate_input.

***Example 4-2.*** Form validation via JavaScript—validator.js

```
function allalphabetic(the_string)
{
    var letters = /^[a-zA-Z ]+$/;
    if (the_string.match(letters))
     {
      return true;
     }
else
     {
      return false;
     }
}


// -------------------------------------------------------------------------------
function validate_dog_name(the_string)
{
        if ((the_string.length > 0) && (allalphabetic(the_string)) && (the_string.length < 21))
        {
          return true;
        }
        else
        {
          return false;
        }
}
// -------------------------------------------------------------------------------
function validate_dog_breed_color(the_string)
{
    if ((the_string.length > 0) && (allalphabetic(the_string)) && (the_string.length < 35))
        {
          return true;
        }
        else
        {
          return false;
        }
}
function validate_dog_weight(the_string)
{
    if ((the_string > 0 && this_string <= 120) && (!isNaN(the_string)))
        {
          return true;
        }
```

```
        else
        {
            return false;
        }
}
// -------------------------------------------------------------------------------------
function validate_input(form)
{
            var error_message = "";
                    if (!validate_dog_name(form.dog_name.value))
            {
                        error_message += "Invalid dog name. ";
            }

        if (!validate_dog_breed_color(form.dog_breed.value))
        {
            error_message += "Invalid dog breed. ";
        }
        if (!validate_dog_breed_color(form.dog_color.value))
        {
            error_message += "Invalid dog color. ";
                    }
        if (!validate_dog_weight(form.dog_weight.value))
        {
            error_message += "Invalid dog weight. ";
        }
        if (error_message.length > 0)
        {
        alert(error_message);
        return false;
        }
        else
        {
        return true;
        }
}

          if (!validate_dog_breed_color(form.dog_color.value))
        {
            error_message += "Invalid dog color. ";
                    }
        if (!validate_dog_weight(form.dog_weight.value))
        {
            error_message += "Invalid dog weight. ";
        }
        if (error_message.length > 0)
        {
        alert(error_message);
        return false;
        }
```

```
        else
        {
        return true;
        }
}

<script src="validator.js"></script>
```

In Example 4-1, the JavaScript file `validator.js` is attached to the `lab.html` file in the head section via an HTML `script` tag. By placing the JavaScript validation in a separate file, you have simplified the HTML file. The JavaScript file is dependent on the HTML file for display. Error messages are passed to an alert box (`alert(error_message);`) near the bottom of the method.

> *Programming suggestion—By passing only a status (error message) back to a calling program, you allow for flexibility. The calling program can then determine how to display the information. This also allows you to easily reuse the method for other HTML forms.*

Let's work backward in reviewing the JavaScript code (Example 4-2). In the HTML file, the `onSubmit` parameter of the `form` tag calls the `validate_input` JavaScript method. This method controls all the validation of each text box on the form. The method uses a series of `if` statements to call methods that will validate the different types of text boxes. The format of each `if` statement is very similar.

```
if (!validate_dog_name(form.dog_name.value))
```

Each method called will return a true response if the validation passes and a false response if the validation fails. (In JavaScript, the constants `true` and `false` are lowercase. In PHP they are uppercase.)

By **passing** form into the `validate_input` function, all the parameters and values in the HTML form are passed at the same time. You can select which parameter to use by using dot notation.

In the previous example, `form.dog_name.value` will pull the value that was entered in the dog_name text box. The value that the user entered in this text box is passed into the `validate_dog_name` method.

```
if (!validate_dog_name(form.dog_name.value))
{
    error_message += "Invalid dog name. ";
}
```

The ! symbol in front of the function name means not. An `if` statement normally executes if the response from a method (or comparison) is `true`. However, you want to save an error message in the `error_message` property if the response returned from the method (`validate_dog_name`) is `false` (it did not validated correctly). The ! symbol causes the `if` statement to do the reverse of what's normal and execute if the function returns a false value.

Each of the other validation methods works in similar ways. The methods check to see if the information entered was in the correct format. If the information was correct, the method returns `true`. If the information was not correct, the method returns `false`.

> *For more information on the JavaScript if conditional statement, visit*
>
> *https://www.thenewboston.com/videos.php?cat=10&video=16960*
>
> *For more information on JavaScript functions (methods), visit*
>
> *https://www.thenewboston.com/videos.php?cat=10&video=16952*

```
function validate_dog_name(the_string)
{
        if ((the_string.length > 0) && (allalphabetic(the_string)) && (the_string.length <= 20))
        {
          return true;
        }
        else
        {
          return false;
        }
}
```

Each method accepts the value from the particular text box by passing it into the the_string property (function validate_dog_name(the_string)). The if statement in each method does most of the work. In the validate_dog_name method, the if statement attempts to check three requirements for the dog name. The first part of the statement uses the length method to make sure the length of the string is greater than zero. If the length of the string is not greater than zero, the user did not enter anything in the text box. Next, the if statement passes the_string to an allalphabetic method to determine if the text box contains only alphabetic characters (you will look at the function shortly). Finally the if statement checks the string length again to make sure it has not exceeded 20 characters. The && symbol is an AND symbol that requires that all three of these checks be true for the complete if statement to be considered true. If all three are true, the if statement returns true to the validate_input method. If any of the three are false, the if statement returns false to the validate_input method.

> *Programming note—JavaScript strings include built-in methods that automatically exist once a variable has been created and set with a string value. In the examples in this chapter, you use both the* length *method and the* match *method. The* length *method returns the length of the string. The* match *method determines if the string contains a set of characters that has been passed into the method (see the next example).*

dog_name, dog_breed, and dog_color all require that only alphabetic characters be allowed. So you created the allalphabetic method that can be called by each validation method instead of repeating the same code.

```
function allalphabetic(the_string)
{
    var letters = /^[a-zA-Z ]+$/;
    if (the_string.match(letters))
    {
      return true;
    }
    else
    {
      return false;
    }
}
```

The allaphabetic method uses a *regular expression* to check for alphabetic characters. Most program languages (including PHP) enable the programmer to create a regular expression that will check a string for a required format.

```
var letters = /^[a-zA-Z ]+$/;
```

This line sets up the expression to determine if the string only has lowercase and/or uppercase alphabetic characters (a though z, A through Z). You will work more in detail with regular expressions within PHP in a later chapter.

> *For more information on JavaScript regular expressions, visit*
>
> `https://developer.mozilla.org/en-US/docs/Web/JavaScript/Guide/Regular_Expressions`
>
> *For more information on the JavaScript* match *method, visit*
>
> `http://www.w3schools.com/jsref/jsref_match.asp`

One of the methods that exists in all JavaScript strings is the match method. This method compares the contents of the string (the_string) to the regular expression (alphabetic characters in this example). If the string meets the requirements of the expression (only contains alphabetic characters), then the method will return true. Otherwise, it will return false. In this example, if the string is alphabetic, true is returned to the if statement in the validate_dog_name (or validate_dog_color or validate_dog_breed) method. If any part of the string contains something other than alphabetic characters, a false is returned to the if statement (which in turn will make the results of the if statement false even if the string size is correct).

Going back to the bottom of the JavaScript code, you determine what to return to the HTML program (lab.html).

```
if (!validate_dog_weight(form.dog_weight.value))
    {
        error_message += "Invalid dog weight. ";
    }
    if (error_message.length > 0)
    {
    alert(error_message);
    return false;
    }
    else
    {
    return true;
    }
```

Each if statement at the bottom of the validate_input method will build an error message (such as "Invalid dog weight.") and place it in the error_message property if the validation fails (If a false is returned from the if statement). The += symbol concatenates what is currently in the property with what is being placed into the property (so you don't overwrite any messages that are already there).

The last if statement (if (error_message.length > 0) checks the length of the error_message property. If it is greater than zero (error messages have been passed into the property), the program will display the messages in an alert box and return false to the HTML program (lab.html). If the length is zero, there were no error messages; true is passed back to the HTML program.

```
<form method="post" action="lab.php" onSubmit="return validate_input(this)">
```

In Example 4-1, the format of the form tag will automatically cause a response if a `true` or `false` is returned from the `validate_input` method. If `true` is returned (there were no validation problems), the HTML program will send the form properties and values to the `lab.php` program on the web server. If `false` is returned (there was at least one validation problem), the HTML program will not pass the information and will stay visible in the browser. The alert box will display for the user to see what errors have occurred. When the user closes the alert box, they will still be on the HTML page (with the information they had previously entered). They can correct any incorrect information and click the Submit button (again) to revalidate the information they have entered.

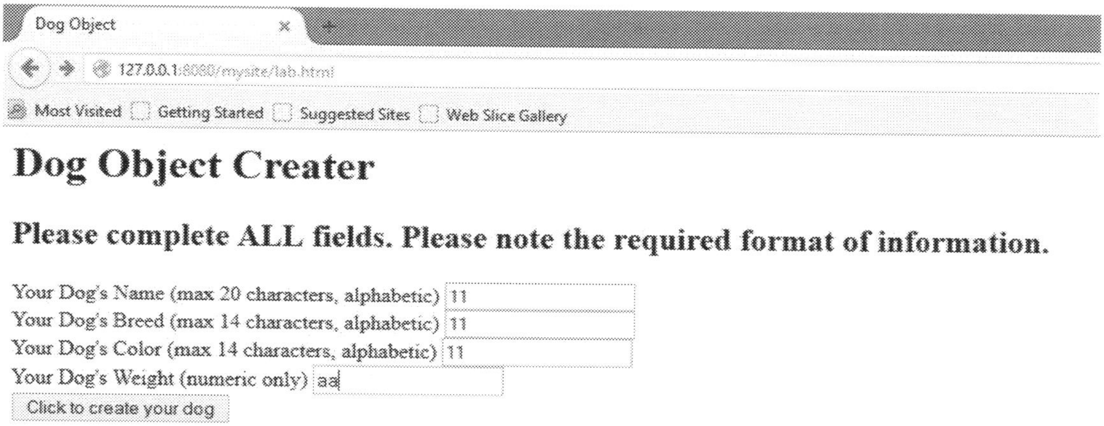

*Figure 4-2.* *The lab.html file with incorrect entries*

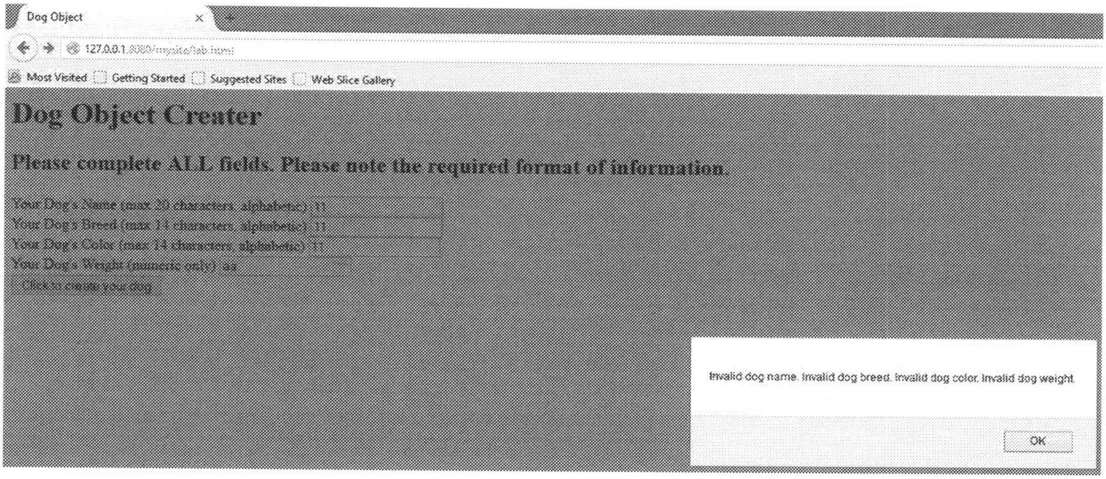

*Figure 4-3.* *The lab.html file after failing JavaScript verification*

---

■ **Note**    Different browsers react in different ways to JavaScript code. Internet Explorer tries to block JavaScript code by default. If you see no results and are sure your code is correct, yet are receiving error messages about missing methods (such as validate_input) it may be that your browser's ability to execute JavaScript is turned off. Either turn it on in the settings of the browser or try a different browser that allows JavaScript to run.

---

*Security and performance—Although you have verified input on the HTML page, the data could still cause harm to the system. The user could try to send HTML, JavaScript, and even PHP code that could to cause harm. This could occur from bad information entered in the HTML page, a packet sniffing program intercepting the data transferring to the PHP page, or a program trying to bypass the HTML page altogether. No matter which of these activities produced the harmful information, the PHP program will need to detect it and handle the problem. Therefore, the receiving program (lab.php) must try to filter (clean and remove harmful code) the data.*

## Do It

1.   Adjust Example 4-2 to validate the gender text box from the first Do It. Make sure to include an error message to indicate the problem(s). Also make sure the error message is added to the $error_message property to be displayed with all other error messages. Make sure to test your code for all possible problems with the user entering data. Don't forget to test if they do not enter any data.

# PHP Filtering

It's time to look at the changes required to the php file (lab.php). You need to be able to accept in the properties and values (dog_name, dog_breed, dog_color, and dog_weight) from the HTML program. However, you need to be concerned that someone might try to send information that could affect the operation of the program or even crash the system in which it is operating.

   This section takes two approaches to help reduce the possibility of harmful data. First, you will determine if you have received all required information. If not, you will ask the user to return to the HTML page (lab.html) to enter the information. This will, at least, make sure that you have all data and it meets the validation provided by the HTML5 page and/or JavaScript program (validator.js). Second, you will use some existing PHP methods to filter out HTML, JavaScript, and PHP syntax from the data received. This will reduce the chance that an executable statement will be passed into the program.

*Example 4-3.*    Partial listing of the top of lab.php with the clean_input method

```php
<?php
require_once("dog.php");
function clean_input($value)
{
$bad_chars = array("{", "}", "(", ")", ";", ":", "<", ">", "/", "$");
$value = str_ireplace($bad_chars,"",$value);
// This part below is really overkill because the string replace above removed special characters
$value = htmlentities($value); // Removes any html from the string and turns it into &lt; format
```

```
$value = strip_tags($value); // Strips html and PHP tags
        if (get_magic_quotes_gpc())
        {
                $value = stripslashes($value); // Gets rid of unwanted quotes
        }
return $value;
}
if ((isset($_POST['dog_name'])) && (isset($_POST['dog_breed'])) && (isset($_POST['dog_
color'])) && (isset($_POST['dog_weight'])))
{
$dog_name = clean_input($_POST['dog_name']);
$dog_breed = clean_input($_POST['dog_breed']);
$dog_color = clean_input($_POST['dog_color']);
$dog_weight = clean_input($_POST['dog_weight']);
$lab = new Dog($dog_name,$dog_breed,$dog_color,$dog_weight);
list($name_error, $breed_error, $color_error, $weight_error) = explode(',', $lab);
...
```

> For more information on the PHP function isset, visit
>
> Examples: http://php.net/manual/en/function.isset.php
>
> Videos: https://www.thenewboston.com/videos.php?cat=11&video=17087
>
> For more information on $_POST, visit
>
> Examples: http://php.net/manual/en/reserved.variables.post.php
>
> Videos: https://www.thenewboston.com/videos.php?cat=11&video=17087

At the top of lab.php, you are adding several items to provide more secure code.

```
if ((isset($_POST['dog_name'])) && (isset($_POST['dog_breed'])) &&
(isset($_POST['dog_color'])) && (isset($_POST['dog_weight'])))
```

This if statement uses the isset method and $_POST to verify that all four properties (dog_name, dog_breed, dog_color, and dog_weight) have been passed into the program with the POST method. If all items have been passed, you then will filter (clean) those items. If any of them have not been passed, an else statement (that you will look at later) will request the user go back to the lab.html page to enter all needed information.

```
$dog_name = clean_input($_POST['dog_name']);
```
Each property is passed to the clean_input method (after it has been retrieved using the $_POST method) to remove harmful tags. In this example, the $dog_name property (on the left side of the = sign) will receive the cleaned information.
```
function clean_input($value)
{
$bad_chars = array("{", "}", "(", ")", ";", ":", "<", ">", "/", "$");
$value = str_ireplace($bad_chars,"",$value);
$value = strip_tags($value); // Strips html and PHP tags
$value = htmlentities($value); // Removes any html from the string and turns it into &lt; format
```

```
if (get_magic_quotes_gpc())
        {
                $value = stripslashes($value); // Gets rid of unwanted quotes
        }
return $value;
}
```

---

▓ **Note**   set_magic_quotes_runtime and magic_quotes_runtime has been removed since PHP 5.4. Magic quotes (since PHP 5.4) can no longer be set at runtime.

---

*For more information on the str_ireplace method, visit*

*http://php.net/manual/en/function.str-ireplace.php*

The clean_input method creates an array $bad_chars that contains a list of all special characters you want to remove from the string (you will look at arrays in more detail later in this chapter and future chapters). The str_ireplace method ($value = str_ireplace($bad_chars,"",$value);) will replace all these characters with "" (nothing, it removes them) from the $value property and place what is left into $value. There may be occasions that you do want some of these special characters (for example in an SQL statement). However, you do not need any of these for the input in this example, so you can remove them.

---

▓ **Note**   It would be effective and efficient for this example to just remove the characters that are not valid. In a real-world situation, you would not need to also include the stripslashes, htmlentities, and string_tags methods (shown in the method). They are included here to demonstrate their use and why, in other situations, you might use them.

---

The three PHP methods (stripslashes, htmlentities, and strip_tags) are used to convert harmful code so it cannot be executed. The stripslashes method removes backslashes from quotes (which actually can also done by the str_ireplace method). The htmlentities method converts HTML characters to their equivalent HTML entity (for example a is converted to &#039;). The strip_tags method removes any PHP or HTML tags. If you were using SQL to update a database, you need to add additional functions to disable any harmful SQL statements.

*For more information on stripslashes, htmlentities, and strip_tags, visit*

*Examples – stripslashes: http://php.net/manual/en/function.stripslashes.php*

*Examples – htmlentities: http://php.net/manual/en/function.htmlentities.php*

*Examples – strip-tags: http://php.net/manual/en/function.strip-tags.php*

*Video – magic quotes and stripslashes: https://www.youtube.com/watch?v=NUqkUjbGuPY*

*Video – htmlentities: https://www.thenewboston.com/videos.php?cat=11&video=17058*

*Video – strip_tags: https://www.youtube.com/watch?v=rn_dnQFLt3U*

*Security and performance—It is extremely important that the program filter out any possible harmful information received from outside the application. It is much easier to remove the harmful data initially, or reject the data initially, before it has been used or saved. With major breaches in security today, this is an absolute MUST DO.*

You could have also restricted which programs called the PHP program. The $__SERVER global variable can assist you.

```
if($__SERVER['HTTP_REFERER'] == 'http://www.mysite.com/lab.html')
{ //  code executed if valid location }
else {exit;}
```

*For more information on the $__SERVER array, visit*
*Examples: http://php.net/manual/en/reserved.variables.server.php*
*Video: https://www.thenewboston.com/videos.php?cat=11&video=17047*

This example code would reject any program that calls the lab.php program (except for the lab.html program that is located at the site). The exit; command closes the program if it is not called from the correct HTML page.

The filter methods demonstrated will not keep someone from entering "asabsbabsa" as a dog name. However, these methods will keep any entry from being harmful.Example 4-4. Partial list of the bottom of lab.php with the clean_input method

```
else
{
print "<p>Missing or invalid parameters. Please go back to the lab.html page to enter valid
information.<br />";
print "<a href='lab.html'>Dog Creation Page</a>";
}
```

The true part of the if statement mentioned includes all the active code in the lab.php file. If one or more parameters is missing, the else section (at the bottom of the lab.php file) will request that the user go back to the lab.html page to properly enter the information.

## Do It

Adjust the code in the new lab.php file (download it from the book's web site). Add code to filter for bad gender code and make sure that gender information has been received from the HTML file. Make sure to pass your property through the clean_input method to remove any harmful data.

# Additional HTML Input Security

As you can see from all the code you have seen in this chapter so far, whenever a text box is used on an HTML form, additional code in several areas must be included to validate what the user has typed. Text boxes are necessary when you need to allow the user flexibility in what they can enter (such as a form that includes name and address). However, you can use other form objects when you want to limit the user's response to a particular list of possible values (such as two-letter abbreviations for states). This would provide more valid data because the user won't be able to enter a typo or enter invalid data.

# HTML5 Select List Box and Radio Buttons

One item that you can change from the original HTML file is the entry of the dog breed. The American Kennel Club currently has over 150 breeds listed on its web site. You can type an option value line for each breed in the HTML file. However, this would be time consuming. Also, if a breed changed, you will have to go back and adjust the list. A better option is to place the breeds in a file and then use that file to populate a select **list**. If a breed changes or is added, you simply update the one file in one place and all programs that use it will access the new list automatically. If this file is hosted on the web server, you can also use the same file in the dog.php code to verify that a correct breed has been passed to the web server from the user.

***Example 4-5.*** The breeds.xml file

```
<?xml version="1.0" encoding="UTF-8"?>
<breeds>
<breed>Affenpinscher</breed>
<breed>Afghan Hound</breed>
<breed>Airedale Terrier</breed>
<breed>Akita</breed>
<breed>Alaskan Malamute</breed>
<breed>American English Coonhound</breed>
<breed>American Eskimo Dog</breed>
<breed>American Foxhound</breed>
<breed>American Staffordshire Terrier</breed>
...
</breeds>
```

> *Security and performance—Providing the user a list of possible values to choose from on an HTML form provides more validity and security than using text boxes. If the user can only pick from a list, they cannot choose incorrectly, nor enter invalid or harmful information.*

The breeds.xml file contains simple **XML** code (two tags—breeds and breed) listing all breeds. If you were creating a true dog breed site, you probably would want to include more information in this file. You could add more information later without it affecting this program.

You now want to use the XML file (from Example 4-5) to populate a select list box. Since this file will reside on the server, you need to create a program on the server to call and retrieve the information. You will assume that this file has been secured on the server for read-only access. You will not attempt to update or delete any information in the file itself.

You can create a PHP program that will retrieve the information you need with just a few lines of code.

> *Security and performance—Remember, security is a team effort. Not only does the program need to be secured, but the web server and its file structure must also be properly secured.*

***Example 4-6.*** The getbreeds.php file

```
<?php
$breed_file = simplexml:load_file("breeds.xml");
$xmlText = $breed_file->asXML();
print "<select name='dog_breed' id='dog_breed'>";
print "<option>Select a dog breed</option>";
```

```
foreach ($breed_file->children() as $name => $value)
{
print "<option value='$value'>$value</option>";
}
print "</select>";
?>
```

PHP can complete many powerful tasks with just a few lines of code. The first line of Example 4-6 opens the breeds.xml file, places the contents into a property ($breed_file), and then closes the breeds.xml file.

Skipping to the foreach statement:

```
foreach ($breed_file->children() as $name => $value)
```

XML data is treated with a parent-child relationship. The parent can contain children (and the children can have children). In the XML file, the initial parent is breeds. The children that exist under breeds all have the label breed.

```
<breed>Affenpinscher</breed>
```

The value in each breed (child) in this example is the text that exists between the breed tags (for example, Affenpinscher).

$breed_file->children() directs the foreach statement to loop through each child (breed in this file). The as $name=> $value part of the statement tells the system to place each child label name (in this example it is always breed, but you can have different children) in $name. It also directs the system to place the value contained in the child (Affenpinscher) in $value.

```
print "<option value='$value'>$value</option>";
```

Inside the foreach **loop,** the print statement places the contents of $value in two places—the value parameter of the option tag and between the option tags. For the first child, it would produce

```
Option value='Affenpinscher'>Affenpinscher</option>
```

The foreach loop automatically loops through the file until there are no more records in the file. Similar lines would be created for each of the breeds in the file. These lines, with the other print lines in the file, create an HTML select box dynamically from the contents of the XML file.

> For more information on the foreach loop, visit
>
> Examples: http://php.net/manual/en/control-structures.foreach.php
>
> Video: https://www.thenewboston.com/videos.php?cat=11&video=17027
>
> For more information on reading XML files, visit
>
> Video: https://www.thenewboston.com/videos.php?cat=11&video=17090

You need to now call this program from within the HTML file. You can do this using the example JavaScript file from Chapter 2, which uses AJAX. This will allow you to retrieve the select box by only updating the section of the page that will display the box. The only line that needs to be changed from the Chapter 2 example is the line that calls the PHP program.

```
xmlHttp.open("GET", "get_breeds.php", true);
```

You simply replace the existing file name with the program that retrieves the select box (get_breeds.php). You can then rename the file (get_breeds.js).You could also pass the name of the program you want to run into the JavaScript method (you will do that later in this chapter).

You now need to make a few changes to the HTML file to use get_breeds.js and to create a div tag for the area that will hold the select box.

***Example 4-7.*** The lab.html file with a dynamic select box

```
<!DOCTYPE html>
<html lan="en">
<head>
<title>Dog Object</title>
<script src="get_breeds.js"></script>
<script src="validator.js"></script>
<style type="text/css">
#JS { display:none; }
</style>
<script>
function checkJS() {
document.getElementById('JS').style.display = "inline";
}
</script>
</head>

<body onload="checkJS();">
<h1>Dog Object Creater</h1>
<div id="JS">
<form method="post" action="lab.php" onSubmit="return validate_input(this)">
<h2>Please complete ALL fields. Please note the required format of information.</h2>
Enter Your Dog's Name (max 20 characters, alphabetic) <input type="text" pattern="[a-zA-Z]*"
title="Up to 20 Alphabetic Characters" maxlength="20" name="dog_name" id="dog_name" /><br
/><br />
Select Your Dog's Color:<br />
<input type="radio" name="dog_color" id="dog_color" value="Brown">Brown<br />
<input type="radio" name="dog_color" id="dog_color" value="Black">Black<br />
<input type="radio" name="dog_color" id="dog_color" value="Yellow">Yellow<br />
<input type="radio" name="dog_color" id="dog_color" value="White">White<br />
<input type="radio" name="dog_color" id="dog_color" value="Mixed">Mixed<br /><br />
Enter Your Dog's Weight (numeric only) <input type="number" min="1" max="120"
name="dog_weight" id="dog_weight" /><br /><br />
<script>
AjaxRequest();
</script>
<div id="AjaxResponse"></div><br />
<input type="submit" value="Click to create your dog" />
</form>
</div>
<noscript>
<div id="noJS">
<form method="post" action="lab.php">
<h2>Please complete ALL fields. Please note the required format of information.</h2>
```

```
Enter Your Dog's Name (max 20 characters, alphabetic) <input type="text" pattern="[a-zA-Z
]*"  title="Up to 20 Alphabetic Characters" maxlength="20" name="dog_name" id="dog_name"
/><br /><br />
```
**Select Your Dog's Color:<br />**
**<input type="radio" name="dog_color" id="dog_color" value="Brown">Brown<br />**
**<input type="radio" name="dog_color" id="dog_color" value="Black">Black<br />**
**<input type="radio" name="dog_color" id="dog_color" value="Yellow">Yellow<br />**
**<input type="radio" name="dog_color" id="dog_color" value="White">White<br />**
**<input type="radio" name="dog_color" id="dog_color" value="Mixed">Mixed<br /><br />**
```
Enter Your Dog's Weight (numeric only) <input type="number" min="1" max="120"
name="dog_weight" id="dog_weight" /><br /><br />
Enter Your Dog's Breed (max 35 characters, alphabetic) <input type="text" pattern="[a-zA-Z
]*" title="Up to 15 Alphabetic Characters" maxlength="35" name="dog_breed" id="dog_breed"
/><br />
<input type="submit" value="Click to create your dog" />
</form>
</div>
</noscript>
</body>
</html>
```

The only true changes related to creating the dynamic select box are highlighted in **bold** in Example 4-7.

```
<script src="get_breeds.js"></script>
```

The `script` tag is added near the top of the code to pull in the JavaScript file that contains AJAX to call the PHP program (`get_breeds.php`) that will display the select box.

```
<script>
AjaxRequest();
</script>
<div id="AjaxResponse"></div><br />
```

A script area has been placed in the JS section of the code (the section that will execute if JavaScript is enabled in the browser.) It includes just one line (`AjaxRequest();`) to execute the AJAX JavaScript code (from the `get_breeds.js` file). `<div id="AjaxResponse"></div>` is placed below the closing script tag. This line should look familiar. It is the same line that was included in the Chapter 2 AJAX example. The output of the `AjaxRequest()` method places the response that is returned from the web server between the `div` tags with the ID of AjaxResponse. In this example, the dynamically created select box is placed in that location.

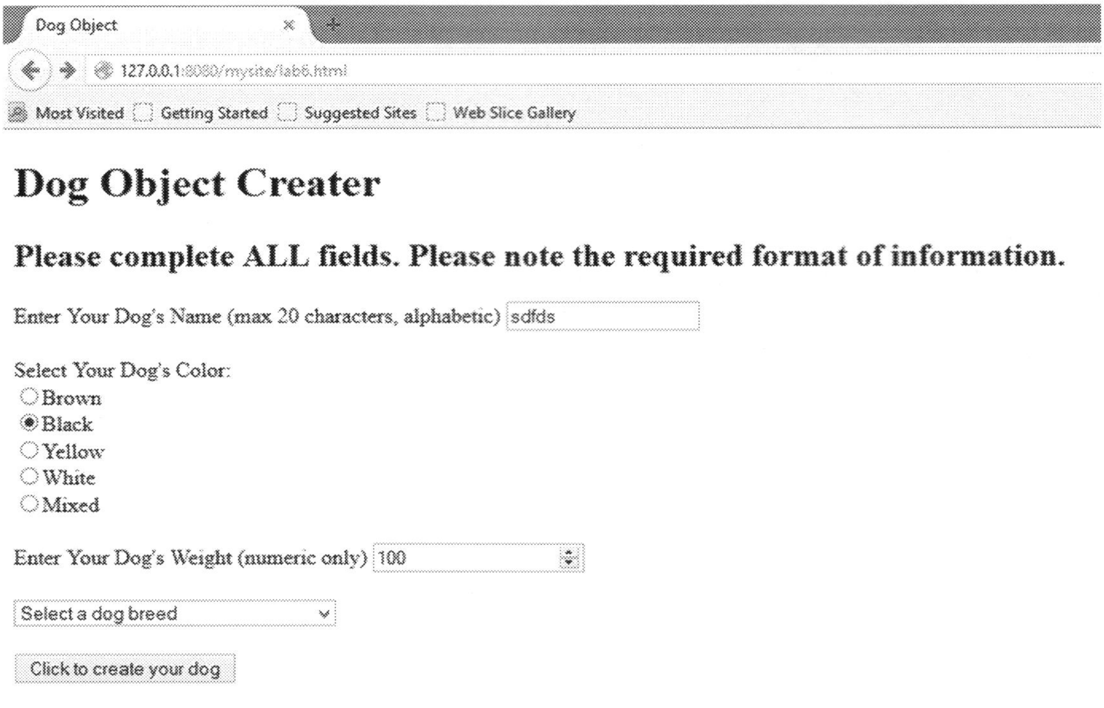

**Figure 4-4.** *The lab.html file with dynamic select box and radio buttons*

You have also replaced the color text box with a static selection of radio buttons. There are just a few possible color combinations for dogs (OK, pretend I am right), and these color combinations are not likely to change, so you don't need a dynamic list. It makes sense to just hard code the selections in the HTML file.

If the user does not have JavaScript enabled, the original dog breed text box will be displayed (from the NJ section of the code). However, since you did not use JavaScript to create the radio buttons, you include the radio buttons in both sections to provide some better secure coding for non-enabled JavaScript browsers.

The Interface of the program (lab.html) now greatly reduces the possibility of invalid data being entered by reducing the number of text boxes used. The users (assuming they have JavaScript enabled) have no choice but to pick a breed from the select box and to pick a color from the radio buttons.

You can also now use the same XML file to validate that you have received a valid breed name from the users on the server side.

## Do It

Adjust the lab.html file from Example 4-7 to include radio buttons (instead of a text box) to accept the gender from the users. Make sure the new lab.html file works with your lab.php file from the previous Do It.

## Validating Input with an XML File

You can add just a few lines of code in the dog.php file to validate that the user has not only sent a correctly formatted string, but has also sent a breed listed by the AKC.

***Example 4-8.*** The validator_breed function (in dog.php)

```php
private function validator_breed($value)
{
$breed_file = simplexml:load_file("breeds.xml");
$xmlText = $breed_file->asXML();

if(stristr($xmlText, $value) === FALSE)
{
return FALSE;
}
else
{
return TRUE;
}
}
```

You can create a private function (only to be used inside the class) to check on the proper breed. This function will accept a value passed into the $value property. The function will then use $breed_file = simplexml:load_file("breeds.xml"); to dump the contents of the XML file into $breed_file. The next line ($xmlText = $breed_file->asXML();) converts the contents of $breed_file into a well formatted string.

```php
if(stristr($xmlText, $value) === FALSE)
```

The stristr method compares the contents of its second parameter (in this case $value) to see if it exists in the string in the first parameter ($xmlText). If it does not exist, it returns FALSE. If it does exist, it returns the location of the string. For your needs you just need to know if it exists. If it does not, you return FALSE. If it does, you return TRUE.

> *For more information on the* stristr *method, visit*
>
> `http://php.net/manual/en/function.stristr.php`

***Example 4-9.*** The complete dog class with validation

```php
<?php
class Dog
{
// ---------------------------------------- Properties ----------------------------------------
private $dog_weight = 0;
private $dog_breed = "no breed";
private $dog_color = "no color";
private $dog_name = "no name";
private $error_message = "??";
// ------------------------------ Constructor ----------------------------------------
function __construct($value1, $value2, $value3, $value4)
{
if (method_exists('dog_container', 'create_dog_app')) {
$name_error = $this->set_dog_name($value1) == TRUE ? 'TRUE,' : 'FALSE,';
$breed_error = $this->set_dog_breed($value2) == TRUE ? 'TRUE,' : 'FALSE,';
$color_error = $this->set_dog_color($value3) == TRUE ? 'TRUE,' : 'FALSE,';
$weight_error= $this->set_dog_weight($value4) == TRUE ? 'TRUE' : 'FALSE';
```

```php
$this->error_message = $name_error . $breed_error . $color_error . $weight_error;
}
else
{
exit;
}
}
//----------------------------------toString-----------------------------------------
public function __toString()
{
        return $this->error_message;
}

// ------------------------------- Set Methods -------------------------------------
function set_dog_name($value)
{
$error_message = TRUE;
(ctype_alpha($value) && strlen($value) <= 20) ? $this->dog_name = $value :
$this->error_message = FALSE;
return $this->error_message;
}
function set_dog_weight($value)
{
$error_message = TRUE;
(ctype_digit($value) && ($value > 0 && $value <= 120)) ? $this->dog_weight = $value :
$this->error_message = FALSE;
return $this->error_message;
}
function set_dog_breed($value)
{
$error_message = TRUE;
((preg_match("/[a-zA-Z ]+$/", $value)) && ($this->validator_breed($value) === TRUE) &&
strlen($value) <= 35) ? $this->dog_breed = $value : $this->error_message = FALSE;
return $this->error_message;
}
function set_dog_color($value)
{
$error_message = TRUE;
(ctype_alpha($value) && strlen($value) <= 15) ? $this->dog_color = $value : $this->error_
message = FALSE;
return $this->error_message;
}
// ---------------------------------------- Get Methods ----------------------------------
function get_dog_name()
{
return $this->dog_name;
}
function get_dog_weight()
{
return $this->dog_weight;
}
```

```php
function get_dog_breed()
{
return $this->dog_breed;
}
function get_dog_color()
{
return $this->dog_color;
}
function get_properties()
{
return "$this->dog_weight,$this->dog_breed,$this->dog_color.";
}
// ----------------------------General Method----------------------------------------------

private function validator_breed($value)
{

$breed_file = simplexml:load_file("breeds.xml");
$xmlText = $breed_file->asXML();

if(stristr($xmlText, $value) === FALSE)
{
return FALSE;
}
else
{
return TRUE;
}
}

}
?>
//--------------------------------toString--------------------------------------------
public function __toString()
{
        return $this->error_message;
}
// ------------------------------ Set Methods -------------------------------------
function set_dog_name($value)
{
$error_message = TRUE;
(ctype_alpha($value) && strlen($value) <= 20) ? $this->dog_name = $value :
$error_message = FALSE;
return $error_message;
}
function set_dog_weight($value)
{
```

```
$error_message = TRUE;
(ctype_digit($value) && ($value > 0 && $value <= 120)) ? $this->dog_weight =
$value : $error_message = FALSE;
return $error_message;
}
function set_dog_breed($value)
{
$error_message = TRUE;
((ctype_alpha($value)) && ($this->validator_breed($value) === TRUE) && strlen($value) <= 35)
? $this->dog_breed = $value : $error_message = FALSE;
return $error_message;
}


{
$error_message = TRUE;
(ctype_alpha($value) && strlen($value) <= 15) ? $this->dog_color = $value : $error_message = FALSE;
return $error_message;
}
// ---------------------------------------- Get Methods ----------------------------------
function get_dog_name()
{
return $this->dog_name;
}
function get_dog_weight()
{
return $this->dog_weight;
}
function get_dog_breed()
{
return $this->dog_breed;
}
function get_dog_color()
{
return $this->dog_color;
}
function get_properties()
{
return "$this->dog_weight,$this->dog_breed,$this->dog_color.";
}
// -----------------------------General Method----------------------------------------------

private function validator_breed($value)
{
$breed_file = simplexml:load_file("breeds.xml");
$xmlText = $breed_file->asXML();

if(stristr($xmlText, $value) === FALSE)
{
return FALSE;
}
```

```php
else
{
return TRUE;
}
}
}
?>
function set_dog_color($value)
{
$error_message = TRUE;
(ctype_alpha($value) && strlen($value) <= 15) ? $this->dog_color = $value : $error_message =
FALSE;
return $error_message;
}
// -------------------------------------- Get Methods ---------------------------------
function get_dog_name()
{
return $this->dog_name;
}
function get_dog_weight()
{
return $this->dog_weight;
}
function get_dog_breed()
{
return $this->dog_breed;
}
function get_dog_color()
{
return $this->dog_color;
}
function get_properties()
{
return "$this->dog_weight,$this->dog_breed,$this->dog_color.";
}
// ----------------------------General Method--------------------------------------------

private function validator_breed($value)
{
$breed_file = simplexml:load_file("breeds.xml");
$xmlText = $breed_file->asXML();

if(stristr($xmlText, $value) === FALSE)
{
return FALSE;
}
else
{
return TRUE;
}
```

```
}
}
?>
/ ---------------------------General Method---------------------------------------
private function validator_breed($value)
{
$breed_file = simplexml:load_file("breeds.xml");
$xmlText = $breed_file->asXML();

if(stristr($xmlText, $value) === FALSE)
{
return FALSE;
}
else
{
return TRUE;
}
}
}
}
?>
```

You can now make a slight change to the code line that checks the validity of the dog_breed value (see the **bold** highlighted line in Example 4-9).

```
((ctype_alpha($value)) && ($this->validator_breed($value) === TRUE) && strlen($value) <= 35)
? $this->dog_breed = $value : $error_message = FALSE;
```

The statement passes $value into validator_breed ($this->validator_breed($value)). If a TRUE is returned then that part of the if statement would be true. Otherwise it would be false. If the complete if statement is TRUE then the dog_breed property is set to the breed found in the XML file ($this->dog_breed = $value). If it is false, then FALSE is passed into the $error_message property ($error_message = FALSE).

> *Programming note—When you call a function in the same object, you must use the $this pointer ($this->validator_breed($value) === TRUE)).*

You have now completed a program that much more secure. Users cannot enter any invalid information. The only field they can attempt to do so is in the dog_name field. However, even if they try to enter program code, or other code, the server-side program will strip out the special characters so the code becomes harmless. If a packet sniffing program tries to change the data before it is received by the server-side program, the validation and/or filtering methods will either cause the data to be rejected or will, again, make the data harmless.

This program is efficient as it tries to validate the information before it is sent to the server. It reduces the amount of communication back and forth between the server and the user. The completed program has two tiers (interface, business rules) and can be expanded to include a third tier (data) without major changes to the current code.

> *Programming recommendation—For small web applications that are used infrequently it is not necessary to break the program apart, as is done in this example. However, as mentioned, if it is an application that might expand in the future, or might gain significant users in the future, the program should initially be created with this in mind, by breaking the program into tiers.*

## Do It

Go to the book's web site and run the example program. See if you can "break" the security built into the program. Remember, you can only attempt to be as secure as possible, nothing is 100% secure. Were you able to send harmful information to the program that affected the program? If so, what did you do? What might be missing from the program that allowed this to happen? If not, what stopped your harmful data from corrupting the program? What changes might you make to this program that would require you to include a data tier? What inefficiencies still exist in the program? What can you do to fix them?

# Dependency Injection

As you have seen, when programs are created, a developer goes through many iterations before the final application has been completed. Along the way, experience programmers will keep different versions of their programs. This allows the programmers to back up to a previous version, quickly, if the version they are working on has too many significant problems. Otherwise, they would have to attempt to strip out the "bad" code without doing harm to the good code. Applications have many files (HTML, JavaScript, CSS, PHP classes, and PHP libraries). Keeping track of which version works with which, or easily changing one part of the program to use a new version of another part, can become confusing. Especially when the file names and class names are coded in the code of the program itself.

Chapter 2 briefly discussed *dependency injection*. It allows the program (client) that will use a block of code (such as a class) to not know the actual implementation of the block of code it will be using. The client program does not know the actual class name.

You can use this idea to help the development process. The example you are about to look at is not for large-scale applications. However, it does give you a chance to look at the benefits of dependency injection. Large-scale applications should use a MVC (Model-View-Control) model or an established tier (or component) system that provides more efficient communication between components.

> *Security and performance—Many times there is a trade-off between being as secure as possible and having a program that has the best performance possible. The example that follows will make multiple system calls when it checks to see if a program exists and then uses require_once to load the program. The check for file existence allows the program to handle missing files rather than the program just crashing. In a later chapter, you will look at using try/catch blocks to allow the program to capture any problems without crashing the program. This would reduce the number of system calls (you would no longer need to check for the existence of the files), giving the program better performance.*

The dog application uses classes and methods contained in different files. This requires the code to also include require_once statements to pull the files into the program. The current design places the actual file name in the require_once statement. This does not allow you to change different versions of the files, unless you change the code. You will now remove these dependencies to provide more flexibility for future development of the application.

Before you get too bogged down with the code, Figure 4-5 shows the flow of the relationship with the programs.

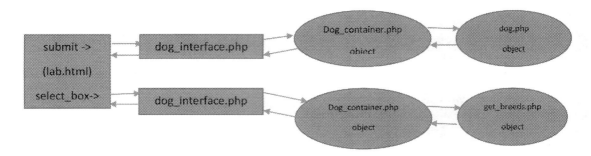

***Figure 4-5.*** *Data flow for the dog application*

The dog_interface.php program will provide the interface for all parts of the dog application. In addition it provides security and filtering as you have already designed in the previous examples. Along with these other activities, dog_interface creates and uses the dog_container object to contain, create, and pass any other objects needed (without knowing the name of the objects). The dog_container object uses an XML file (not shown) to discover the location and name of files containing the classes it will create (providing dependency injection).

The application will always use the dog_interface program to access the other classes. The dog_interface program will determine what classes are needed to accomplish a particular task. Whenever a class is needed, the dog_interface will use the dog_container to determine the name and location of the class (via the XML file), and to create an instance of the class (object). By using an XML file to list the class file names and locations, changes can be made without causing any code changes to programs in the application.

When the breed select box is requested from the lab.html page, the dog_interface program is called. It will create a dog_container object. The dog_container object will discover the location and file name of the get_breeds class file and the breeds XML file. Once it is discovered, the dog_container object will create a get_breeds object. The get_breeds object will then build the code for the select box; eventually returning the code to the form in lab.html for display to the user. All objects (dog_container and get_breeds) are then destroyed (removed from memory).

When the Submit button is clicked on the lab.html form (assuming all validation is passed), it will call the dog_interface program. This program will create the dog_container object. The dog_container object will then discover the location and file name of the dog.php class file. Once discovered, the dog_container object will create the dog object. The dog object will behave exactly as it has in previous examples (validating properties and displaying properties). Once the dog object has completed, the objects (dog_container and dog) are destroyed (removed from memory). This design allows complete independence of the objects providing both two-tier design (interface and business rules) and dependency injection.

***Example 4-10.*** The dog_applications.xml file

```
<?xml version="1.0" encoding="UTF-8"?>
<dog_applications>
<application>
<type ID="dog">
<location>dog3.php</location>
</type>
</application>
<application>
<type ID="selectbox">
<location>get_breeds2.php</location>
</type>
</application>
```

```
<application>
<type ID="breeds">
<location>breeds.xml</location>
</type>
</application>
</dog_applications>
```

In Example 4-10, you have created a simple XML file that will be used for version changes of the significant files in the PHP application. Each `application` tag identifies the type of file (dog, select box, breeds). Each `location` tag within the `application` tag provides the file name and location (although in this example you have all files in the same location). Once you adjust the program to use this file, you will have the flexibility to change the file names (such as the example using dog3.php instead of dog.php) and the location without having to change any program code. This can help you to swap versions in/out of the application during the development process.

You will now create a `Dog_container` class that will contain two methods. `get_dog_application` will be used to "fetch" the name and location of any of the files listed in the XML file. The `create_object` method will create an instance of either the dog class or the get_breeds class.

***Example 4-11.*** The dog_container.php file

```php
<?php
class Dog_container
{
private $app;
private $dog_location;
function __construct($value)
{
if (function_exists('clean_input'))
{
$this->app = $value;
}
else
{
exit;
} }
public function set_app($value)
{
$this->app = $value;
}
public function get_dog_application()
{
$xmlDoc = new DOMDocument();
if ( file_exists("dog_applications.xml") )
{
$xmlDoc->load( 'dog_applications.xml' );
$searchNode = $xmlDoc->getElementsByTagName( "type" );
foreach( $searchNode as $searchNode )
{
    $valueID = $searchNode->getAttribute('ID');
    if($valueID == $this->app)
```

```php
        {
        $xmlLocation = $searchNode->getElementsByTagName( "location" );
        return $xmlLocation->item(0)->nodeValue;
        break;
        }
    }
}
    return FALSE;
}
function create_object($properties_array)
{
    $dog_loc = $this->get_dog_application();
    if(($dog_loc == FALSE) || (!file_exists($dog_loc)))
    {
        return FALSE;
    }
    else
    {
        require_once($dog_loc);
        $class_array = get_declared_classes();
            $last_position = count($class_array) - 1;
            $class_name = $class_array[$last_position];
            $dog_object = new $class_name($properties_array);

            return $dog_object;
            }
    }
}
?>
```

First, at the top of the class (dog_container), you declare two private properties—$app and $dog_location. These properties are declared as private, instead of public, to keep their values only known within this class.

In the constructor, $value accepts a name of an application type that you want to find in the XML file (such as selectbox). Later in the code, you will compare $value to the type ID in the XML file to see if you can find the application type and a file associated with it. The constructor places $value into the $app property. However, the method also includes an if statement that uses the method function_exists to determine if the clean_input function exists.

Why? At the beginning of the chapter, you briefly looked at code that allowed you to restrict the use of a program to a specific application that has called it. In this example, you look at another technique to restrict which programs can use this class. The if statement demands that any program that makes an instance of this class must also have a clean_input method. If someone tries to make an instance of the program using another program that does not already contain a clean_input method, the else part of the statement will execute, which will cause the object not to be created and will close the program.

> *Security and performance—Any time a program is accepting information from the Internet, or across a network, it is a good idea to determine the source of the information. In addition to determining application and function names, PHP programs can also look at the source IP addresses.*

138

```php
public function get_dog_application()
{
$xmlDoc = new DOMDocument();
if ( file_exists("dog_applications.xml") )
{
$xmlDoc->load( 'dog_applications.xml' );
$searchNode = $xmlDoc->getElementsByTagName( "type" );
```

The first part of the get_dog_application method should look familiar. This code opens the dog_applications.xml file (after making sure it exists). Then it loads the contents into $xmlDoc. The last line calls the PHP method getElementsByTagName. This method searches for all occurrences of "type" in $xmlDoc and places each occurrence in $searchNode.

```php
foreach( $searchNode as $searchNode )
{
    $valueID = $searchNode->getAttribute('ID');
    if($valueID == $this->app)
    {
    $xmlLocation = $searchNode->getElementsByTagName( "location" );
    return $xmlLocation->item(0)->nodeValue;
    break;
    }
}
```

The foreach loop looks at each line contained in $searchNode. It uses the PHP method getAttribute to place the next line with an ID XML attribute into the property $valueID. Once it is placed in $valueID, the value in this property (dog, selectbox, or breeds) is compared to $this->app. (The property app was loaded with a value in the constructor.) If the ID is found in the XML file, getElementsByTagName will search for the next line that contains a location XML tag. The return line then takes the value in the location tag (the file name and its location) and returns it to the program that called this method. The break statement is used to break out of the loop early because you have already returned the value needed in the previous line of code. The else part of the method (shown in Example 4-11) will return FALSE if the XML file does not exist.

```php
function create_object($properties_array)
```

The create_object method is used to create the dog and get_breeds objects. The dog object constructor was expecting four values (dog_name, dog_weight, dog_breed, and dog_color) in its constructor. The get_breeds app was not accepting any values in its constructor. In order to provide more efficient code in dog_container, you change the signature of the constructor (the top line of the function) of each class to accept an array, instead of individual values. This will allow you to pass any number of items into either constructor.

```php
function __construct($properties_array)
{ // dog class constructor
if (method_exists('dog_container', 'create_object')) {
$name_error = $this->set_dog_name($properties_array[0]) == TRUE ? 'TRUE,' : 'FALSE,';
$breed_error = $this->set_dog_breed($properties_array[1]) == TRUE ? 'TRUE,' : 'FALSE,';
$color_error = $this->set_dog_color($properties_array[2]) == TRUE ? 'TRUE,' : 'FALSE,';
$weight_error= $this->set_dog_weight($properties_array[3]) == TRUE ? 'TRUE' : 'FALSE';
```

This requires changing these lines in the dog.php file to accept an array and then use the values in the array to set each property.

Notice that $properties_array in the first line does not have anything that declares it as an array (except the name). Remember that PHP properties determine what data type they are by what is passed in the property. The same is true with arrays. If an array is passed into $properties_array, it becomes an array.

The address of the array is passed into the method. The property that accepts the address ($properties_array) actually points to the location of the array in memory. This is very efficient. If you needed to pass 50 items into a method, you could pass them all one at a time with different properties declared in the methods signature for each of these 50 items. However, instead, you can create an array that holds the 50 items and pass the array. You are only passing one value using this approach, which is the address of the array in memory. Also, as noted with this example, using an array allows you to be flexible in the amount of items you want to pass into a method signature.

```
$name_error = $this->set_dog_name($properties_array[0]) == TRUE ? 'TRUE,' : 'FALSE,';
```

To copy an item from an array, you refer to the item using the array's name ($properties_array) and the position that the item exists in the array ([0]). Notice that you use [ ] brackets for declaring the position. The position is commonly called the *subscript*. Arrays subscripts begin with position 0, not position 1.

```
class GetBreeds {
function __construct($properties_array)
{ //get_breeds constructor
if (!(method_exists('dog_container', 'create_object')))
{
exit;
}
}
```

You must adjust the get_breeds program. GetBreeds is now a class. You also create the signature of the GetBreeds constructor to accept an array. However, as you can see from this code, you actually will ignore anything that is passed into the array. This allows you to use the same method in dog_container to create an object of either class (or actually of any class that accepts an array). All you need to find is the name of the class (dog or GetBreeds) so you can make an instance of it.

```
function create_object($properties_array)
{
  $dog_loc = $this->get_dog_application();
  if(($dog_loc == FALSE) || (!file_exists($dog_loc)))
  {
    return FALSE;
  }
```

The create_object method then calls the get_dog_application method and places the value returned (the location of the file and file name) into $dog_loc. If the value in $dog_loc is FALSE or is not an existing file, the method returns FALSE to the program that called it.

```
else
  {
    require_once($dog_loc);
    $class_array = get_declared_classes();
        $last_position = count($class_array) - 1;
```

```
        $class_name = $class_array[$last_position];
        $dog_object = new $class_name($properties_array);
        return $dog_object;
        } } }
?>
```

If the path and file name are valid, the else portion of the code will execute. The value in $dog_loc is used in the require_once statement (which pulls the contents of the file into this method).

You must now determine the name of the class that exists in the file (dependence injection requires you to not only discover the file names and file path, but also the class names).

The PHP method get_declared_classes returns an array of all the classes that currently exist in the program. The classes are in order from first to last. Thus, since you just included the file with a class (either the dog or get_breeds class), you can hunt for the last entry in the array created. You have placed the array created by get_declared_classes in $class_array. You can now determine the size of the array. The PHP method count will return the size of an array. Remember the size of an array is the number of items in the array not the last position. If an array has a size of ten, the actual subscripts are 0 through 9, not 1 through 10.

```
$last_position = count($class_array) - 1;
```

> For more information on get_declared_classes, visit
> http://php.net/manual/en/function.get-declared-classes.php

With this in mind, this statement determines the size of $class_array and then subtracts 1 from the size and places that value in $last_position. Thus, if the array had a size of 10, the number 9 would be stored in $last_position (since the array subscripts would be 0 through 9, not 10).

```
$class_name = $class_array[$last_position];
```

You can then use the value in $last_position to pull the last class created from the array and place it into $class_name. As you can see, you can actually pass the property $last_position between the [ ] subscript brackets to indicate to the program you want the value of whatever is in the position located in $last_position. This allows you to be able to pull the information from the last position in any size array (since you have no idea of the size of the $class_array).

You can now create an instance of the class, because you have the class name in $class_name.

```
$dog_object = new $class_name($properties_array);
```

This line of code will now create an instance of any class (that accepts an array into the constructor) that has just been included (require_once) in the program. The method will create an instance of either the dog class or getBreeds class.

```
return $dog_object;
```

Finally, the object (which is either a dog object or a getBreeds object) is returned to the program that called the method. By returning the object, the calling program has complete access to the object and its properties and methods, even though it did not actually create the object (dog_interface can use the object even though dog_container created it).

The object's location in memory is returned in a similar way as the array's location was passed into the constructor in the previous example. You can think of it as the new object is temporarily "contained" within the dog_container object. However, the object is returned (to dog_interface).

*Programming note—What? What really happens is that the address in memory of the $dog_object is passed to the calling program (dog_interface). This allows the calling program to have access to the object, along with the $dog_container object. Thus, there is only one copy of the $dog_object in memory but two different program blocks can use it. If one of the blocks (dog_container or dog_interface) closes, the other object still has access to it, until it also closes. Then the garbage collector will remove the $dog_object from memory.*

***Example 4-12.*** The get_breeds class

```php
<?php
class GetBreeds {
function __construct($properties_array)
{ //get_breeds constructor
if (!(method_exists('dog_container', 'create_object')))
{ exit;}}
private $result = "??";
public function get_select($dog_app)
{ if (($dog_app != FALSE) && ( file_exists($dog_app))) {
    $breed_file = simplexml:load_file($dog_app);
    $xmlText = $breed_file->asXML();
    $this->result = "<select name='dog_breed' id='dog_breed'>";
    $this->result = $this->result . "<option value='-1' selected>Select a dog breed</option>";
    foreach ($breed_file->children() as $name => $value)
    {    $this->result = $this->result . "<option value='$value'>$value</option>";  }
      $this->result = $this->result . "</select>";
            return $this->result;
    } else {
            return FALSE;
    }
}
}
?>
```

As you can see from Example 4-12, only minor changes were needed. As mentioned, a class was declared and a constructor was added. The constructor verifies that this class was created from a program that contains both the dog_container and create_breed_app methods. This security attempts to keep other programs from knowing that the file names and locations for the Dog application that reside in the dog_application.xml file.

***Example 4-13.*** The dog_interface.php file

```php
<?php
function clean_input($value) {
$bad_chars = array( "{", "}", "(", ")", ";", ":", "<", ">", "/", "$" );
$value = str_ireplace($bad_chars,"",$value);
 $value = htmlentities($value);
$value = strip_tags($value);
```

```
            if (get_magic_quotes_gpc())
            { $value = stripslashes($value); }
$value = htmlentities($value);
return $value;
}
function error_check_dog_app($lab) {
list($name_error, $breed_error, $color_error, $weight_error) = explode(',', $lab);
print $name_error == 'TRUE' ? 'Name update successful<br/>' : 'Name update not successful<br/>';
print $breed_error == 'TRUE' ? 'Breed update successful<br/>' : 'Breed update not successful<br/>';
print $color_error == 'TRUE' ? 'Color update successful<br/>' : 'Color update not successful<br/>';
print $weight_error == 'TRUE' ? 'Weight update successful<br/>' : 'Weight update not successful<br/>';
}
function get_dog_app_properties($lab) {
print "Your dog's name is " . $lab->get_dog_name() . "<br/>";
print "Your dog weights " . $lab->get_dog_weight() . " lbs. <br />";
print "Your dog's breed is " . $lab->get_dog_breed() . "<br />";
print "Your dog's color is " . $lab->get_dog_color() . "<br />";
}
//----------------Main Section------------------------------------
if ( file_exists("dog_container.php"))
{  require_once("dog_container.php"); }
 else { print "System Error #1"; exit; }
if (isset($_POST['dog_app']))
  {
if ((isset($_POST['dog_name'])) && (isset($_POST['dog_breed'])) && (isset($_POST['dog_
color'])) && (isset($_POST['dog_weight'])))
{     $container = new dog_container(clean_input($_POST['dog_app']));
    $dog_name = clean_input(filter_input(INPUT_POST, "dog_name"));
    $dog_breed = clean_input($_POST['dog_breed']);
    $dog_color = clean_input($_POST['dog_color']);
    $dog_weight = clean_input($_POST['dog_weight']);
    $properties_array = array($dog_name,$dog_breed,$dog_color,$dog_weight);
    $lab = $container->create_object($properties_array);
        if ($lab != FALSE) {
    error_check_dog_app($lab);
    get_dog_app_properties($lab);  }
        else { print "System Error #2"; }
}
else {
print "<p>Missing or invalid parameters. Please go back to the dog.html page to enter valid
information.<br />";
print "<a href='dog.html'>Dog Creation Page</a>";
}
}
else
{
    $container = new dog_container("selectbox");
    $lab = $container->create_breed_app();
```

```
if ($lab != FALSE) {
        $container = new dog_container("selectbox");
        $properties_array = array("selectbox");
        $lab = $container->create_object($properties_array);
if ($lab != FALSE) {
        $container->set_app("breeds");
        $dog_app = $container->get_dog_application();
        $method_array = get_class_methods($dog_data);
        $last_position = count($method_array) - 1;
        $method_name = $method_array[$last_position];
        $result = $dog_data->$method_name($dog_app);
                if ( $result == FALSE) {
            print "System Error #3"; //select box not created
          }
          else
          {
              print $result; //pass back select box
          }
        }
        else
        {
        print "System Error #4";
        }
      }
?>
```

The dog_interface program is actually the lab.php program with code changes in the main section. None of the methods from lab.php have changed.

```
if ( file_exists("dog_container.php"))
{   require_once("dog_container.php"); }
 else { print "System Error #1"; exit; }
if (isset($_POST['dog_app']))
```

First the program determines if the dog_container exists by using the PHP file_exists method. If it does, it pulls the code into the program using require_once. If dog_container does not exist, the program prints an error message ("System Error #1") and then closes (exit;).

Next, the program uses isset to determine if a value for $dog_app has been provided by the calling program. If this value has been passed, it is an indication that the calling program wants to create a Dog object.

```
$container = new dog_container(clean_input($_POST['dog_app']));
$dog_name = clean_input(filter_input(INPUT_POST, "dog_name"));
$dog_breed = clean_input($_POST['dog_breed']);
$dog_color = clean_input($_POST['dog_color']);
$dog_weight = clean_input($_POST['dog_weight']);
$properties_array = array($dog_name,$dog_breed,$dog_color,$dog_weight);
    $lab = $container->create_object($properties_array);
        if ($lab != FALSE)
        {
    error_check_dog_app($lab);
    get_dog_app_properties($lab);
```

```
        } else {
        print "System Error #2";
        } else {
print "<p>Missing or invalid parameters. Please go back to the lab.html page to enter valid
information.<br />";
print "<a href='lab.html'>Dog Creation Page</a>";
} }
```

The program then creates an instance of dog_container ($container) that passes the value in $dog_app into the $container object. Each of the properties of the Dog object are filtered using the clean_input method. Then the properties are passed into the $properties_array array. The array is then passed into the create_object method of the dog_container object ($container). If the Dog object ($lab) is created successfully then the error_check_dog_app method is called to verify that each property has valid information. The get_dog_app_properties method is called to display each property.

If any of the properties needed for the Dog object are missing, the user is requested to return to the lab.html page to re-enter the required information.

```
else
{ //get breeds
    $container = new dog_container("selectbox");
    $properties_array = array("selectbox");
    $lab = $container->create_object($properties_array);
if ($lab != FALSE)
        {
    $container->set_app("breeds");
    $dog_app = $container->get_dog_application();
    $method_array = get_class_methods($lab);
     $last_position = count($method_array) - 1;
     $method_name = $method_array[$last_position];
    $result = $lab->$method_name($dog_app);
        if ( $result == FALSE) // select box not created
        {
          print "System Error #3";
        }
        else
        {
           print $result; // select box created!
        }
    }
    else
    {
    print "System Error #4";
    }
```

If the $dog_app value is not passed in to the class, the else statement is executed. It is assumed that the user wants to create a getBreeds object. An instance of the dog_container is created ($container) and it passes the value selectbox. (If the object can't be created, "System Error #4" will display). The words "selectbox" are passed into the array $properties_array (Note: The array keyword must be used or you would be creating a property not an array.) The container object ($container) will then call the create_object (passing the $properties_array to create an instance of the getBreeds class ($lab). If the getBreeds object is successfully created ($lab !=FALSE) you then need to find the location of the get_breeds.xml file (which contains the list of breeds). So you reset the app property (by calling set_app) in the container to "breeds". This tells the container program you are a getBreeds object, not a dog object. You then use the get_dog_application method of the container to find the location of the breeds XML file.

> *For more information on arrays, visit*
>
> *Examples: http://php.net/manual/en/function.array.php*
>
> *Videos: https://www.thenewboston.com/videos.php?cat=11&video=17024*

The PHP method get_class_methods is used to create an array of methods contained in getBreeds. Since the get_select method is the only method (besides the constructor), it is also the last method in the array. Its name is pulled from the array and then it is called using the property $method_name ($result = $dog_data->$method_name($dog_app) ). This allows the getBreed class to be completely independent of the dog_interface. The developer can change the name of the get_select method and everything would still work (as long as it's the last method in the class). This provides a complete split between the interface tier and the business rules tier.

The location of the XML file is passed into the get_select method of the getBreeds object ($lab), which uses the XML file for the data to create the select list box. The code for the select list box is dropped into $result. If the code did get dropped into $result, the code is displayed (print $result) back into the HTML form for the user to select a breed. If the file name was not valid, an error message (print "System Error #3") will display instead of the select box.

The only other changes required are two slight changes to the lab.html and get_breeds.js files.

```
function AjaxRequest($value)
```

In the get_breed.js file, the function header for the AjaxRequest method has been changed to pass the actual file being called (this was not a requirement of this design, but it allows this file to be used for any program that is called via AJAX).

```
xmlHttp.open("GET", $value, true);
```

In addition, the open statement has been adjusted to use $value instead of a file name.

In the lab.html program, there are a couple of additional changes.

```
AjaxRequest('dog_interface.php');
```

The call to the JavaScript function now passes the file name, which has also been changed to the dog_interface.php file.

```
<form method="post" action="dog_interface.php" onSubmit="return validate_input(this)">
```

Finally, the action tag (in both form tag locations) for the HTML form has been changed to call the dog_interface.php program.

Notice that now, whenever you want to use the Dog application you call the interface first. Then the interface determines what you want to accomplish (get the breeds select box or process the properties for the dog you are creating).

You must communicate to all of your classes through the interface. The interface, in turn must create any required objects by using the container (except, of course, for the container itself). This follows the concepts of tier design.

You will not see any different output than previously seen (unless you have some system errors). However, now you can easily change file names and locations (via the XML file) in the application without changing any program code!

## Do It

1. Download the files for this section from the book's web site. Change the file names for the get_breeds.xml file, the get_breeds.php file, and the dog.php file. Try to run the program via the lab.html file. The select box will not display and the program will not run. Now go to the dog_applications.xml file and change the data in the XML file to the new file names you just created. Go back to your lab.html file (reload it). You should now see the select box. Fill in and select the information and click the Submit button. The application should now work.

# Chapter Terms

| | |
|---|---|
| Validate | validator Method |
| JavaScript Hide/Show | HTML onSubmit |
| Form Validation | JavaScript Alert Box |
| HTML Passing "Form" | JavaScript Dot Notation |
| JavaScript if Statements | JavaScript length Method |
| && AND | \|\| OR |
| Regular Expression | JavaScript match Method |
| Filter/Filtering | isset |
| $_POST | str_ireplace |
| Stripslashes | htmlentities |
| strip_tags | $__SERVER |
| exit | else |
| HTML Select List | XML |
| XML Data format | XML Parent-Child |
| foreach Loop | HTML Radio Buttons |
| private Function | stristr |
| Dependency Injection | function_exists |
| break Statement | method Signature |
| getElementsByTagName | getAttribute |
| array | array subscript |
| get_declared_classes | Count |
| Size of an Array | Last Position of an Array |
| array Keyword | Passing Objects |
| get_class_methods | |

# Chapter Questions and Projects

**Multiple Choice**

1. When using form validation, which of the following is true?

    a. The server automatically successfully processes input values with no errors.

    b. A required field is checked to make sure it has content.

    c. A dynamic web page is updated.

    d. All information is sent to the server.

2. Which of the following can be verified with a validator?

    a. E-mails

    b. IP addresses

    c. Integers

    d. All of the above

3. Why must you validate your code?

    a. To see if your browser can complete a task.

    b. To make sure your information is correct and secure.

    c. To make sure that your browser can run JavaScript and HTML5.

    d. To verify that your computer can run the latest version of PHP.

4. The verification code in a PHP file does which of the following?

    a. Compares the information received to an expected standard format

    b. Verifies user program interaction

    c. Checks and eradicates harmful data being entered by the user

    d. Checks for incorrect PHP functions being used

5. `stripslashes` do which of the following?

    a. Remove backslashes from quotes.

    b. Convert HTML characters to their equivalent HTML entity.

    c. Remove any PHP or HTML tags.

    d. All of the above.

6. If the size of an array is 29, what is the subscript range?

    a. 1 through 30

    b. 1 through 29

    c. 0 through 29

    d. None of the above

7. in_array does which of the following?

   a. Searches for the number of empty spaces in an array.

   b. Searches for the number of characters in an array.

   c. Searches for a value in an array.

   d. None of the above.

8. The PHP method count will return which of the following of an array?

   a. `last_position`

   b. `subscript`

   c. `size`

   d. None of these

9. Which method will produce a variable that you can use to refer to the last position of the array?

   a. `$last_position=count($class_array) - 1;`

   b. `$class_array=$last_position(count - 1);`

   c. `$count=$last_position - 1($class_array);`

   d. `$last_position=$class_array -1 (count);`

10. The exit command does which of the following?

    a. Automatically directs the user to a new page.

    b. Closes the program if it is not called from the correct HTML page.

    c. Turns off your computer.

    d. None of the above.

11. What is not true in relation to the foreach command?

    a. Works only with arrays and objects.

    b. Used to parse through each key/value pair in an array.

    c. Can be iterated by reference.

    d. The equivalent to an if/then statement.

12. The break statement does which of the following?

    a. Ends execution of the for, foreach, do-while, and/or switch structure(s).

    b. Executes the for, foreach, do-while, and/or switch structure(s).

    c. Ensures the execution of for, foreach, do-while, and/or switch structure(s).

    d. Breaks the for, foreach, do-while, and/or switch structure(s) before they are executed.

13. Using the `getAttribute` will do which of the following?

    a. Return the value of the attribute.

    b. Print a list of data.

    c. Load a new HTML page.

    d. None of these.

14. Which function converts HTML tags into their entities versions?

    a. `strlen`

    b. `htmlentities`

    c. `explode`

    d. `getAttribute`

15. Which is a commonly used function to find the length of a string?

    a. `strlen`

    b. `getLength`

    c. String concatenation

    d. `__toString`

**True/False**

1. The `count` function returns the number of elements in an array.

2. When using an array, the index must not exceed the size of the array.

3. A subscript is the name given to position where the item currently exists in the array and is usually contained in [ ].

4. A *private* function is an event in PHP to network for a job.

5. One purpose of `exit` is to end the program.

6. The `getElementsByTagName` searches for occurrences that correspond to a specific XML tag.

7. `get_declared_classes` returns an array of all classes that currently exist in a program in order from first to last.

8. Dependency injection allows the program client to enter a block of code to know the implementation of the block of code it will be using.

**Short Answer/Essay**

1. Why should you validate user input both within the interface tier and business rules tier?

2. Why should input received in the business rules tier be filtered? What are the different ways you can filter the information?

3. Explain how you can reduce errors from user input by the type of HTML objects (such as radio buttons) used to accept information.

4. What causes the example code shown in the dependency injection section of this chapter inefficient? How does this code help a developer with version changes to the application?

**Projects**

1. Create an application that registers a runner for the local 5K road race. The interface should accept all necessary personal information (name, address, gender, age, and T-shirt size). Whenever possible, use HTML objects that restrict input (such a select object for T-shirt size and state). Validate all information in the interface tier using both HTML5 and JavaScript. If the information is valid, pass the information to the business rules tier. The business rules tier will validate the information received and filter out any harmful information. Once all information has been accepted, the program will display the cost of entering the race ($25). Any shirts over XL will add an additional charge of $2. Any runner 65 or older will be charged $5 less.

2. Develop the application described in #1 to use dependency injection to allow the developer to change file name and locations without requiring code changes to the application itself.

**Term Project**

1. Update the Chapter 3 Term Project to validate all information as it is entered into an HTML form (via HTML and JavaScript as shown in Chapter 4) in the interface tier. After the information is validated it is passed to the business rules tier. The business rules tier will validate the information received and filter out any harmful information. Once the information is accepted (and stored in the properties) the application will display all fields of the product stored in the warehouse of the ABC Computer Parts Company. The interface tier and the business rules tier must be separated using dependency injection (via an XML file), as shown. Your completed project should use logic similar to the examples shown in this chapter.

# CHAPTER 5

# Handling and Logging Exceptions

*"The education of a man is never completed until he dies." —Robert E. Lee (As quoted in Peter's Quotations: Ideas for Our Time (1977) by Laurence J. Peter, p. 175)*

## Chapter Objectives/Student Learning Outcomes

After completing this chapter, the student will be able to:

- Explain the difference between errors and exceptions
- Create a PHP program that can handle general exceptions
- Create a PHP program that can create, raise, and handle user exceptions
- Explain and use a `switch` and/or embedded `if`/`else` statement
- Create a PHP program that uses the `while` loop and/or `for` loop
- Create a program that reads/updates a text file using a two-dimensional array
- Create a PHP program that logs exceptions and e-mails support personnel

## Handling Exceptions

As a programmer, you want to do everything possible to ensure that your program will not crash. Anyone using your application will get a bad taste in their mouths if they have to deal with system crashes. You have probably dealt with this situation too. As a user, you may have chosen one application over another because of bad reviews. Once an application has been determined to be "buggy," it's difficult to convince customers to use the product, even if newer versions have corrected some or all of the problems. An application must be created to handle every possible unanticipated event.

A program must look at each scenario and decide if it can continue or if it must shut down. There will always be a possibility that the application cannot continue to operate due to an unexpected event. Properly developed programs will let the user know that there is a problem without the program crashing. Users are more likely to understand when an application asks them to "try again later" (assuming the problem is fixed before they return to the web site).

---

**Electronic supplementary material**  The online version of this chapter (doi:10.1007/978-1-4842-1730-6_5) contains supplementary material, which is available to authorized users.

S. Prettyman. *Learn PHP 7*. DOI 10.1007/978-1-4842-1730-6_5

*Errors* are program events that are handled by the system that cause the program to shut down. In some cases, the system can shut down the program and display an error message. Some errors immediately cause the program to crash (such as the server itself crashing). Errors are usually events beyond the control of the program and not directly caused by code (or lack of code) in the program. For example, insufficient memory will cause application errors.

*Exceptions* are events that are not part of the normal flow of the program logic. All exceptions should be handled by the program. Exceptions can be "raised" when the application anticipates a problem (a missing file) or when the user does something out of the ordinary (tries to enter invalid information). The program should "catch" all the exceptions. It can then examine the exception and determine if it can be corrected, ignored, or if the application must shut down. If a program does not catch exceptions, the system will display the exception message and then shut down the application.

PHP produces a mixture of errors and exceptions depending on the circumstances. Before PHP 5, exception handling did not exist. Thus, some older PHP commands produced errors (which shut down the program) instead of exceptions. In PHP 7 exception handling is the "rule". PHP 7 Errors can be handled with exception handling techniques. If exceptions are not handled with program code, the program will halt as if it were a fatal error.

Any time an application is dependent on something external, it is probable that at some point that action will not take place. For example, in the Dog application, the user is expected to enter the proper information. The application must anticipate that not all users will enter correct information. The application is also dependent on several files existing on server (dog_interface, dog_container, dog_applications, and get_breeds). If any of these files are missing, the application cannot continue to function properly.

Most object-oriented programming languages use a standard format for handing exceptions. The current version of PHP also uses this approach. As you explore PHP examples on the Internet, you will discover existing PHP code that does not use this standard format. While this code will still execute in the current version of PHP, it is recommend that the standard techniques be used. The standard approach uses the try-catch **block**.

```
try {
// code that might cause an exception
}
catch(Exception $e) {
// code that executes if there is an exception
}
catch(Error $e) {
// PHP 7+ capture and handle errors
}
```

Any code that could cause an exception should be included in the try block. In addition, you may also want to consider placing other conditions (such as math calculations) in the try block.

```
try {
$result = $firstNumber / $secondNumber;
}
catch(Exception $e) {
// code that executes if there is an exception
}
catch(Error $e) {
// PHP 7+ capture and handle errors
}
```

This example might produce an exceptiwon if $secondNumber contains a zero (dividing by zero). If the exception occurs, the code would jump to the catch block. Any code in the block will then be executed. The statement $e->getMessage(); will display any system message related to the exception (in this case a message about the attempt to divide by zero). However, you do not have to use the system message; you can use echo or print to display messages to the users.

```
try {
$result = $firstNumber /$secondNumber;
}
catch(Exception $e) {
echo "You entered zero for the second number. Your entry must be greater than zero";
}
```

However, there is a problem with these examples. If you were trying to catch more than one type of exception in the try block, all exceptions would go into the one catch block. Any exception would display the same message. There are a couple of different ways you can handle this.

One way is by throwing your own exception instead of having the system throw it.

```
try {
        if ($secondNumber == 0)
{ throw new Exception("Zero Exception"); }
else { $result = $firstnumber / $secondnumber; }
// other code with exceptions }
catch(Exception $e) {
        switch ($e->getMessage()) {
                case "Zero Exception":
                        echo "The value of second number must be greater than zero";
                        break;
                case "Some other exception":
                        echo "You did something else wrong";
                        break;
                default:
                        echo $e->getMessage();
}
```

*Programming note—In addition to getMessage method, the Exception and Error objects include:*

*getCode()—Displays the code causing the exception*

*getFile()—Displays the file name containing code that threw the exception*

*getLine()—Displays the line number that threw the exception*

*getTrace() and getTraceAsString()—Displays backtrace (exception flow through the program) information*

*In some circumstances it might be appropriate to display the Exception or Error message to the users. However, the other methods should only be used for debugging or log entries. Providing code information to the users is usually unnecessary and is a breach of security.*

In this example, a `switch` statement was used in the `catch` block to look at all possible exception messages. A `switch` statement accomplishes the same task as an embedded `if` statement. You could have used:

```
If($e->getMessage == "Zero Exception")
{ echo "The value of second number must be greater than zero"; }
else if($e->getMessage == "Some other exception")
{ echo "You did something else wrong"; }
else
{ echo $e->getMessage(); }
```

For some, the `switch` statement is easier to understand when looking at multiple possible values for the same property (variable) or the result of executing a method (as in this example). The default section of the `switch` statement (or the last `else` statement in the embedded `if` statement) catches anything you did not anticipate. In this example, you simply display the exception message for other exceptions.

As stated earlier, it's very important that you handle all exceptions and errors. By including the default code you are able to handle exceptions and errors you may have never anticipated. Notice that each `case` section must include a `break` as the last statement. This keeps the code from following through into the next case statement.

```
Catch(Exception $e) {
        switch($e->getMessage()) {
                case "Zero Exception":
                        echo "The value of second number must be greater than zero";
                case "Some other exception":
                        echo "You did something else wrong";
                        break;
                default:
                        echo $e->getMessage():
        }
```

In this example, if the Zero Exception occurred, both of the messages ("The value of the second number must be greater than zero" and "You did something else wrong") would be displayed. The use of the `switch` statement is very common in `catch` blocks. However, as stated earlier, you can use the embedded `if` statement if you prefer.

Another way you can handle multiple exceptions is to create your own exceptions, throw them, and then catch them. You will need to create a class for your own exception.

```
class zeroException extends Exception {
   public function errorMessage() {
        $errorMessage = "Second Number cannot be " . $this->getMessage();
        return $errorMessage;
        }
 }
try {
if ($secondNumber == 0)
{ throw new zeroException("Zero"); }
else
```

```
{ $result = $firstnumber / $secondnumber; }
// other code with exceptions }
catch(zeroException $e) {
        echo $e->errorMessage();
}
catch(Exception $e) {
        Echo $e->getMessage();
}
```

The zeroException class *extends* the class Exception. The extends keyword is used to inherit all of the functionality of the Exception **class**. *Inheritance* is another key component of object-oriented programming (along with encapsulation and polymorphism). A *child* **class** (like zeroException) can inherit all the properties and methods of its *parent* class (Exception). The child class then can add methods (such as the function errorMessage) specific to the class. Since zeroException inherited Exception, it is treated the same as any other exception. The zeroException can be thrown (throw new zeroException("Zero")) and it can be caught (catch(zeroException $e)).

> *Program note—Programmer-created exception classes inherit from Exception. Thus, all the functionality of the Exception class is available from within any new exception class.*
>
> *Class zeroException extends Exception { }*
>
> *The previous code creates a valid new zeroException class with no new methods.*
>
> *catch(zeroException $e) { echo $e->getMessage(); }*
>
> *This catch block will be called by the new exception and display the exception message generated by the Exception class.*

For each exception or error class that is created and thrown, there must be a catch block to catch the exception or error. In the example, there are two catch blocks; one catches the zeroException and the other catches any other exceptions that might occur. Just like the previous example using a switch default or if else statement, you should always have the last catch blocks handle any remaining exceptions or errors. If the generic catch block is listed first, all exceptions would be caught by that block and not the specific block for the exception.

As stated, the developer should make every attempt to keep the application from crashing. Errors, however, are designed to display messages and shut down programs with an error code (what you consider to be "crashing" the program). Before PHP 7, in some cases, you could override this functionality by creating a method that will handle errors.

```
function errorHandler($severity, $message, $file, $line) {
    throw new errorException($message, 0, $severity, $file, $line); }
set_error_handler('errorHandler');
// set_error_handler() doesn't work with all fatal errors, some can't be thrown as Exceptions.
try { trigger_error( "User Error", E_USER_ERROR);
    }
catch(errorException $e)
{ echo $e->getMessage(); }
catch(Exception $e)
{ echo $e->getMessage(); }
// Code placed here would execute after an error with this handler. It would not execute if
// there was not a handler.
```

In this example, the `set_error_handler` method redirects all errors (that can be redirected) to the method errorHandler. When the method `trigger_error` causes `E_USER_ERROR` to occur, the handling of the error is redirected to the `errorHandler` method. This method then gathers the information from the error to throw an exception (errorException). The exception is captured by the `catch(errorException $e)` method, which causes the message `"User Error"` to be displayed.

In PHP 7, the Error object captures potential system errors as exceptions.

```
try {
call_method(null); // no such method!
} catch (Error $e)
{ echo $e->getMessage; }
```

Previously, the call to a non-existent function would cause a fatal error. Using the `EngineException` object allows the programmer to handle the error. The example shown previously (before PHP 7) would only capture some errors; this new technique is designed to allow the programmer much more control over errors. If this `catch` block is not included, any "error" would cause the program to crash with the `"Fatal error: Uncaught exception"` message.

If you have PHP 7 installed, use the new `Error` object along with the `Exception` object to avoid fatal errors whenever possible.

> *Security and performance—Usually the use of throwing and catching exceptions can reduce the amount of code needed in a program. However, there is a trade-off. Several studies of different object-oriented program languages have concluded that exception handling is less efficient (performance) than using developer created routines. The developer should use exceptions as true "exceptions" to the normal flow of the application. For more frequently occurring situations, the developer should create situation handling routines in the application.*

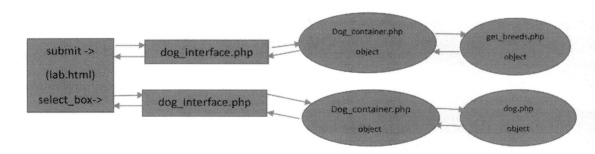

***Figure 5-1.*** *Data flow for the dog application*

In the Dog application, the information flows between many different programs. Each of these programs must be able to handle exceptions properly. However, message handling should all occur in the interface. Any objects that are part of the business rules tier (dog_container, dog, and get_breeds) should pass any exception messages to the interface to handle. At first this may sound like a complex and confusing task. However, the hierarchy of exception handling will greatly simplify this task. As you are about to see, using exception handling will reduce the amount of code necessary.

When exceptions are thrown, the environment will look in the program (or class) itself to determine if there is a `catch` block that can handle the exception. If there is not a `catch` block, it will go up one level in the hierarchy and check any calling program (or program that has made an instance of the class) for a `catch` block. This process will continue until either a catch block has been discovered or it has been determined that the environment itself must handle the exception.

Using this process, you can throw exceptions in the dog_container, dog, and get_breeds modules without using catches. In the dog_interface, you can create a try block around calls to these files. Multiple catch blocks (or one with a switch statement) could be created in the interface to handle the exceptions from both the interface and all the other modules. This satisfies one of the requirements of three-tier programming. The business rules tier (and data tier) pass messages to the interface tier. The interface tier then determines how to handle those messages. It could display them to the users, place them in a log file (which you will look at later in this chapter), or ignore them (if it does not adversely affect the operation of the application).

Before you change the Dog application code, let's look at an example of exceptions being handled by the hierarchy.

***Example 5-1.*** testerror.php with error and exception-producing methods

```php
<?php
class testerror {
    function produceerror() {
        trigger_error( "User Error", E_USER_ERROR);
        echo "This line will not display";  }
    function throwexception() {
        throw new userException("User Exception");
        echo "This line will not display";  }  }
?>
```

***Example 5-2.*** The handleerror.php file captures error or exception

```php
<?php
function errorHandler($severity, $message, $file, $line) {
        throw new errorException($message, 0, $severity, $file, $line);
    }
class userException extends Exception { }
Set_error_handler('errorHandler');
try {
require_once("testerror.php");
$tester = new testerror();
$tester->produceerror();
echo "This line does not display";
$tester->throwexception(); // will not execute if produceerror() is executed
echo "This line does not display"; }
catch (errorException $e ){
        echo $e->getMessage(); }
catch (userException $e) {
  echo $e->getMessage(); }
catch (Exception $e) {
        echo $e->getMessage(); }
echo "This line will display";
?>
```

The `testerror` class (in Example 5-1) includes a method to cause an error (`produceerror`) and a method that throws an exception (`throwexception`). However, the class does not have `try` or `catch` blocks. It does not have the ability to react to any exceptions or errors that might occur.

The `handleerror` program (in Example 5-2) includes a method that will handle user errors (`errorHandler`), along with the `set_error_handler` command to redirect errors to this method. It also includes a class (`userException`) that can react when the `userException` exception is thrown in the `try` block. The `require_once` statement is included in the `try` block in an attempt to capture the error if the file is missing. However, this happens to be a system error (not a user error) which cannot be redirected. To capture system errors in PHP 7, the Error class must be used within a `catch` block as previously shown.

After the `require_once` statement, an instance of class `testerror` is created. If this class is missing, the system will also error with a fatal message. The block calls the `produceerror` method, which causes a user error. This error is redirected to the `errorHandler`, which throws an exception (`errorException`). The `catch` block receives the exception and displays the error message. Since exceptions do not shut down the program (like fatal errors), the flow of the program jumps to the first line after all the `catch` blocks and executes the echo statement (`echo "This line will display";`). The reaction to the error will cause the program to skip any remaining code in the `try` block. In this example, the `throwexception` method call would be ignored.

If the `$tester->produceerror()` line is commented out, the `throwexception` method call can take place. The `userException` is thrown in the method. The `userException` class inherits the `Exception` class. No special methods have been included in `userException`. The flow of the program will jump to the `catch` block for `userException`. This block uses the `Exception` class `getMessage` method to display the message. The logic then jumps to the first line of code after the `catch` blocks and executes the echo `"This line will display"` statement.

> *Program note—try/catch can also include a finally block after all catch blocks. The finally block will execute for all caught exceptions after the associated catch block has executed. PHP allows the finally block to exist without any catch blocks (but the try block must still exist). One of the most common uses of the finally block is to close files and/or databases when an exception has occurred. A program should not close before files and databases have been properly closed. If not closed properly, the data may become corrupt and not be accessible.*

## Do It

1.  Go to the book's web site and download the files for Examples 5-1 and 5-2. Adjust the `testerror` program to only create an error. Create an additional `testexception` program (with a `testexception` class) to throw an exception. Now adjust the `handleerror` program to create an instance of both programs. The `handleerror` program should now be able to handle errors or exceptions from either program (class).

# Exception and Error Handling vs. If/Else Conditions

A programmer can always choose to handle exceptions and errors using `If/else` conditional statements as shown in the dog application files from Chapter 4. It is not any less efficient to handle errors in this way (it might even be more efficient). However, as you are about to discover, the *attitude* of the code in the business rules tier (and data tier) changes if you use exception handling. When you use `if/else` statements, the flow of the program spends a lot of time being pessimistic by preparing for the worst (errors and/or exceptions). In many cases, by using exception handling, the coding for most of the business rules tier (and data tier) becomes optimistic including code which handles the normal operation of the program. The application relies on the interface tier to handle any problems.

***Example 5-3.*** The dog.class with exception handling

```php
<?php
class Dog
{
// --------------------------------- Properties ----------------------------------------
private $dog_weight = 0;
private $dog_breed = "no breed";
private $dog_color = "no color";
private $dog_name = "no name";
private $error_message = "??";
private $breedxml = "";
// --------------------------------- Constructor ----------------------------------------
function __construct($properties_array)
{
  if (method_exists('dog_container', 'create_object')) {
  $this->breedxml = $properties_array[4];
  $name_error = $this->set_dog_name($properties_array[0]) == TRUE ? 'TRUE,' : 'FALSE,';
  $color_error = $this->set_dog_color($properties_array[2]) == TRUE ? 'TRUE,' : 'FALSE,';
  $weight_error= $this->set_dog_weight($properties_array[3]) == TRUE ? 'TRUE' : 'FALSE';
  $breed_error = $this->set_dog_breed($properties_array[1]) == TRUE ? 'TRUE,' : 'FALSE,';
  $this->error_message = $name_error . $breed_error . $color_error . $weight_error;
  if(stristr($this->error_message, 'FALSE'))
  {
        throw new setException($this->error_message);
  }
}
    else { exit; }
}

function set_dog_name($value) {
  $error_message = TRUE;
  (ctype_alpha($value) && strlen($value) <= 20) ? $this->dog_name = $value : $this->error_
  message = FALSE;
  return $this->error_message; }
function set_dog_weight($value) {
  $error_message = TRUE;
  (ctype_digit($value) && ($value > 0 && $value <= 120)) ? $this->dog_weight = $value :
  $this->error_message = FALSE;
  return $this->error_message; }
function set_dog_breed($value) {
  $error_message = TRUE;
  ($this->validator_breed($value) === TRUE) ? $this->dog_breed = $value : $this->error_
  message = FALSE;
  return $this->error_message; }
function set_dog_color($value) {
  $error_message = TRUE;
  (ctype_alpha($value) && strlen($value) <= 15) ? $this->dog_color = $value : $this->error_
  message = FALSE;
  return $this->error_message; }
```

```
// --------------------------------Get Methods----------------------------------------
function get_dog_name() {
  return $this->dog_name; }
function get_dog_weight() {
  return $this->dog_weight; }
function get_dog_breed() {
  return $this->dog_breed; }
function get_dog_color() {
  return $this->dog_color; }
function get_properties() {
  return "$this->dog_name,$this->dog_weight,$this->dog_breed,$this->dog_color."; }
// --------------------------------General Method--------------------------------------
  private function validator_breed($value)
  {
    $breed_file = simplexml:load_file($this->breedxml);
    $xmlText = $breed_file->asXML();
    if(stristr($xmlText, $value) === FALSE)
  {
    return FALSE;
  }
  else
    {
      return TRUE;
    }
  }
}
?>
```

Comparing Example 4-8 to Example 5-3, you will notice only a couple of slight changes to the code. The __toString method has been removed and replaced by an if statement that checks to see if FALSE exists anywhere in the error_message string. If it does exist, a setException message is raised, passing the error_message string to the exception handler. This causes a logical change in the flow of the overall application. Instead of the dog_interface program (in Example 4-12) checking for user entry errors by calling the __toString method, the Dog class notifies the dog_interface (via a thrown exception) when user errors occur. Previously the interface had to pull the errors from the Dog class. In this example, the Dog class pushes the errors to the interface class. As you will see, this will eliminate code from the dog_interface program, since it no longer has to ask if there are any errors.

> *Security and performance—The __toString method "exposes" whatever it returns to any program that makes an instance of the class in which it exists. Using this method to pass error messages might allow a hacker to determine what incorrect information they are sending into a program. In the dog.class example from Chapter 4, __toString passes back the error_message string containing 'TRUE' or 'FALSE' responses. This is more secure than returning error messages. However, by replacing the __toString method with throwing a special exception, you provide even better security. Hackers must now not only know what the error_message means, but they must also know the name of the exception (setException) in order to capture it in their own programs.*

*Example 5-4.* The getbreeds.class with exception handling

```php
<?php
class GetBreeds {
    function __construct($properties_array) {
        if (!(method_exists('dog_container', 'create_object')))
            { exit; }
    }
      private $result = "??";
  public function get_select($dog_app)
  {
            if (($dog_app != FALSE) && ( file_exists($dog_app)))
            {
                $breed_file = simplexml:load_file($dog_app);
                $xmlText = $breed_file->asXML();
                $this->result = "<select name='dog_breed' id='dog_breed'>";
                 $this->result = $this->result . "<option value='-1' selected>Select a dog
                breed</option>";
                foreach ($breed_file->children() as $name => $value)
                {
                        $this->result = $this->result . "<option value='$value'>$value</option>";
                }
                $this->result = $this->result . "</select>";
                 return $this->result;
            }
            else
            {
                    throw new Exception("Breed xml file missing or corrupt");
            }
    }
}
?>
```

Comparing the previous GetBreeds class (in Example 4-11) with Example 5-4 shows only one change. It returns 'FALSE' and throws a general exception indicating that the breed.xml file is missing or corrupt. Again, the GetBreeds class pushes any exceptions to the interface. The interface no longer has to determine if there are any exceptions. Even though missing file errors cannot be redirected to be handled as exceptions, the code uses file_exists to throw an exception if the file is missing.

*Example 5-5.* The dog_container.php file with exception handling

```php
<?php
class dog_container
{
  private $app;
  private $dog_location;
  function __construct($value) {
      if (function_exists('clean_input')) {
          $this->app = $value;
      } else { exit; }
  }
```

```php
    public function set_app($value) {
        $this->app = $value; }
public function get_dog_application($search_value) {
        $xmlDoc = new DOMDocument();
        if ( file_exists("e5dog_applications.xml") ) {
            $xmlDoc->load( 'e5dog_applications.xml' );
            $searchNode = $xmlDoc->getElementsByTagName( "type" );
            foreach( $searchNode as $searchNode )  {
                $valueID = $searchNode->getAttribute('ID');
                if($valueID == $search_value)    {
                    $xmlLocation = $searchNode->getElementsByTagName( "location" );
                     return $xmlLocation->item(0)->nodeValue;
                break;    }
    } }
        throw new Exception("Dog applications xml file missing or corrupt"); }
    function create_object($properties_array) {
        $dog_loc = $this->get_dog_application($this->app);
        if(($dog_loc == FALSE) || (!file_exists($dog_loc))) {
            throw new Exception("File $dog_loc missing or corrupt.");   }
    else
     {
        require_once($dog_loc);
        $class_array = get_declared_classes();
        $last_position = count($class_array) - 1;
        $class_name = $class_array[$last_position];
        $dog_object = new $class_name($properties_array);
        return $dog_object;
    }
 }
}
?>
```

The dog_container in Example 5-5 replaces returning 'FALSE' from Example 4-10 when the dog_application.xml file, dog.class file, and/or the get_breeds file is missing. Instead, an exception is thrown indicating which file is missing.

***Example 5-6.*** The dog_interface.php file with exception handling

```php
<?php
  function clean_input($value)
 {
    $value = htmlentities($value);
    $value = strip_tags($value);
    if (get_magic_quotes_gpc())
     {
        $value = stripslashes($value);
    }
    $value = htmlentities($value);
    $bad_chars = array( "{", "}", "(", ")", ";", ":", "<", ">", "/", "$" );
    $value = str_ireplace($bad_chars,"",$value);
    return $value;
  }
```

```
class setException extends Exception {
    public function errorMessage() {
        list($name_error, $breed_error, $color_error, $weight_error) = explode(',',
        $this->getMessage());
        $name_error == 'TRUE' ? $eMessage = '' : $eMessage = 'Name update not successful<br/>';
        $breed_error == 'TRUE' ? $eMessage .= '' : $eMessage .= 'Breed update not successful<br/>';
        $color_error == 'TRUE' ? $eMessage .= '' : $eMessage .= 'Color update not successful<br/>';
        $weight_error == 'TRUE' ? $eMessage .= '' : $eMessage .= 'Weight update not successful<br/>';
        return $eMessage;
    }
}
function get_dog_app_properties($lab)
{
print "Your dog's name is " . $lab->get_dog_name() . "<br/>";
print "Your dog weights " . $lab->get_dog_weight() . " lbs. <br />";
print "Your dog's breed is " . $lab->get_dog_breed() . "<br />";
print "Your dog's color is " . $lab->get_dog_color() . "<br />";
}
//---------------Main Section-------------------------------------
try {
        if ( file_exists("e5dog_container.php"))
        {   Require_once("e5dog_container.php"); }
        else
        {    throw new Exception("Dog container file missing or corrupt"); }
                if (isset($_POST['dog_app'])) {
if ((isset($_POST['dog_name'])) && (isset($_POST['dog_breed'])) && (isset($_POST['dog_
color'])) &&  (isset($_POST['dog_weight'])))
        {
            $container = new dog_container(clean_input($_POST['dog_app']));
            $dog_name = clean_input(filter_input(INPUT_POST, "dog_name"));
            $dog_breed = clean_input($_POST['dog_breed']);
            $dog_color = clean_input($_POST['dog_color']);
            $dog_weight = clean_input($_POST['dog_weight']);
            $breedxml = $container->get_dog_application("breeds");
            $properties_array = array($dog_name,$dog_breed,$dog_color,
            $dog_weight,$breedxml);
            $lab = $container->create_object($properties_array);
            print "Updates successful<br />";
            get_dog_app_properties($lab); }
        else {
            print "<p>Missing or invalid parameters. Please go back to the lab.html page to
            enter valid information.<br />";
                    print "<a href='dog.html'>Dog Creation Page</a>";
            }
        } else // select box {
                    $container = new dog_container("selectbox");
                    $properties_array = array("selectbox");
                    $lab = $container->create_object($properties_array);
                    $container->set_app("breeds");
                    $dog_app = $container->get_dog_application("breeds");
```

```
                $result = $lab->get_select($dog_app);
                print $result;
            }
    } // try
  catch(setException $e)
  {
        echo $e->errorMessage();
  }
  catch(Exception $e)
  {
        echo $e->getMessage();
  }
  catch(Error $e) // PHP 7+ only
  {
        echo $e->getMessage();
  }
?>
```

When comparing Example 4-12 to Example 5-6, the amount of code needed to handle exceptions is less than using if/else conditional statements. The logical flow of the program is easier to follow with very few else statements. This occurs because the exceptions thrown from all the files in this application are handled by the catch blocks in dog_interface. The user errors are thrown to a special setException exception. The system errors are captured by the Error catch block. The error_check_dog_app method (in Example 4-12) has been replaced by the setException class. The code in the class is very similar to the code in the error_check_dog_app. The display of individual update messages in the $eMessage string is removed, since this class reacts to user errors, not successful updates. A general print line has been added in the main body of the code to let the users know that all updates have been successful. The try block has been added around all the code in this interface. This helps to capture any problems in any part of this application. Notice that an exception is also thrown if the dog_container file cannot be found.

Only three catch blocks are required for this application. The setException catch block calls the errorMessage method from the setException class, which determines what user errors have occurred. The information is then displayed back to the user. The Exception catch block handles all other exceptions. It currently displays this information to the user. However, the Exception and Error catch blocks are currently providing the user too much information. It is a violation of security to inform the user what other problems the application maybe experiencing. You should just tell them that the system is not currently available and ask them to check back later. Displaying detailed errors is okay when you're testing. However, it's not good for the real world. You will resolve this breach of security in the next section.

*For more information on exception handling, visit*
*Examples: http://www.w3schools.com/php/php_exception.asp*
*Video: https://www.thenewboston.com/videos.php?cat=11&video=17171*

## Do It

1. Examine the code from this section. Are there any areas in which error checking could have been converted to exception handling? Go to the book's web site and download the code for this section. Make the potential changes to the existing code to use additional exception handling.

# Logging Exceptions

Applications must have an ability to notify systems analysts when problems occur. However, specific messages about errors should not be displayed to the user of the application. The user should be notified that the system is not currently operational. The systems analyst should be notified of the specific problem that has occurred.

The easiest way to provide this ability is to place error messages into a log file. PHP applications can log messages into the default PHP error file or in an application specific file. The php.ini file can be edited (see Chapter 1 for location) to specify the location and name of the default error log file. Once the php.ini file is open in an editor, search for error_log. If a semicolon is located at the beginning of the line, the location has been commented out. Just remove the semicolon and specify a location, such as:

```
error_log = c:/temp/php_errors.log
-or-
error_log = http://www.asite.com/temp/php_errors.log
```

When writing to the default error log, PHP will insert a *timestamp* along with the error message that you submit. Your default time zone may not be set correctly in the php.ini file. Search for date.timezone. The valid time zone settings for the continental United States are:

```
date.timezone = "America/New_York"
date.timezone = "America/Chicago"
date.timezone = "America/Los_Angeles"
For all other American time zones visit: http://www.php.net/manual/en/timezones.america.php
For worldwide time zones visit: http://php.net/manual/en/timezones.php
```

The Apache httpd config file (see Chapter 1 for location) can override the settings in the php.ini file. You should also open this file and search for date.timezone. Replace the existing line with a format similar to the following.

```
php_value date.timezone "America/New_York"
```

Once you have updated and saved the php.ini and/or apache.httpd files, you must reload your Apache server for the changes to take place (see Chapter 1).

---

▓ **Note** The time zone can also be set with program code. PHP 7 does not support the datefmt_set_timezone_id method. The datefmt_set_timezone method can be used for PHP 5.2+. For more information on setting the time zone with program code, visit http://php.net/manual/en/datetime.settimezone.php.

---

```php
<?php
error_log("error message");
?>
```

Enter this code and save it in a test file. Test it in your environment. If your settings are correct, PHP will create the error log at the location specified in the error_log parameter. Don't create the file yourself. PHP will not log information to a log file that it did not create. The format of the message sent to your log file should be similar to the following:

```
[25-Jun-2015 17:01:12 America/New_York] error message
```

With only the simple one line of code, PHP created the text-based file in the location specified and placed the message in the file.

If you do not have access to these files, you can specify a specific location in the PHP application to send your messages. This ability also allows you to set up multiple application log files. It is common for an application to have informational log files, authentication (login) log files, error log files, and security log files. By separating each type of message, it's easier to scan for a specific type of message in a log file.

Let's assume you want to log user errors in one file and other errors in a different file.

```php
<?php
const USER_ERROR_LOG = 'User_Errors.log';
const ERROR_LOG = 'Errors.log';
// sending a user error
error_log("A user error",3,USER_ERROR_LOG);
// sending all other errors
error_log("A general error",3,ERROR_LOG);
<?php
```

This code will use the **constants** (USER_ERROR_LOG and ERROR_LOG) to direct the error messages to the correct location. Notice that a second parameter of 3 is used to let the error_log method know that a different location will be used to log the error. A standard format should be used for sending messages to your log(s). The format should include the time/date (if not already included by the environment as mentioned previously), the type of message (if there is more than one message type in the file), the error message, and any other pertinent information. By default, the message size is limited to 120 characters. However this can be changed in the php.ini file.

```php
$date = date('m.d.Y h:i:s');
// For more info on data time format go to: http://php.net/manual/en/function.date.php
$errormessage = "This is the error";
$eMessage =  $date . " | User Error | " . $errormessage . "\n";
error_log($eMessage,3,USER_ERROR_LOG);
The above code would produce
06.06.2015 03:00:55 | User Error | This is the error
```

A standard text editor (Notepad++ or Notepad) or log-monitoring software (you will create a log reader program later in this chapter) can be used to view the contents of the file.

The system will limit the size of the log file(s). However, assuming that there is not too much logging per day, the application can create logs that are specific for each day.

```php
$USER_ERROR_LOG = "User_Errors" . date('mdy') . ".log";
$ERROR_LOG = "Errors" . date('mdy') . ".log";
...
error_log($eMessage,3,$USER_ERROR_LOG);
```

> *Security and performance—The location of the log files should reside in a different folder than the application. The folder will need to allow write access for the application. However, it should be secured from read access or write access outside the server itself. Only authorized personnel should have access to the logs.*

Note that the constants (USER_ERROR_LOG and ERROR_LOG) must be changed to variables due to the date method creating a possible variable output (different dates). The format would create a file name similar to User_Errors06062015.log or Errors06062015.log.

PHP also makes it very easy to send an e-mail alert when something has been written to a log file. The webserver must include an e-mail server. Your local machine may not have this capability. However, usually, a web host provider (that has PHP capability) includes an e-mail service. To use this ability, you can add an error_log statement:

```php
error_log("Date/Time: $date - Serious System Problems with Dog Application. Check error log
for details", 1, "noone@helpme.com", "Subject: Dog Application Error \nFrom: System Log
<systemlog@helpme.com>" . "\r\n");
```

> *Security and performance – While it is tempting to inform the associate receiving the e-mail message of the exact problem that has occurred in the application, do not. By default, e-mail is not encrypted. Sending an unencrypted e-mail with detailed information about your application is inviting hackers to corrupt your application. You should, however, provide enough information in the message (such as a date/time stamp and maybe an error number) to help the associate locate the error message(s) in the log file(s).*

The first parameter specifies the message of the e-mail. The second parameter informs error_log to e-mail this information. The third parameter provides the "To" e-mail address. The fourth parameter is an extra header field. This field is commonly used to include the subject of the e-mail and the e-mail address that sent the message. The "From" address must be included or the message will not be sent. The "From" address does not, however, need to be an existing address.

> *For more information on logging errors, visit*
> *Examples: http://php.net/manual/en/function.error-log.php*
> *Examples: http://www.w3schools.com/php/php_error.asp*

In the Dog application, you can provide the ability to log exceptions and e-mail major errors by adjusting the catch blocks of the dog_interface (from Example 5-6).

***Example 5-7.*** The dog_inteface.php file with exception logging and e-mail

```php
<?php
const USER_ERROR_LOG = "User_Errors.log";
const ERROR_LOG = "Errors.log";

function clean_input($value)
{
 $value = htmlentities($value);
               // Removes any html from the string and turns it into &lt; format
               $value = strip_tags($value);
        if (get_magic_quotes_gpc())
        {
               $value = stripslashes($value);          // Gets rid of unwanted slashes
        }
               $value = htmlentities($value);          // Removes any html from the string
                                                       and turns it into &lt; format
        $bad_chars = array( "{", "}", "(", ")", ";", ":", "<", ">", "/", "$" );
        $value = str_ireplace($bad_chars,"",$value);
               return $value;
}
class setException extends Exception {
    public function errorMessage() {
         list($name_error, $breed_error, $color_error, $weight_error) = explode(',', $this->getMessage());
         $name_error == 'TRUE' ? $eMessage = '' : $eMessage = 'Name update not successful<br/>';
         $breed_error == 'TRUE' ? $eMessage .= '' : $eMessage .= 'Breed update not successful<br/>';
         $color_error == 'TRUE' ? $eMessage .= '' : $eMessage .= 'Color update not successful<br/>';
         $weight_error == 'TRUE' ? $eMessage .= '' : $eMessage .= 'Weight update not successful<br/>';
       return $eMessage;
           } }
 }

function get_dog_app_properties($lab)
{

print "Your dog's name is " . $lab->get_dog_name() . "<br/>";
print "Your dog weights " . $lab->get_dog_weight() . " lbs. <br />";
print "Your dog's breed is " . $lab->get_dog_breed() . "<br />";
print "Your dog's color is " . $lab->get_dog_color() . "<br />";

}
//---------------Main Section-----------------------------------
try {
        if ( file_exists("e5dog_container.php"))
        {
               Require_once("e5dog_container.php");
        }
        else
```

```
    {
            throw new Exception("Dog container file missing or corrupt");
    }

    if (isset($_POST['dog_app']))
    {

            if ((isset($_POST['dog_name'])) && (isset($_POST['dog_breed'])) &&
            (isset($_POST['dog_color'])) && (isset($_POST['dog_weight'])))
            {

                    $container = new dog_container(clean_input($_POST['dog_app']));

                    $dog_name = clean_input(filter_input(INPUT_POST, "dog_name"));
                    $dog_breed = clean_input($_POST['dog_breed']);
                    $dog_color = clean_input($_POST['dog_color']);
                    $dog_weight = clean_input($_POST['dog_weight']);
                    $breedxml = $container->get_dog_application("breeds");

                    $properties_array = array($dog_name,$dog_breed,$dog_color,
                    $dog_weight,$breedxml);
                    $lab = $container->create_object($properties_array);
                    print "Updates successful<br />";
                    get_dog_app_properties($lab);
            }

            else
            {

            print "<p>Missing or invalid parameters. Please go back to the dog.html page
            to enter valid information.<br />";

            print "<a href='dog.html'>Dog Creation Page</a>";

            }
    }
    else // select box
    {

            $container = new dog_container("selectbox");

            $properties_array = array("selectbox");

            $lab = $container->create_object($properties_array);
    $container->set_app("breeds");
    $dog_app = $container->get_dog_application("breeds");
```

```php
                $result = $lab->get_select($dog_app);

            print $result;
        }
    }
    catch(setException $e)
    {
                echo $e->errorMessage(); // displays to the user

                $date = date('m.d.Y h:i:s');
                $errormessage = $e->errorMessage();
                $eMessage =  $date . " | User Error | " . $errormessage . "\n";
                error_log($eMessage,3,USER_ERROR_LOG); // writes message to user error log file


    }
    catch(Exception $e)
    {

                echo "The system is currently unavailable. Please try again later.";
                // displays message to the user

                $date = date('m.d.Y h:i:s');
                $errormessage = $e->getMessage();
                $eMessage = $date . " | User Error | " . $errormessage . "\n";
                error_log($eMessage,3,ERROR_LOG); // writes message to error log file

                error_log("Date/Time: $date - Serious System Problems with Dog Application.
Check error log for details", 1, "noone@helpme.com", "Subject: Dog Application Error \nFrom:
System Log <systemlog@helpme.com>" . "\r\n");
        // e-mails personnel to alert them of a system problem

    }
    catch (Error $e)
    {

                echo "The system is currently unavailable. Please try again later.";
                // displays message to the user

                $date = date('m.d.Y h:i:s');
                $errormessage = $e->getMessage();
                $eMessage = $date . " | Fatal System Error | " . $errormessage . "\n";
                error_log($eMessage,3,ERROR_LOG); // writes message to error log file

                error_log("Date/Time: $date - Serious System Problems with Dog Application.
Check error log for details", 1, "noone@helpme.com", "Subject: Dog Application Error \nFrom:
System Log <systemlog@helpme.com>" . "\r\n");
        // e-mails personnel to alert them of a system problem

    }
```

At the top of the Example 5-7 code, the constants USER_ERROR_LOG and ERROR_LOG have been created to pinpoint the name and location of the log files. Locating constants that might be subject to change (such as a tax rate) at the top of the code provides easy access for quick changes by a programmer who is charged with supporting the application. As stated previously, the location of the log file must be in a folder that allows application write access. It is recommended that log files be centrally located in a common folder, with other log files, for easy access by data center personnel (or systems analysts).

The other code changes are located in the catch blocks. The setException catch block returns the error message generated by the setException class to the users. This message lets the users know what properties (Name, Breed, Color, and Weight) were not updated. Errors that caused this exception could have come from the user, or by corruption when the information was transmitted from the client machine to the server. These messages only provides information about the requirements of the properties, which the user already should have known. The catch block also writes a similar message to the user error log. A user error is not an urgent error that needs to be addressed by the analyst. However, tracking trends of user problems can provide an indication of possible changes needed to ensure the user has the best experience possible with the application.

The Exception and Error catch blocks captures all non-user generated exceptions. The messages caused by these exceptions might reveal information that would break the security of the application. Therefore a generic message (such as "The system is currently unavailable. Please try again later.") should be displayed to the user. Detailed information about the exception (error message, file location, coding line that raised the exception) should be placed in the error log for further analysis. Most exceptions caught by these catch blocks will keep the application from running. Therefore, it is important that personnel be informed of the problems occurring. This catch blocks are a good location to send an e-mail to the support personnel to alert them of any problems.

Now that you have built-in exception handling and error handling into the program, you could edit the php.ini file to turn off error reporting to the user. However, you should wait to do this until all development and testing has been completed. Locate the line "display_errors = On" in the php.ini file. If you change this setting to "display_errors = Off", most error messages will not be displayed to the user. This change will not affect any messages sent back by the program to the user via the echo or print methods (including in any catch blocks). This change will give the developer greater control over the type of messages displayed to the users when there are system problems.

# Do It

1. Download the code for this section. Create or use an existing HTML page that does not check for user input errors. Run the program entering values for the name, breed, weight, and color, which should cause user errors. Stop the program and open the contents of the user error log file. Did the errors appear in the file? If not, check the security of the folder that contains the log file to make sure that it allows write access to the log file. Once you are satisfied that it has caught user errors, try to cause other system errors to occur. Hint: Change the file names to nonexistent names in the dog application XML file. Check the error log to determine if the errors have been written to the file. Were you able to cause any errors that are not captured by one of the log files? If so, is there a way to capture those errors?

# Reading Log and Text Files

In the previous section, you discovered that the error_log method writes to a log file using just one line of code. It creates the log file if it does not exist. It appends (adds to the end of the file) any message passed to the contents of the file. It then closes the file. If you were to create your own logging process, it would take several lines of code.

```
$logFile = fopen("error_log.log", "a");
$eMessage = $e->getMessage();
fwrite($logFile, $eMessage);
fclose($logFile);
```

The fopen method will also create the file if it does not already exist. The "a" parameter indicates that anything written to the file should be appended. "w" would indicate that any contents in the file would be lost (written over). The fwrite method will then place the string located in the second parameter ($eMessage) into the file indicated by the first parameter ($logFile). $logFile is a pointer that points to the location of the text file. The fclose method closes the text file.

> For more information on writing to text files, visit
> Examples: visit w3schools at: http://www.w3schools.com/php/php_file_create.asp
> Video: visit "The New Boston" at https://www.thenewboston.com/videos.php?cat=11&video=17063

Since a log file is a text-based file, you can use similar logic to create your own application to open a log file and read its contents.

```
$logFile = fopen("error_log.log", "r");
echo fgets($logFile);
fclose($logFile);
```

This code will open the log file and read the first line (via a fgets method) in the file and close the file. However, it is likely that there is more than one line in the file. You must be able to loop through and display each line in the file. You can do this using the while loop shown here.

```
$logFile = fopen("error_log.log", "r");
while(!feof($logFile))
{
        echo fgets($logFile) . "<br>";
}
fclose($logFile);
```

The while loop will continue to loop as long as the conditional statement is TRUE. Once the statement is FALSE, the code will exit the loop and jump to the next line of code after the end of the loop. In this example the error_log file is open for read only ("r"). The while loop looks at the end of file indicator (feof) of the log file to determine if it has reached the end of the file. If feof returns TRUE, the end of the file has been reached. The loop must continue while you have not reached the end of the file. To cause the conditional statement to produce a TRUE, while there are still records to be read, you must reverse the logic and have feof produce TRUE if there are records and FALSE if there are not records. You can do this by using the ! operator. The ! operator is a NOT operator and it reverses the result. A NOT TRUE is FALSE or a NOT FALSE is

TRUE. Thus, !feof operator will now produce TRUE when there are more records and FALSE when there are no more records. The loop in combination with the fgets method will display each record in the file. Once each record is displayed, it will close the file using fclose.

*For more information on reading text files,*
*Visit w3schools for examples:*
`http://www.w3schools.com/php/php_file_open.asp`
*Visit "The New Boston" for videos:*
`https://www.thenewboston.com/videos.php?cat=11&video=17064`
*For more information on the* while loop:
*Visit w3schools for examples:*
`http://www.w3schools.com/php/php_looping.asp`
*Visit "The New Boston" for videos:*
`https://www.thenewboston.com/videos.php?cat=11&video=17011`

The output produced by the previous example is pretty plain.

```
06.06.2015 03:00:55 | User Error | This is the error
```

This is not providing you any better viewing than just opening the log file in a text editor. You can use a combination of an HTML table, the explode method, and arrays to produce a much better output. You can place each line from the log file into a two-dimensional array using the explode method. The two-dimensional array will have rows and columns just like the HTML table.

```
$dogs = array
  (
  array("Sammy","Lab",18,"Yellow"),
  array("Spot","Mixed",14,"Mixed"),
  array("Princess","Chihuahua",4,"White"),
  array("Max","Boxer",35,"Brown")
  );
```

Two-dimensional arrays are a collection of rows of information. Each **row** has common information in each position (**column**). In the previous example, all dog names are in position 0, dog breeds are in position 1, dog weights are in position 2, and dog colors are in position 3. This associates directly with the positions in a table.

*For more information on the multi-dimensional arrays, visit:*
*examples:* `http://www.w3schools.com/php/php_arrays_multi.asp`
*videos:* `https://www.thenewboston.com/videos.php?cat=11&video=17026`

| | | | |
|---|---|---|---|
| Sammy | Lab | 18 | Yellow |
| Spot | Mixed | 14 | Mixed |
| Princess | Chihuahua | 4 | White |
| Max | Boxer | 35 | Brown |

Each position in the table and the two-dimensional array is referred to by the column and row. In this table, Sammy is in position (0,0). Yellow is in position (0,3). Max is in position (3,0). Brown in in position (3,3). The first position is the column. The second position is the row. In PHP, [ ] are used to define the position (subscript) for an array.

```
echo $dogs[0][0] // displays Sammy
echo $dogs[0][3] // displays Yellow
echo $dogs[3][0] // displays Max
echo $dogs[3][3] // displays Brown
```

You can now adjust the loop to place the log contents in a two-dimensional array. However, you will not know the size of the array. So you can't use the format previously shown. This might cause developers to get a major migraine if they were not using PHP. PHP, however, allows you to dynamically create the array, just like it allows you to create variables (properties) whenever you need them.

```
$logFile = fopen("error_log.log", "r");
$row_Count = 0;
while(!feof($logFile))
{
        print_r ($error_Array[$row_Count] = explode(' | ', fgets($logFile)));
        $row_Count++;
}
fclose($logFile);
```

In the loop in this example, the explode method breaks the incoming line from the text file via the | character (actually a space, |, and a space). It places each separated string into the $error_Array at the row indicated by the value in $row_Count. The first time through the loop, the first line of the log file is placed in $error_Array[0] (the first row of the array). Because the explode command separated the string, this causes columns to be created for each piece.

If the first line of the file contained:

```
A general error | stuff | more stuff
```

then the first row of the array would contain:

```
$error_Array[0][0] = "A general error"
$error_Array[0][1] = "stuff";
$error_Array[0][2] = "more stuff";
```

You can verify this by using the print_r command shown in the example. print_r displays the contents of an array in the following format.

```
Array ( [0] => A general error [1] => stuff [2] => more stuff )
```

This format verifies that each piece of the string has been placed into the proper position in the array.

$row_count is incremented by 1 before the loop continues. This positions the next line of the file to be placed into the next position in the array ($error_Array[1], if it is the second line of the file). You, of course, don't want to use print_r to display the results to the users (it's not very pretty).

However, it is a great tool to help you make sure the program is placing everything properly in the array. You can add code to the loop to build a table.

```
$logFile = fopen("Errors.log", "r");
$row_Count = 0;
echo "<table>";
while(!feof($logFile))
{        echo "<tr>";
         $error_Array[$row_Count] = explode(' | ', fgets($logFile));
         $displayString = "";
         for($I=0; $I < 3; $I++)
                        {
         echo "<td> " . $error_Array[$row_Count][$I] . " </td> ";
 }
             echo "</tr>";
             $row_Count++;
}
echo "</table>";
fclose($logFile);
```

An echo statement is located just before the while loop to open the HTML table. An additional echo statement (echo "<tr>") exists just inside the while loop to create a row of the table.

*For more information on the for loop, visit:*
*Examples: http://www.w3schools.com/php/php_looping_for.asp*
*Videos: https://www.thenewboston.com/videos.php?cat=11&video=17013*

Also in the while loop, a for loop has been created to loop through each of the columns of the row. Since you know that there are four columns, the for loop is a good choice. The for loop is used when you know exactly how many times to loop. The first parameter (before the ;) of the for loop initializes the counting variable ($I=0). This variable ($I) is used to count each loop. The second parameter ($I < 3) includes the comparison to determine if the logical flow will stay in the loop. If the comparison is TRUE, the loop will continue. If it is FALSE, the logical flow jumps to the first statement after the loop (echo "</tr>"). The third parameter ($I++) can increment or decrement the counting variable. The for loop helps the programmer to remember to initialize the variable, check the condition, and increment the variable by requiring all the information in one code line.

The echo statement in the for loop uses the $row_Count and $I variables to pull the information from each column in the current row. The first time in the loop, $row_Count will be 0. The echo statement will display the contents of $errorArray[0][0]. As the for loop continues, the contents of $errorArray[0][1], $errorArray[0][2], and $errorArray[0][3] will be displayed. Each value is placed into a cell in the table using the <td> and </td> tags. Once the for loop completes, the flow drops below the loop and closes the row (echo </tr>). Then the row_Count variable is incremented. If there are more rows (more records in the file), the while loop will continue the process with the next row, until there are no more records in the file. Once the flow jumps out of the while loop, the table is closed (echo "</table>"). Then the file is closed.

Text (log) files are sequential files. As items are added (appended), they are added to the bottom of the list. You may want to sort the information, listing the most current first. This can be accomplished with just a slight change to the code.

```php
$logFile = fopen("Errors.log", "r");
$row_Count = 0;
while(!feof($logFile))
{
        $error_Array[$row_Count] = explode(' | ', fgets($logFile));
        $row_Count++;
}
$row_Count--;
fclose($logFile);
echo "<table>";
for ($J=$row_Count; $J >= 0; $J--)
{        echo "<tr>";
        $displayString = "";
        for($I=0; $I < 3; $I++)
        {
                echo "<td> " . $error_Array[$J][$I] . " </td> ";
        }
        echo "</tr>";
}
echo "</table>";
```

The while loop now loads the array with the records and keeps a count of the number of items in the array. After the loop ends and the file has been closed, a for loop works through the array in reverse order to echo out the rows in the table. The counter variable $J begins with the total number of rows in the array ($row_Count). One is subtracted from $row_Count before the loop because it is incremented in the while loop after the last record has been retrieved, which makes the count one too many. $J is then decremented ($J--) for each loop until the value is less than zero. The internal for loop (for($I=0;$I<3;$I++)) has not changed, as it must still loop through each column of the rows to display the information.

By loading the records into an array, you can modify them if needed. Let's assume that you want to be able to delete a record from the log. As long as you know the row number that is to be deleted you can remove that record from the array. Then you can repopulate the file with the remaining records.

First you will make a slight change to the echo code you have completed to include a link next to the record to be deleted. You then will add a delete method, move the display code to a display method (so it can be called whenever needed), and create a save changes method to update the log file.

**Example 5-8.** The readerrorlog.php file

```php
<?php

function deleteRecord($recordNumber, &$row_Count, &$error_Array) {
        for ($J=$recordNumber; $J < $row_Count - 1; $J++) {
                for($I=0; $I < 3; $I++)
                { $error_Array[$J][$I] = $error_Array[$J + 1][$I]; }
}

        Unset($error_Array[$row_Count]);
        $row_Count--;
        }
function saveChanges($row_Count,$error_Array,$log_File) {
        $logFile = fopen($log_File, "w");
```

```php
        for($I=0; $I < $row_Count; $I++) {
                $writeString = $error_Array[$I][0] . " | " . $error_Array[$I][1] . " | " .
                $error_Array[$I][2];
                fwrite($logFile, $writeString);
        }
        fclose($logFile);
}
function displayRecords($row_Count, $error_Array) {
echo "<html><head>";
echo "<style> table { border: 2px solid #5c744d;}  </style>";
echo "</head><body><table>";
echo "<caption>Log File: " . ERROR_LOG . "</caption>";
echo "<tr><th></th><th>Date/Time</th><th>Error Type</th><th>Error Message</th></tr><tr>";
        for ($J=$row_Count; $J >= 0; $J--) {
                echo "<td><a href='readlogfilea.php?rn=$J'>Delete</a></td>";
                for($I=0; $I < 3; $I++)  {
                        echo "<td> " . $error_Array[$J][$I] . " </td> ";
                }
        echo "</tr>";
}
echo "</table>";
echo "</body></html>";
} // main section

const ERROR_LOG = "Errors.log";

$logFile = fopen(ERROR_LOG, "r");
$row_Count = 0;
while(!feof($logFile))
{
        $error_Array[$row_Count] = explode(' | ', fgets($logFile));
        $row_Count++;
}
fclose($logFile);

if(isset($_GET['rn']))
{

        deleteRecord($_GET['rn'], $row_Count, $error_Array);
        saveChanges($row_Count,$error_Array,ERROR_LOG);
}

displayRecords($row_Count,$error_Array);

?>
```

*Figure 5-2. The readerrorlog.php file with user errors*

In Example 5-8, the displayRecords method contains most of the same code previously shown. Extra CSS code has been added to make the display a little more professional. Also, an HTML href link has been included with each record displayed. The link recalls the program, passing the record number that the user wants to delete.

The set of code in the "main section" (the first lines of code that execute) creates a constant ERROR_LOG to define the location and name of the log file. The file is opened and loaded into the array in the same manner as shown previously.

Once the array is loaded, the program checks to see if it has been called by one of the delete links for each record. If a value has been passed via HTTP GET, the program then calls the deleteRecord method. Once the deleteRecord method is complete, the program calls the saveChanges method. Whether or not a value has been passed into the program, it executes the last statement, which calls the displayRecords method.

> *Program note—The header line of the deleteRecords method (function deleteRecord($recordNumber, &$row_Count, &$error_Array)) uses by reference, instead of by value, to allow $row_Count and $error_Array to be updated in the method. By default, parameters passed into a method cannot be changed by the method (by value). The & indicates that the parameter is passed by reference. This allows the value to be changed. deleteRecords can adjust the count of the number of rows in the array ($row_Count) and the information in the array itself ($error_Array).*
>
> *By value passes the contents (data) that is contained in the parameter into the method. By reference passes the memory address of the parameter into the method, which allows the method to change the value of the parameter in memory.*

The deleteRecords method accepts the record number to be deleted as one of its parameters. Any position in the array above this record number is unchanged. Any position below this record must be shifted up one position. For example, if an array has ten positions (0-9) and the fifth position (4) is to be deleted, then positions 5-9 must now become positions 4-8.

In the following example, position $J+1 is placed into position J for any record after the $recordNumber to be deleted:

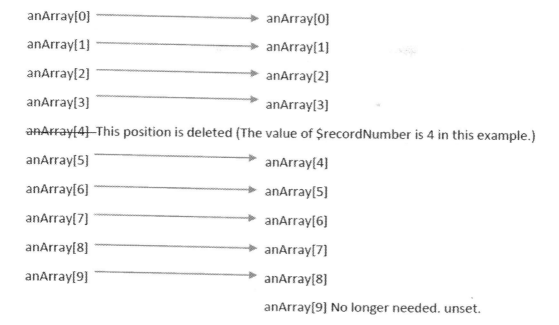

anArray[4] This position is deleted (The value of $recordNumber is 4 in this example.)

anArray[9] No longer needed. unset.

The last position in the array is no longer needed. The last position of the array is released (using unset). This will inform the operating system that the space is memory is no longer needed. The operating system will call its garbage collector to free up the memory location. We will discover an easier way to accomplish this task when we discuss associative arrays in a later chapter. Once the array has been reconfigured, the saveChanges method is called to replace the records in the log file. The code shown is very similar to previous examples in this chapter, with one exception. The fopen method uses the parameter "w". The "w" parameter will erase anything that is already in the file and replace it with what is currently being written to the file. In this example the file will be updated (replaced) with the new set of records that excludes the record that was deleted. The displayRecords method is called anytime the program is called (with or without a record being deleted). This method displays the contents of the log file.

> *Programming note—Programs that retrieve data that will be used throughout the program usually retrieve the information in the initial stages of the code and place it in a data structure (array, list, or dataset). As the data is updated in the program, the information in the data structure is updated. When the data processing has been completed, the information is then returned to the original location (text file or database). Updating the text file or database is usually completed as one of the final stages of the program. The process of a user logging out of a program would provide an event to indicate that the updated data should be saved.*

## Do It

1. Download the code for Example 5-8 from the book's web site. Add a `try catch` block to handle any unexpected problems (such as a nonexistent log file). Test and save your changes.

2. Adjust the Example 5-8 code from either #1 or the book's web site to allow the users to select which log file to read. The program should allow the users to select either the user log file or the general system log file. Test and save your changes.

# Chapter Terms

| | |
|---|---|
| Errors | Exceptions |
| `try/catch` Block | `$e->getMessage();` |
| switch Statement | Embedded if Statement |
| Default Code | `extends` |
| Exception Class | Inheritance |
| Child Class | Parent Class |
| `trigger_error` | Hierarchy of Exception Handling |
| Raising (Throwing) an Exception | Catching an Exception |
| Attitude of the Code | Push the Errors |
| Pull the Errors | Log File |
| Default PHP Error File | `error_log` |
| `Timestamp` | `date.timezone` |
| Application Log Files | Constants |
| E-mail Alerts | `display_errors` |
| Text File | Sequential File |
| `fopen` | `fwrite` |
| Pointer | `fclose` |
| `fgets` | `while` Loop |
| `feof` | `! operator` |
| `EngineException` | `explode` |
| Two-Dimensional Array | Row |
| Column | Subscript |
| Dynamic Arrays | First Row of an Array |
| `print_f` | `increment` |
| decrement | `for` Loop |
| HTML HREF | `unset` |

# Chapter Questions and Projects

**Multiple Choice**

1.  Which of the folowing is true about PHP program errors?

    a.  They are used for all exceptional situations before PHP 5.0.

    b.  They are handled by the operating system.

    c.  They might be displayed to the users.

    d.  All of these.

2.  Which of the folowing is true about PHP program exceptions?

    a.  They are used for all exceptional situations after PHP 5.0.

    b.  They can be handled by the operating system.

    c.  They might be displayed to the users.

    d.  All of these.

3.  The `try/catch` block is used to do which of the following?

    a.  Capture all errors.

    b.  Capture only known errors.

    c.  Capture all exceptions.

    d.  Capture only known exceptions.

4.  Inheritance does which of the following?

    a.  Is part of object-oriented programming.

    b.  Allows the child class to use all the attributes of its parent class.

    c.  Allows the child to create its own methods or properties.

    d.  All of these.

5.  Text files do which of the following?

    a.  Are easy to use in PHP.

    b.  Are more secure than using databases.

    c.  Are non-sequential.

    d.  None of these.

6. PHP log files do which of the following?

   a. Are created by the `error_log` method.

   b. Are updated by the `error_log` method.

   c. Should be located in a different directory than the application.

   d. All of these

7. Which of the following describes two-dimensional arrays?

   a. They are similar to HTML tables. They contain rows and columns.

   b. They should be avoided at all costs. They are inefficient and difficult to use.

   c. They require all columns to be loaded with data before rows.

   d. None of these.

8. Which of the following describes the first position of a two-dimensional array?

   a. It has a subscript of 0.

   b. It has a subscript of 1.

   c. It has a default value.

   d. None of these.

9. Application log files should include which of the folllowing?.

   a. User log files.

   b. Error log files.

   c. Informational log files.

   d. All of these.

10. E-mails generated because of program exceptions should do what?

    a. Include all error information, including the error descriptions.

    b. Include the code lines that caused the error to occur.

    c. Include the date and time the error occurred.

    d. All of these.

**True/False**

1. All exceptions should be displayed to the users.

2. The `for` loop should be used when you know exactly how many loops will occur.

3. The `while` loop will continue to loop until the conditional statement becomes true.

4. `unset` can be used to release a position in an array.

5. All PHP arrays must be declared before being used.

6. A pointer points to the location in memory that an object resides.

7. The ! operator reverses a TRUE result to a FALSE result.

8. print_f can be used to display the contents of an array.

9. Try/Catch blocks should reside in the business rules and data tiers but not the interface tier.

10. Only Exceptions intentionally thrown by program code should be caught.

**Short Answer/Essay**

1. Explain how hierarchy of exception handling works with three-tier applications.

2. What is the difference between an error and an exception?

3. How do you correct the time zone if PHP is providing an incorrect timestamp?

4. How can PHP programmers try to capture errors so they can be treated as if they are exceptions?

5. Why is it important to have multiple log files produced by an application?

**Projects**

1. Adjust the code from project #1 (or #2) from Chapter 4 to include exception handling and logging.

2. Create an application that will register contestants for your favorite game show. Include verification of the data entered using HTML5 and JavaScript. Also validate the data when it is passed to the application. The application should include an interface php program (interface tier) and a registration class (business rules tier). The registration class should include exception handling (both user exceptions and program exceptions). The interface program should handle the exceptions using try/catch blocks as shown in this chapter.

**Term Project**

1. Update the ABC Computer Parts Warehouse Inventory application to include exception handling. The application should attempt to handle all exceptions, and errors, when possible.

   User exceptions should be logged to a user log. All other exceptions should be logged to a system log. If the exception is considered to be extreme (will cause the program to otherwise crash), an e-mail should be sent to the system administrator. Hint: The Try/Catch block should only exist in the interface tier.

# CHAPTER 6

# Data Objects

*"I'm an idealist. I don't know where I'm going, but I'm on my way." —Carl Sandburg, Incidentals (1904)*

## Chapter Objectives/Student Learning Outcomes

After completing this chapter, the student will be able to:

- Create a data class that inserts, updates, and deletes XML or JSON data
- Explain how to create a data class that updates MySQL data using a SQL script
- Create a PHP program that creates a change backup log
- Create a PHP program that can recover data from a previous backup
- Apply changes to create up-to-date valid information
- Use dependency injection to attach a data class to another class in the BR tier
- Create a three-tier PHP application

## The Data Class

The interface and business rules tiers should not store application information. These tiers should not even be aware of how the information is stored (text file, XML, or database) or the location of the stored information. Any information that is stored must be passed from the business rules tier to the data tier. The data tier is also responsible for reacting to requests for information from the business rules tier.

This allows the interface tier and business rules tier to be unaware of any changes in types of storage methods (text file, XML, or database) and the locations of stored items. The signature (parameters accepted) and items returned from the data tier should remain unchanged over the life of the application. As long as these do not change, there should be no changes needed in the other tiers when changes occur in the data tier.

Security and performance—When using databases it may seem logical to build a SQL string in the business rules tier and pass the string to the data tier. This would cause a major security hole in the application. Hackers could pass any SQL string (including a delete string). It may also seem logical to pass SQL update commands (DELETE, UPDATE, and INSERT) into the data tier. Again this provides a major hole. Passing data for a WHERE SQL command is also a bad idea as it might allow hackers to delete or change any combination of data in the database.

---

**Electronic supplementary material**  The online version of this chapter (doi:10.1007/978-1-4842-1730-6_6) contains supplementary material, which is available to authorized users.

S. Prettyman. *Learn PHP 7*. DOI 10.1007/978-1-4842-1730-6_6

A data class should provide complete functionality for manipulating information. This includes the ability to read, insert, update, and delete information. Even if the current application does not require all these commands, logically, they should exist in the data class for future use.

A balance should be achieved between performance and the requirement to store information. While highly important information might require immediate storage, other information can be held in a data structure (list, array, and dataset) in the application until the user has completed any updates. Holding and making changes to information in the memory of the server, instead of the storage location, is much more efficient. Storing the information only after all changes have been completed will reduce several calls to the storage location down to two (initial retrieval of the information and saving of the updated information). Making changes to information in memory is always more efficient than making changes on a storage device (such as a hard drive).

Using a data class provides a logical ability to populate a data structure and to save information in a storage location automatically. Assuming that an instance of the data class will only be created when it is necessary to update information, the constructor of the class can be used to retrieve the information from storage and place it in the memory of the server. When the data object is no longer needed, logically, no more changes are required to the information. The destructor of the class can be used to return the information from memory to storage.

```
class dog_data
{
        function __construct()
        {
                $xmlfile = file_get_contents(get_dog_application("datastorage"));
                $xmlstring = simplexml:load_string($xmlfile);
                $array = (array)$xmlstring;
                print_r($array);
        }
}
```

This example constructor comes very close to providing useful information from an XML file. The PHP file_get_contents method opens a text file, drops the contents into a string, and closes the file. The constructor calls this method along with the get_dog_application method (same method that was used in dog_container in Example 5-5) to determine the file name and location of the XML data file. The contents of the file are then placed in $xmlfile. The PHP simplexml:load_string method then formats the data to allow the SimpleXML data model to traverse the information. At this point, the SimpleXML methods could be used to display and manipulate the data. However, the next line attempts to convert the XML data into an array. The (array) statement tries to use type casting. The print_r statement displays the results.

```
<?xml version="1.0" encoding="UTF-8"?>
<dogs>
<dog>
<dog_name>Woff</dog_name>
<dog_weight>12</dog_weight>
<dog_color>Yellow</dog_color>
<dog_breed>Lab</dog_breed>
</dog>
<dog>
<dog_name>Sam</dog_name>
<dog_weight>10</dog_weight>
<dog_color>Brown</dog_color>
<dog_breed>Lab</dog_breed>
</dog>
</dogs>
```

Assuming that the XML file is formatted as shown here, the output includes:

```
Array ( [dog] => Array ( [0] => SimpleXMLElement Object ( [dog_name] => Woff [dog_weight] => 12
[dog_color] => Yellow [dog_breed] => Lab ) [1] => SimpleXMLElement Object ( [dog_name] => Sam
[dog_weight] => 10 [dog_color] => Brown [dog_breed] => Lab ) ) )
```

A combination of multidimensional arrays and SimpleXML objects have been created. This does not provide useful data that can easily be manipulated. However, you can use JSON methods to trick PHP into creating a multidimensional *associate array*.

```
class dog_data
{
        function __construct()
        {
                $xmlfile = file_get_contents(get_dog_application("datastorage"));
                $xmlstring = simplexml:load_string($xmlfile);
                $json = json_encode($xmlstring);
                print_r($json);
        }
}
{"dog":[{"dog_name":"Woff","dog_weight":"12","dog_color":"Yellow","dog_breed":"Lab"},{"dog_name"
:"Sam","dog_weight":"10","dog_color":"Brown","dog_breed":"Lab"}]}
```

Using the PHP json_encode method changes the data into well-structured JSON data. You could use one of the several PHP techniques to manipulate JSON data or, with one additional statement (json_decode), you can create a well-structured multidimensional associate array.

```
class dog_data
{
        function __construct()
        {
                $xmlfile = file_get_contents(get_dog_application("datastorage"));
                $xmlstring = simplexml:load_string($xmlfile);
                $json = json_encode($xmlstring);
                $dogs_array = json_decode($json,TRUE);
                print_r($dogs_array);
        }
}
Array ( [dog] =>
Array (
[0] => Array ( [dog_name] => Woff [dog_weight] => 12 [dog_color] => Yellow [dog_breed] => Lab )
[1] => Array ( [dog_name] => Sam [dog_weight] => 10 [dog_color] => Brown [dog_breed] => Lab ) ) )
```

As you can see, there is no longer a mixture of arrays and SimpleXML objects. An associate array has been created that uses keywords instead of numerical values for subscripts (indexes). In the previous example, an array called "dog" has been created with two rows (each row is represented by an array). In each row, the columns (cells) are referenced by a column name (dog_name, dog_weight, dog_color, and dog_breed) instead of indexes (0, 1, 2, 3). These rows and columns can be manipulated using some of the techniques you have seen in previous chapters.

Once you have completed all changes to the array (as requested by the business rules tier), you will return the information to the storage location in the destructor.

```
private $dogs_array = array(); // defined as an empty array initially
function __construct()
        {
                $xmlfile = file_get_contents(get_dog_application("datastorage"));
                $xmlstring = simplexml:load_string($xmlfile);
                $json = json_encode($xmlstring);
                $this->dogs_array = json_decode($json,TRUE);
        }
function __destruct()
{
                $xmlstring = '<?xml version="1.0" encoding="UTF-8"?>';
                $xmlstring .= "\n<dogs>\n";
                foreach ($this->dogs_array as $dogs=>$dogs_value) {
                    foreach ($dogs_value as $dog => $dog_value)
                    {
                                $xmlstring .="<$dogs>\n";
                                foreach ($dog_value as $column => $column_value)
                                {
                                $xmlstring .= "<$column>" . $dog_value[$column] . "</$column>\n";
                                }
                                $xmlstring .= "</$dogs>\n";
                    }
        }
$xmlstring .= "</dogs>\n";  file_put_contents(get_dog_application("datastorage"),$xmlstring);
}
```

There are many ways that you can create XML data in PHP. The previous example takes a simplistic approach by supplying the XML tags from the array. As seen in the structure, there are three sets of arrays in this multidimensional array. The first foreach loop is used to flow through the first array (dogs). The second foreach loop handles the dog arrays (rows). Once inside this loop, the third foreach loop controls the columns in each dog array (each row).

The third loop retrieves the column names (from $column) and places them in XML tags. $column is also used to pull the value in the column ($dog_value[$column]). The $xmlstring supplies the same tags and structure as in the original XML file. Note that each line includes a newline character (\n) to display different lines in the file. The structure would work without this addition. However, if makes the file more readable in a text editor.

Once the $xmlstring has been created, the code uses a combination of the PHP file_put_contents method and the get_dog_application method (from Chapter 4) to open the XML file, replace the contents with the string contained in $xmlstring, and close the file.

You need to make one more final adjustment to the constructor to allow it to handle XML parsing errors. A parsing error occurs when something is wrong with the XML structure. The previous dog_breed and dog_application XML files are not updated by the application and are fairly stable. However, the XML file for the dog's information will be updated frequently. You need to handle any problems that may occur. You will raise a general error, which will be treated by dog_interface as an important error that is logged and e-mailed to support personnel. It will also display a "System currently not available please try again later" message to the users.

```
private $dogs_array = array(); defined as an empty array initially
libxml:use_internal_errors(true);
function __construct() {
        $xmlfile = file_get_contents(get_dog_application("datastorage"));
        $xmlstring = simplexml:load_string($xmlfile);
        if ($xmlstring === false) {
                $errorString = "Failed loading XML: ";
                foreach(libxml:get_errors() as $error) {
                        $errorString .= $error->message . " ";  }
                throw new Exception($errorString); }
$json = json_encode($xmlstring);
$this->dogs_array = json_decode($json,TRUE);
}
```

By default, XML parsing errors will cause the system to display the errors to the user and shut down the program. The libxml:user_internal_errors(true) method will suppress the errors. When the string is converted to XML format via the simplexml:load_string method, the XML is parsed to determine if it is valid. If it is not valid, the method will return FALSE instead of the XML information. The if statement shown will create an $errorString and use the foreach statement to loop through each error returned by the libxml:get_errors method (which returns an array containing the errors). Once all errors are collected, it will raise an exception passing the $errorString. The dog_interface program will catch this error and process it, as shown in Chapter 5.

This example does make one bad assumption (which simplifies the example). It assumes that the $errorString does not exceed the maximum capacity of 120 characters for the log file. A very badly formatted file could quickly cause $errorString to exceed this size. This limit can be adjusted in the PHP configuration file.

With the data automatically being saved whenever the data object is removed from memory, the insert, update, and delete methods only need to adjust the contents of the multidimensional associative array. Let's take a first look at creating a delete method since you have already seen an example in Chapter 5.

In the readerrorlog program (in Example 5-8) you created a deleterecord method. The method was used for regular multidimensional arrays. We could make a few adjustments to this routine to create the deleteRecord method for the dog_data class.

```
function deleteRecord($recordNumber) {
        foreach ($this->dogs_array as $dogs=>&$dogs_value) {
                for($J=$recordNumber; $J < count($dogs_value) -1; $J++)
                        {
                        foreach ($dogs_value[$J] as $column => $column_value)
                        {
                                $dogs_value[$J][$column] = $dogs_value[$J + 1][$column];
                        }
                }
        }
unset ($dogs_value[count($dogs_value) -1]);
        }
}
```

In the previous deleterecord method, the number of rows in the array and the array itself were passed into the method. The array in dog_data class is populated by the XML file containing the dog information. There is no property set with the number of records. This is not a problem. The PHP method **count** will return the size of an array. You can access and update the dogs_array (which is a protected private property) using the $this pointer. Methods in classes can use the this pointer to access and update protected properties; it is not necessary to pass them into a method. The only property you need to pass to the deleteRecord method is the record number ($recordNumber) to delete.

The associate array has three dimensions. The outer dimension is related to the dogs tag from the XML structure. Although there is only one "row" for dogs, a loop is still needed to move into the next array (dog). The foreach loop penetrates the dogs array and provides access to the dog array (which was created from the dog tags in the XML file). $dogs will contain the number of the dog row currently used. $dogs_value will contain the contents of the row (an array with the values in dog_name, dog_weight, dog_color, and dog_breed).

To move through each row (array) contained in the dog array, the method uses a for loop. The conditional statement ($J < count($dogs_value) -1) uses the count method to determine the size of the dog array. The count method returns the size of the array, not the last position of the array. Thus the loop count must be less than (<) the size returned from count. One is subtracted from this value. As stated in Chapter 5, any row after a deleted row must be moved up one from its current position. The last position of the array will no longer be needed, which reduces the number of loops needed by one.

In the Chapter 5 example, a for loop was used to pull each column from the row and place it in the row above. With an associate array, you use a foreach loop. The $column parameter contains the column name ($J contains the row number) to place the values in the columns into the proper locations. After the values in the rows have been moved, the last position of the array is removed using the PHP **unset** method.

Similar logic can be used in almost any program language. However, PHP associate arrays allow index numbers to be skipped. Unlike other languages which would place a NULL value in a missing index, PHP associate arrays just skip the actual index. Thus any array could have indexes of 0, 1, 2, 4, 5 and a foreach loop would properly loop through the array. With this in mind we can greatly simplify the previous example delete example to only contain one line of code, just the unset command shown. The unset command would remove the index passed into the method from the dog_array. Any for loop using the dog_array would still properly loop through the array. The example code contained in the demo website provides this ability.

You can also make a few adjustments to the displayRecords method from Chapter 5 to return any record(s) that a calling program (such as the Dog class) requests.

```
function readRecords($recordNumber) {
if($recordNumber === "ALL") {
                return $this->dogs_array["dog"];
}
else {
                return $this->dogs_array["dog"][$recordNumber];
        } }
```

As you can see the readRecords method is more simplistic that the displayRecords method. All formatting of the results of this method are left to the calling program (if needed). Remember that displaying and formatting of output occurs in the interface tier, not the data tier (or business rules tier).

This method allows the calling program to request all records or a specific record. In either case it returns an array with either one row (the specific record requested) or all rows. When all rows are returned, the top array (representing the rows XML tag) is removed to keep the number of dimensions (two) the same for either selection.

The insertRecords method accepts an associate array with the subscript names previously mentioned. However, in order to allow for dependency injection and flexibility in the tag names for the XML file, the calling program does not need not know the tag names until an instance of the dog_data class is created. This can be accomplished by using the readRecords method to pull the first record and then have the calling program examine the subscript names returned from that record.

```
function insertRecords($records_array)
{
        $dogs_array_size = count($this->dogs_array["dog"]);
        for($I=0;$I< count($records_array);$I++)
        {
                $this->dogs_array["dog"][$dogs_array_size + $I] = $records_array[$I];
        }
}
```

---

▓ **Note**   The process of creating the dog_array using the JSON functions shown previously will create one inconsistency in creating the dog_array. If the dog_data.xml file contains only one record, the JSON functions will not create a numeric index (such as '0'). When more than one record is contained in the xml file the numeric indexes will be created (such as '0', '1'). An alternative solution to which handles these differences is provided in the demo files on the textbook website.

---

In the insertRecords method, all records are added to the end of the array (the calling program can sort them if needed). The current size of dogs_array is determined by the count method and stored into $dogs_array_size. The count method is also used inside the for structure to determine the size of the $records_array and to determine the number of loops. Since the results of the count method produces the size of the array, which is one more than the last subscript position, the result of count also gives the next position available to insert a record.

In the first loop, $I is 0. The first record of $records_array is placed into $dogs_array_size plus 0, or $dogs_array_size (the first open row to place a record). The next time through the loop, the second record of $records_array ($I was incremented by the loop) is placed into position $dogs_array_size plus 1. This is the next position available after the first record has been inserted. The loop will continue until there are no more records in the $records_array. By the way, this method also works well with just one record to insert (as long as it is passed as an associate array). The loop will execute only once.

The last method you need to examine is an update method. This method is a very simple form of the destructor method.

```
function updateRecords($records_array)
{
        foreach ($records_array as $records=>$records_value) {
                foreach ($records_value as $record => $record_value) {
                        $this->dogs_array["dog"][$records] = $records_array[$records];
                }
        }
}
```

This little tiny method will take any size associate array and update the dogs array. It is based on PHP's ability to dynamically build arrays.

```
$records_array = Array (
0 => Array ( "dog_name" => "Jeffrey", "dog_weight" => "19", "dog_color" => "Green",
"dog_breed" => "Lab" ),
2 => Array ( "dog_name" => "James", "dog_weight" => "21", "dog_color" => "Black",
"dog_breed" => "Mixed" ));
```

*Dynamically built* arrays are not required to have values for every position in the array. If the dynamic array shown previously is passed into the updateRecords method, records 0 and 2 would be updated with the new information. The value in position 1 in the dogs array would remain untouched.

Take a moment to look at these methods. There are only two XML tags that have been coded in the methods (dogs and dog). Even those two could have been retrieved from the XML file. However, the assumption that these tags will always exist in a valid dog XML file makes logical sense. By dynamically pulling all of the other tags (dog_name, dog_weight, dog_color, and dog_breed) from the XML file, changes can be made to the file without causing any code changes. Additional tags can be added, removed, and/or changed.

Let's put it all together.

***Example 6-1.*** The dog_data.php file

```php
<?php
class dog_data
{
private $dogs_array = array(); //defined as an empty array initially
private $dog_data_xml = "";
function __construct() {
        libxml:use_internal_errors(true);
        $xmlDoc = new DOMDocument();
        if ( file_exists("e5dog_applications.xml") )         {
        $xmlDoc->load( 'e5dog_applications.xml' );
        $searchNode = $xmlDoc->getElementsByTagName( "type" );
                foreach( $searchNode as $searchNode )
                {
                        $valueID = $searchNode->getAttribute('ID');
                        if($valueID == "datastorage")
                        {
                                $xmlLocation = $searchNode->getElementsByTagName( "location" );
                                $this->dog_data_xml = $xmlLocation->item(0)->nodeValue;
                                break;
                        }
                } }
        else { throw new Exception("Dog applications xml file missing or corrupt"); }
$xmlfile = file_get_contents($this->dog_data_xml);
        $xmlstring = simplexml:load_string($xmlfile);

        if ($xmlstring === false) {
                $errorString = "Failed loading XML: ";
                foreach(libxml:get_errors() as $error) {
                        $errorString .= $error->message . " " ;  }
                throw new Exception($errorString); }
        $json = json_encode($xmlstring);
        $this->dogs_array = json_decode($json,TRUE);
        }
function __destruct()
{
        $xmlstring = '<?xml version="1.0" encoding="UTF-8"?>';
        $xmlstring .= "\n<dogs>\n";
        foreach ($this->dogs_array as $dogs=>$dogs_value) {
```

```php
                foreach ($dogs_value as $dog => $dog_value)
                {
                        $xmlstring .="<$dogs>\n";
                                foreach ($dog_value as $column => $column_value)
                                {
                                $xmlstring .= "<$column>" . $dog_value[$column] . "</$column>\n";
                                }
                        $xmlstring .= "</$dogs>\n";
                }
        }
        $xmlstring .= "</dogs>\n";
        file_put_contents($this->dog_data_xml,$xmlstring);
}

function deleteRecord($recordNumber)
{
        foreach ($this->dogs_array as $dogs=>&$dogs_value) {
                for($J=$recordNumber; $J < count($dogs_value) -1; $J++) {

                        foreach ($dogs_value[$J] as $column => $column_value)
                        {
                                $dogs_value[$J][$column] = $dogs_value[$J + 1][$column];
                        }

        }

        unset ($dogs_value[count($dogs_value) -1]);
        }
 }
function readRecords($recordNumber)
 {
        if($recordNumber === "ALL") {
                return $this->dogs_array["dog"];
        }
        else
        {
                return $this->dogs_array["dog"][$recordNumber];
        }
}

function insertRecords($records_array)
{
        $dogs_array_size = count($this->dogs_array["dog"]);
        for($I=0;$I< count($records_array);$I++)
        {
                $this->dogs_array["dog"][$dogs_array_size + $I] = $records_array[$I];
        }
}
```

```
function updateRecords($records_array)
{
        foreach ($records_array as $records=>$records_value)
        {
                foreach ($records_value as $record => $record_value)
                {
                        $this->dogs_array["dog"][$records] = $records_array[$records];
                }
        }
}
}
?>
```

---

⬛ **Note**   An alternative solution which handles associate arrays with missing indexes, and the possibility that the dog_data.xml file may contain one or zero records, is provided on the textbook website.

---

The only change in this final version of the dog_data class is the inclusion of get_dog_application method code in the constructor to retrieve the location and name of the XML file holding the dog data.

***Example 6-2.***  The testdata.php file

```
<?php
include("dog_data.php");
$tester = new dog_data();
$records_array = Array (
0 => Array ( "dog_name" => "Sally", "dog_weight" => "19", "dog_color" => "Green",
"dog_breed" => "Lab" ));
$tester->insertRecords($records_array);
print_r ($tester->readRecords("ALL"));
print("<br>");

$records_array = Array (
1 => Array ( "dog_name" => "Spot", "dog_weight" => "19", "dog_color" => "Green",
"dog_breed" => "Lab" ));

$tester->updateRecords($records_array);
print_r ($tester->readRecords("ALL"));
print("<br>");

$tester->deleteRecord(1);
print_r ($tester->readRecords("ALL"));
$tester = NULL; // calls the destructor and saves the xml records in the file
?>
```

Example 6-2 tests some of the possible scenarios of using the dog_data class. Notice the last line of code calls the destructor (to save the data). This is accomplished by setting the pointer to the object ($tester) to NULL, which releases the object. This will inform the garbage collector of the operating system that the object should be removed from memory. This will cause the destructor to execute, which will update the XML file and remove the object from the memory of the server.

# JSON Data

Let's take a second to back up and look at the ability to read and write JSON data. Using the example code shown in this chapter, only the constructor and destructor will need to be adjusted when you use other forms of data besides XML. Accessing and using JSON data is even easier than using XML data.

```
...
$json = file_get_contents($this->dog_data_JSON);
$this->dogs_array = json_decode($json,TRUE);
if ($this->dogs_array === null && json_last_error() !== JSON_ERROR_NONE)
{
     throw new Exception("JSON error: " . json_last_error_msg());
}
...
```

In the constructor, after the `if else` structure that retrieves the location of the data from the `dog_application.xml` file, the multiple lines accessing and formatting the XML data can be replaced by the lines shown previously. The `json_decode` method (as shown previously) will attempt to format the data from the text file into the associate array format. If the data is not a valid JSON format, an exception is thrown passing the error message. Since the `Exception` class is used, the `dog_interface` program would log this information in the error log, e-mail the support personnel, and display a general message to the users.

```
$json = json_encode($this->dogs_array);
file_put_contents($this->dog_data_JSON,$json);
```

The complete code for the destructor requires only two lines. The `json_encode` method will convert the associate array data into JSON format. The `file_put_contents` method will then save the information to the proper location of the JSON file (`$this->dog_data_JSON`). No changes are required to any of the other methods in dog_data. Note: An example application using JSON data is available on the book's web site under Chapter 6.

# MySQL Data

This book is intended as an introduction to the PHP language. Thus, you will not spend much time learning about database usage. However, this is a good time to give a brief example of adjustments you can make to the constructor and destructor methods to access and update database information.

---

■ **Note**    mysql has been removed since PHP5.5. It is recommended that you use mysqli or pdo_mysql.

---

```
$mysqli =mysqli_connect($server, $db_username, $db_password, $database);

if (mysqli_connect_errno())
  {
        throw new Exception("MySQL connection error: " . mysqli_connect_error());
  }

$sql="SELECT * FROM Dogs";
$result=mysqli_query($con,$sql);
```

```
If($result===null)
{
        throw new Exception("No records retrieved from Database");
}

$this->dogs_array = mysqli_fetch_assoc($result);

mysqli_free_result($result);

mysqli_close($con);
```

Most of the code required for the constructor method is associated to connecting, retrieving, and disconnecting from the database. The mysqli_connect method uses the server location ($server), database user ID ($db_username), database password ($db_password), and database name ($database) to connect to the database. If mysqli_connect_errno contains any errors an Exception is thrown describing the error. If there are no errors, a SQL SELECT statement ($sql) is used to retrieve all the records from the Dogs table in the database. If no records are retrieved, another exception is thrown. If records are retrieved, the mysqli_ fetch_assoc method will convert the data into an associate array. The mysqli_free_result statement releases the data from $result. The mysqli_close method closes access to the database.

The destructor takes a little more coding. However, the looping is similar to saving the XML data.

```
$mysqli = new mysqli($server, $db_username, $db_password, $database);
if ($mysqli->connect_errno)
{
        throw new Exception("MySQL connection error:" . $mysqli->connect_error);
}
If( (!$mysqli->query("DROP TABLE IF EXISTS Dogs") ||
   (!$mysqli->query("CREATE TABLE IF NOT EXISTS Dogs (dog_id CHAR(4), dog_name CHAR(20),
   dog_weight CHAR(3), dog_color CHAR(15), dog_breed CHAR(35)") )
{
throw new Exception("Dog table can't be created or deleted. Error: " . $mysqli->error);
}
foreach ($this->dogs_array as $dogs=>$dogs_value) {
        foreach ($dogs_value as $dog => $dog_value)
        {
                $dog_id = $dog_value["dog_id"];
                $dog_name = $dog_value["dog_name"];
                $dog_weight = $dog_value["dog_weight"];
                $dog_color = $dog_value["dog_color"];
                $dog_breed = $dog_value["dog_breed"];
                If(!$mysqli->query("INSERT INTO Dogs(dog_id, dog_name, dog_weight, dog_color,
                dog_breed) VALUES ('$dog_id', '$dog_name', '$dog_weight', '$dog_color',
                '$dog_breed')"))
                {
                        throw new Exception("Dog Table Insert Error: " . $mysqli->error);
                }
        }
}
...
```

The destructor method attempts to connect to the database. If the connection is successful, the method removes any preexisting Dogs table and creates a new one with the required fields. (Note: It would probably be better to rename the old one and create a new one.). If the old table can be removed and the new table created, then the method attempts to insert rows into the table. The SQL INSERT statement places the values from $dog_name, $dog_weight, $dog_color, and $dog_breed into a row in the table. The foreach loops retrieve each row from the associate array to be placed into the table. If any of the inserts are not successful, an exception is thrown. An example program is located under Chapter 6 on the book's web site.

*Programming note—The Apache server must be properly configured and MySQL must be properly installed to run this (or a similar) database example. $server must be set to the URL, "localhost", or "127.0.0.1". $db_username must be set to the user ID name to access the database ('root' if a user ID has not been configured). $db_password must be set to the database password (or '' if there is no password). $database must be set to the database name. There is a large varieties of ways to access and manipulate databases in the PHP language.*

## Do It

1.  Download the example files for this section from the book's web site. Adjust the deleteRecords method to allow the ability to delete multiple records. However, also include a check to limit the amount of records that can be deleted. It would not be very secure to allow all records to be deleted. If an attempt is made to delete all records (or too many records), an exception should be raised. The exception should cause the calling program (eventually dog_interface) to write an error message to the main log file, e-mail the support personnel, and display the general message to the users (shown in Chapter 5). Adjust the testdata program to test the ability to delete multiple records and catch the exceptions.

2.  Download the example files for this section from the book's web site. Adjust the testdata program to test all remaining scenarios that have not already been tested. These are related to inserting, updating (more than one), reading, and deleting records. Be sure to test improperly formatted information. Create a try catch block in the testdata program to capture any exceptions. You can use the try catch block from dog_interface in Chapter 5 as an example.

# Backup and Recovery

There is always a possibility that something can go wrong when changes are made to stored information. While a well-developed application must filter and clean data before it is saved; it must also be prepared to handle the possibility that bad data may still flowed through and corrupt the information. In addition to intentional corruption, unforeseen problems (such as system crashes) may occur. An application must provide the ability to recover without the loss of data. This can be accomplished by logging change requests and backing up valid information. Recovery can be accomplished by using a valid backup and reapplying valid changes to the backup files to produce up-to-date information.

You can make just a few minor changes to the dogdata file (Example 6-1) to create a change log and to provide backup and recovery capability. First, you will create a main method (processRecords) that will interpret any data passed into the class. This function will simplify the recovery process by allowing the recovery program to pass all change log information into one method. This will also make dependency injection easier to accomplish.

```
function processRecords($change_Type, $records_array)
{
switch($change_Type)
{
        case "Delete":
                $this->deleteRecord($records_array);
                break;
        case "Insert":
                $this->insertRecords($records_array);
                break;
        case "Update":
                $this->updateRecords($records_array);
                break;
        case "Display":
                $this->readRecords($records_array);
                Break;
        default:
                throw new Exception("Invalid XML file change type: $change_Type");
}
}
```

All requests for changes will now be passed through this method. The method accepts a change type (Insert, Delete, Update, or Display) and the array (for Insert or Update) or the record number (for Delete or Update). The values are passed into $record_array. $record_array is dynamically created as either an array or a string. This allows the processRecords method to provide *polymorphism* (the ability for the same method call to accept different parameters), which is one of the requirements of an object-oriented language (along with encapsulation and inheritance). The switch statement looks at $change_Type to determine which method to call. It then calls the related method. If an invalid type is passed, an exception is thrown.

> *Security and performance—In a 'live' environment, it would be more secure to pass "codes" into this type of method instead of using a value that indicates the action that will take place. For example, 101 could be used to indicate an update. The switch statement could easily be adjusted to examine the codes to determine which method to call.*

Each of the methods that you have examined previously (except for the constructor and destructor) are now set to 'private'. This makes the process much more secure; changes can only occur by using the processRecords method. Three code lines have also been added to the end of each of the three methods to provide backup and recovery capabilities.

```
...
$change_string = date('mdYhis') . " | Delete | " . $recordNumber . "\n";
$chge_log_file = date('mdYhis') . $this->change_log_file;
error_log($change_string,3,$chge_log_file); // might exceed 120 chars
...
```

The first line formats a string for a change log file. The format used is similar to the format you look at in Chapter 5. In the previous example, the record number is passed as required for the delete method.

```
$change_string = date('mdYhis') . " | Update | " . serialize($records_array) . "\n";
```

For update and insert, the arrays are passed. However, an array cannot be placed into a string. The serialize method transforms an array into a string format similar to the following.

```
a:1:{i:0;a:4:{s:8:"dog_name";s:7:"Spot";s:10:"dog_weight";s:2:"19";s:9:
"dog_color";s:5:"Green";s:9:"dog_breed";s:3:"Lab";}}
```

The data in a serialized string can be returned to an array format (or another format) using the unserialize method. The second line creates a string ($chge_log_file), which uses the date method and the log file name located in the dog_applications XML file to create a backup file name (and location). The string created is then passed to this log using the error_log method. The contents of the log file will look similar to the following.

```
07142015042510 | Insert | a:1:{i:0;a:4:{s:8:"dog_name";s:7:"tester1";s:10:
"dog_weight";s:2:"19";s:9:"dog_color";s:5:"Green";s:9:"dog_breed";s:3:"Lab";}}
07142015042510 | Update | a:1:{i:1;a:4:{s:8:"dog_name";s:7:"tester2";s:10:
"dog_weight";s:2:"19";s:9:"dog_color";s:5:"Green";s:9:"dog_breed";s:3:"Lab";}}
07142015042510 | Delete | 1
```

This format provides all the information needed to help with the recovery process. If the current version of the dog data file is corrupted, the change log file can be used to apply changes to a good version of the file to develop a new current version.

The only other changes needed to the data class are a few additional code lines in the destructor.

```
$new_valid_data_file = preg_replace('/[0-9]+/', '', $this->dog_data_xml);
// remove the previous date and time if it exists
$oldxmldata = date('mdYhis') . $new_valid_data_file;
if (!rename($this->dog_data_xml, $oldxmldata))
        {
            throw new Exception("Backup file $oldxmldata could not be created.");
        }
file_put_contents($new_valid_data_file,$xmlstring);
```

Before the destructor uses the file_put_contents method to apply changes to the XML file, a *backup* should be created in case the changes cause corruption to the current data. The recovery process will allow the support personnel to select which data file contains good data and which change file(s) will be applied to the data to produce the correct current version of the data.

Because this process may use a backup file of the data, which includes a file name with a date and time, the preg_replace method is used to remove any numerical information from the data file name. The regular expression (/[0-9]+/) in the first parameter directs the method to search for all occurrences of numbers in $this->dog_data_xml. If any occurrence is found, it is replaced with the value in the second parameter (''). In this case, nothing. The new file name is then placed in $new_valid_data_file. This will not cause any change to a "normal" non-backup file name because it does not contain any numerical information. A new backup file name is created using the file name in $new_valid_data_file with the date and time information. The new backup file name is stored in $oldxmldata.

Now the last valid data can be moved to the new backup file using the rename method. The data in $this->dog_data_xml (the location of the good data without changes) is copied to the new backup file location ($oldxmldata). If the file cannot be renamed, an exception is thrown.

Finally the valid changed data (located in $xmlstring) can be placed into the new location of the valid data (which is the same file name without any date information) contained in the $new_valid_data_file property.

For example, if 07142015042510dog_data.xml contains the last valid data available, 07152015001510dog_data.xml might be the new location of this data before any changes are applied. dog_data.xml would be the location of the valid data after changes have been applied. The last coding change to the dog data class is the inclusion of a set method.

```
function setChangeLogFile($value)
{
$this->dog_data_xml = $value;
}
```

To allow the recovery application to use the last valid data, the application must have the ability to change the location of the valid data. The setChangeLogFile method changes the value in $this->dog_data_xml. This property was originally set from locating information in the dog application XML file. However, that might not currently be the location of valid data. The code added to the destructor will use the new location of the valid data, apply the changes needed, and place valid data back into the original data file. There is no need to make any changes to the data_application XML file. After the destructor completes, the data file will now contain the most up-to-date valid data.

***Example 6-3.*** The dogdata.php file with logging as well as backup and recovery processes

```php
<?php
class dog_data {
private $dogs_array = array(); //defined as an empty array initially
private $dog_data_xml = "";
private $change_log_file = "change.log";
function __construct() {
        libxml:use_internal_errors(true);
        $xmlDoc = new DOMDocument();
        if ( file_exists("e5dog_applications.xml") )          {
        $xmlDoc->load( 'e5dog_applications.xml' );
        $searchNode = $xmlDoc->getElementsByTagName( "type" );
                foreach( $searchNode as $searchNode )           {
                        $valueID = $searchNode->getAttribute('ID');
                        if($valueID == "datastorage") {
                                $xmlLocation = $searchNode->getElementsByTagName( "location" );
                                $this->dog_data_xml = $xmlLocation->item(0)->nodeValue;

                                break;
                        }

                }
        }

        else { throw new Exception("Dog applications xml file missing or corrupt"); }
        $xmlfile = file_get_contents($this->dog_data_xml);
        $xmlstring = simplexml:load_string($xmlfile);
        if ($xmlstring === false) {
                $errorString = "Failed loading XML: ";
                foreach(libxml:get_errors() as $error) {
                        $errorString .= $error->message . " " ;  }
                throw new Exception($errorString); }
        $json = json_encode($xmlstring);
        $this->dogs_array = json_decode($json,TRUE);
}

function __destruct() {
        $xmlstring = '<?xml version="1.0" encoding="UTF-8"?>';
        $xmlstring .= "\n<dogs>\n";
        foreach ($this->dogs_array as $dogs=>$dogs_value) {
                foreach ($dogs_value as $dog => $dog_value) {
                        $xmlstring .="<$dogs>\n";
                        foreach ($dog_value as $column => $column_value)
```

```
                             {
                                       $xmlstring .= "<$column>" . $dog_value[$column] . "</$column>\n";
                             }
                             $xmlstring .= "</$dogs>\n";
              }  }
$xmlstring .= "</dogs>\n";
$new_valid_data_file = preg_replace('/[0-9]+/', '', $this->dog_data_xml);
// remove the previous date and time if it exists
$oldxmldata = date('mdYhis') . $new_valid_data_file;
if (!rename($this->dog_data_xml, $oldxmldata)) {    throw new Exception("Backup file
$oldxmldata could not be created."); }
file_put_contents($new_valid_data_file,$xmlstring);
}
private function deleteRecord($recordNumber)
{
foreach ($this->dogs_array as $dogs=>&$dogs_value) {
                for($J=$recordNumber; $J < count($dogs_value) -1; $J++) {
                        foreach ($dogs_value[$J] as $column => $column_value)
                        {
                                  $dogs_value[$J][$column] = $dogs_value[$J + 1][$column];
                        }
}
        unset ($dogs_value[count($dogs_value) -1]);
        }
        $change_string = date('mdYhis') . " | Delete | " . $recordNumber . "\n";
        $chge_log_file = date('mdYhis') . $this->change_log_file;
        error_log($change_string,3,$chge_log_file); // might exceed 120 chars
 }
private function readRecords($recordNumber)
 {
        if($recordNumber === "ALL") {
                return $this->dogs_array["dog"];
        } else {
        return $this->dogs_array["dog"][$recordNumber];
        }
}
private function insertRecords($records_array)
{
        $dogs_array_size = count($this->dogs_array["dog"]);
        for($I=0;$I< count($records_array);$I++) {
                $this->dogs_array["dog"][$dogs_array_size + $I] = $records_array[$I];
        }
        $change_string = date('mdYhis') . " | Insert | " . serialize($records_array) . "\n";
        $chge_log_file = date('mdYhis') . $this->change_log_file;
        error_log($change_string,3,$chge_log_file); // might exceed 120 chars
}
private function updateRecords($records_array)
{
        foreach ($records_array as $records=>$records_value)
        {
                foreach ($records_value as $record => $record_value)
```

```
                          {
                                      $this->dogs_array["dog"][$records] = $records_array[$records];
                          }
              }
$change_string = date('mdYhis') . " | Update | " . serialize($records_array) . "\n";
$chge_log_file = date('mdYhis') . $this->change_log_file;
          error_log($change_string,3,$chge_log_file); // might exceed 120 chars
}
function setChangeLogFile($value)
{
          $this->dog_data_xml = $value;
}
function processRecords($change_Type, $records_array)
{
switch($change_Type)
{
          case "Delete":
                    $this->deleteRecord($records_array);
                    break;
          case "Insert":
                    $this->insertRecords($records_array);
                    break;
          case "Update":
                    $this->updateRecords($records_array);
                    break;
          default:
                    throw new Exception("Invalid XML file change type: $change_Type");
} } }
```

---

▓ **Note**   An alternative solution is provided on the textbook website which will allow associate arrays with missing indexes and one or no records within the dog_data.xml file.

---

Now that you have the ability to provide backup and recovery, let's make some adjustments to the readerrorlog file (in Example 5-8). The new application will need to allow the support personnel to select (and modify) any valid change log file, select the most valid data file available, and apply the changes from the change log file to produce a new valid data XML file.

```
if(isset($_POST['data_File']))
{
          update_XML_File_Process();
}
else if(isset($_GET['rn']))
{
          delete_Process();
}
else if(isset($_POST['change_file']))
{
          display_Process();
}
```

```
else
{
        select_File_Process();
}
```

Since the code has grown in length, it will be much easier to follow the logical flow (and to modify the code when necessary) if much of the work is done in methods. As with many applications, the main flow of the program becomes one embedded if else statement.

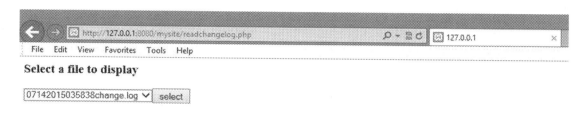

***Figure 6-1.*** *The readchangelog.php file requesting selection of a change log file*

Upon opening the application, a list box will allow the users to select which valid change log file to use (and possibly update). The else portion of the statement will direct the program to select_File_Process, which will handle this request.

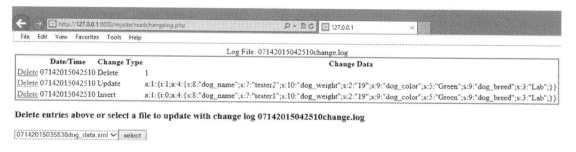

***Figure 6-2.*** *The readchangelog file displaying the selected log and requesting the valid data file*

Once the user has selected a change file, the contents of the file will be displayed in the same manner as shown in Chapter 5. The display_Process method will provide this information. The user can decide to remove some entries in the change file selected. If deletions are needed, the delete_Process method will complete the process, using the same techniques shown in Chapter 5. In addition, the same method will allow the user to select the most recent valid data file to apply changes.

Once the data file has been selected, update_XML_File_Process will apply the changes to the file using the dogdata program (in Example 6-3). The process will display a changes completed message to the user.

The select_File_Process method uses similar logic as found in the getbreeds.php program (in Example 4-5).

```
function select_File_Process()
{
$directory = "";
$files = glob($directory . "*change.log");
echo "<form id='file_select' name='file_select' method='post' action='readchangelog.php'>";
echo "<h3>Select a file to display</h3>";
echo "<select name='change_file' id='change_file'>";
foreach($files as $file)
{
        echo "<option value='$file'>$file</option>";
}
echo "</select>";
echo "<input type='submit' id='submit' name='submit' value='select'>";
echo "</form>";
}
```

The PHP glob method places all file names in a given directory ($directory) into an array ($files). Setting $directory to "" indicates that the current directory will be searched. The second parameter provides the ability to filter the file types retrieved. *change.log directs the method to pull all files with the ending change.log. The * (asterisk) is a wildcard character that accepts any characters. This combination will pull all the change log files produced by the dog_data class. The remaining lines create an HTML drop-down list displaying the file names retrieved. A submit will cause the program to call itself again with the selected file residing in the change_file property.

```
function display_Process()
{
$change_Array = load_Array();
$row_Count = count($change_Array) -1;
displayRecords($row_Count, $change_Array, $_POST['change_file']);
}
```

display_Process is called when a change file has been selected. This method calls the load_Array method.
```
function load_Array()
{
$change_File = $_POST['change_file'];
$logFile = fopen($change_File, "r");
$row_Count = 0;
while(!feof($logFile))
{
            $change_Array[$row_Count] = explode(' | ', fgets($logFile));
            $row_Count++;
}
$row_Count--;
fclose($logFile);
return $change_Array;
}
```

The load_Array method is very similar to the constructor in the dog_data class. This method retrieves the value in change_file and places it in $change_File. This file is then opened and all entries in the file are placed into $change_Array. The explode method will produce three columns (date/time, change type, array or string used for the change). It returns this array to the calling program (display_Process).

The array is returned to $change_Array in display_Process. The count method determines the size of this array. Its value is placed in $row_count. displayRecords is called, passing the row_count, the change_Array, and the change_file into displayRecords.

```php
function displayRecords($row_Count, $change_Array, $change_File)
{
echo "<html><head>";
echo "<style> table { border: 2px solid #5c744d;}  </style>";
echo "</head><body>";
echo "<table>";
echo "<caption>Log File: " . $change_File . "</caption>";
echo "<tr><th></th><th>Date/Time</th><th>Change Type</th><th>Change Data</th></tr><tr>";
for ($J=$row_Count -1; $J >= 0; $J--)
{
        echo "<td><a href='readchangelog.php?rn=$J&change_File=$change_File'>Delete</a></td>";
        for($I=0; $I < 3; $I++)
                {
                echo "<td> " . $change_Array[$J][$I] . " </td> ";
                }
        echo "</tr>";
}
echo "</table>";
echo "</body></html>";


$directory = "";
$files = glob($directory . "*dog_data.xml");
echo "<form id='data_select' name='data_select' method='post' action='readchangelog.php'>";
echo "<h3>Delete entries above or select a file to update with change log $change_File</h3>";
echo "<select name='data_File' id='data_File'>";
foreach($files as $file)
{
        echo "<option value='$file'>$file</option>";
}
echo "</select>";
echo "<input type='hidden' id='change_file' name='change_file' value='$change_File'>";
echo "<input type='submit' id='submit' name='submit' value='select'>";
echo "</form>";
}
```

displayRecords displays the contents of the change log file using almost exactly the same logic used in the displayRecords method of the readerrorlog program (in Example 5-8). It also uses almost the same logic as the selectFileProcess (explained previously) to display the data files for the user to select the last uncorrupted file.

If the user decides to delete some records from the change log, the delete_Process is called.

```php
function delete_Process()
{
$change_Array = load_Array();
deleteRecord($_GET['rn'], $row_Count, $change_Array);
saveChanges($row_Count,$change_Array,$change_File);
displayRecords($row_Count,$change_Array,$change_File);
}
```

The delete_Process method will place the change file records into $change_Array using the same change_Array as shown before. It will pass the record number to be deleted ($_GET['rn']), the number of rows in the array ($row_Count), and the array ($change_Array) into the deleteRecord method. The deleteRecords method will use the same logic as shown in the deleteRecord method from the readerrorlog (in Example 5-8) program. The delete_Process will then call the saveChanges method, passing in the row_count, change_Array, and change_File information.

```
function saveChanges($row_Count,$change_Array,$change_File)
{
        $changeFile = fopen($change_File, "w");
        for($I=0; $I < $row_Count; $I++)
        {
            $writeString = $change_Array[$I][0] . " | " . $change_Array[$I][1] . " | " .
            $change_Array[$I][2];
          fwrite($changeFile, $writeString);
        }
        fclose($changeFile);
}
```

The saveChanges method builds the date/time-changetype-changedata format, seen previously, from the change_Array. This information is saved in $writeString and is used to replace the change log file with the updated version (minus the record that was deleted).

The delete_Process method then recalls the displayRecords method (described earlier) to display the updated change log (minus the record deleted) and the data file drop-down list.

Once the user selects the data file to be changed, the update_XML_File_Process method is called.

```
function update_XML_File_Process()
{
$change_Array = load_Array();
require_once("dog_data.php");
$data_Changer = new dog_data();
$row_Count = count($change_Array) -1;
for($I=0;$I < $row_Count; $I++)
{
   if($change_Array[$I][1] != "Delete")
        {
                $temp = unserialize($change_Array[$I][2]);
        }
        else
        {
                $temp = (integer)$change_Array[$I][2];
        }
        $data_Changer->processRecords($change_Array[$I][1], $temp);
}
```

The method calls the load_Array method to return the changes into $change_Array. The dog_data file is imported into the method to prepare for the changes to the data file selected by the user. An instance of the data_data class is created ($data_Changer).

A for loop is used to peruse the change array and to pass each change into the processRecords method of the data class. However, before the records are passed, the serialized data must be returned to an associate array format using the unserialize method. If the change request is Delete, type casting must occur to change the data (record number) into an integer. This is one of the few times that PHP requires type casting. Serialized data is not considered a data type. The data must be transformed by either unserializing it or type casting it. The change type (Update, Delete, or Insert) is passed into the first parameter of the processRecords method. The change array or the record number is passed into the second parameter of the method. All changes are made to the data, the file is backed up, and a new change log is created, in case there are more corruption problems.

***Example 6-4.*** The displaychangelog.php file

```php
<?php
function displayRecords($row_Count, $change_Array, $change_File) {
echo "<html><head>";
echo "<style> table { border: 2px solid #5c744d;}  </style>";
echo "</head><body><table><caption>Log File: " . $change_File . "</caption>";
echo "<tr><th></th><th>Date/Time</th><th>Change Type</th><th>Change Data</th></tr><tr>";
for ($J=$row_Count -1; $J >= 0; $J--) {
        echo "<td><a href='readchangelog.php?rn=$J&change_File=$change_File'>Delete</a></td>";
        for($I=0; $I < 3; $I++) {
                echo "<td> " . $change_Array[$J][$I] . " </td> ";
        }
        echo "</tr>";
}
echo "</table>";
echo "</body></html>";
echo "</table>";
echo "</body></html>";
$directory = "";
$files = glob($directory . "*dog_data.xml");
echo "<form id='data_select' name='data_select' method='post' action='readchangelog.php'>";
echo "<h3>Delete entries above or select a file to update with change log $change_File</h3>";
echo "<select name='data_File' id='data_File'>";
foreach($files as $file) {
            echo "<option value='$file'>$file</option>";
}
echo "</select>";
echo "<input type='hidden' id='change_file' name='change_file' value='$change_File'>";
echo "<input type='submit' id='submit' name='submit' value='select'>";
echo "</form>";
}
function deleteRecord($recordNumber, &$row_Count, &$change_Array) {
for ($J=$recordNumber; $J < $row_Count - 1; $J++) {
        for($I=0; $I < 3; $I++) {
                $change_Array[$J][$I] = $change_Array[$J + 1][$I];
        }
}
unset($change_Array[$row_Count]);
$row_Count--;
}
```

209

```php
function saveChanges($row_Count,$change_Array,$change_File)
{
        $changeFile = fopen($change_File, "w");
        for($I=0; $I < $row_Count; $I++)
        {
            $writeString = $change_Array[$I][0] . " | " . $change_Array[$I][1] . " | " .
            $change_Array[$I][2];
                fwrite($changeFile, $writeString);
        }
        fclose($changeFile);
}
function delete_Process() {
$change_Array = load_Array();
deleteRecord($_GET['rn'], $row_Count, $change_Array);
saveChanges($row_Count,$change_Array,$change_File);
displayRecords($row_Count,$change_Array,$change_File);
}
function load_Array() {
$change_File = $_POST['change_file'];
$logFile = fopen($change_File, "r");
$row_Count = 0;
while(!feof($logFile)) {
            $change_Array[$row_Count] = explode(' | ', fgets($logFile));
            $row_Count++;    }
$row_Count--;
fclose($logFile);
return $change_Array;
}
function display_Process() {
$change_Array = load_Array();
$row_Count = count($change_Array) -1;
displayRecords($row_Count, $change_Array, $_POST['change_file']);
}
function select_File_Process() {
$directory = "";
$files = glob($directory . "*change.log");
echo "<form id='file_select' name='file_select' method='post' action='readchangelog.php'>";
echo "<h3>Select a file to display</h3>";
echo "<select name='change_file' id='change_file'>";
foreach($files as $file) {
echo "<option value='$file'>$file</option>";
}
echo "</select>";
echo "<input type='submit' id='submit' name='submit' value='select'>";
echo "</form>";
}
function update_XML_File_Process() {
$change_Array = load_Array();
require_once("dog_datad.php");
$data_Changer = new dog_data();
$row_Count = count($change_Array) -1;
```

```php
for($I=0;$I < $row_Count; $I++) {
        if($change_Array[$I][1] != "Delete") {
            $temp = unserialize($change_Array[$I][2]);
        } else {
            $temp = (integer)$change_Array[$I][2];
        }
        $data_Changer->processRecords($change_Array[$I][1], $temp);
}
$data_Changer->setChangeLogFile($_POST['data_File']);
$data_Changer = NULL;
echo "Changes completed";
}
// main section
if(isset($_POST['data_File'])) {
        update_XML_File_Process();
} else if(isset($_GET['rn'])) {
        delete_Process();
} else if(isset($_POST['change_file'])) {
        display_Process();
} else {
select_File_Process();
}
?>
```

# JSON Backup and Recovery

What changes are needed to provide backup and recovery for JSON data instead of XML data? Actually, no changes at all. As long as the changes from the first section of this chapter are implemented, the displaychangelog program and the changes to the dog_data class will handle JSON in the same manner as XML data.

# MySQL Backup and Recovery

As you might be guessing, as long as the changes from the second section of this chapter are implemented, no additional changes will be required for backup and recovery of MySQL data. However, you can take a moment to look at an alternative way of handling MySQL data.

It is a common practice to create a SQL script file to execute against a database. A script file contains all the SQL code necessary to update the database. Using this type of file will allow you to do proper INSERT, UPDATE, and DELETE SQL commands instead of only an INSERT as previously shown. The previous example required creating an INSERT command for every record in the associate array. This includes records that were not changed. This would be inefficient for medium to large databases. You only need to update the record that changed.

You can develop the scripting file from records in the associate array that have changed. You can use the change log as the script file, as the SQL script lists all changes that have been requested. It can be rerun to fix any corrupted data.

211

For example, in the updateRecords method, you can create any required SQL UPDATE commands.

```
private function updateRecords($records_array)
{
        $chge_log_file = date('mdYhis') . $this->change_log_file;
        $chge_string = "";
        foreach ($records_array as $records=>$records_value)
        {
                $this->dogs_array["dog"][$records] = $records_array[$records];
                $chge_string .=  "UPDATE Dogs ";
                $chge_string .= "SET dog_name='" . $records_array[$records]['dog_name'] ."', ";
                $chge_string .= "dog_weight='" . $records_array[$records]['dog_weight'] ."',
                $chge_string .= "dog_color='" . $records_array[$records]['dog_color'] ."', ";
                $chge_string .= "dog_breed='" . $records_array[$records]['dog_breed'] ."' ";
                $chge_string .= "WHERE dog_id='" . $records_array[$records]['dog_id'] . "';\n";
        }
        $chge_log_file = date('mdYhis') . $this->change_log_file;
        error_log($chge_string,3,$chge_log_file); // might exceed 120 chars
}
```

These changes would build all the update requirements from the associate array. Similar changes could also be done to the insert and delete methods.

```
private function deleteRecord($recordNumber)
{
        foreach ($this->dogs_array as $dogs=>&$dogs_value) {
                for($J=$recordNumber; $J < count($dogs_value) -1; $J++) {
                        foreach ($dogs_value[$J] as $column => $column_value)
                        {
                                $dogs_value[$J][$column] = $dogs_value[$J + 1][$column];
                        }
                }
        unset ($dogs_value[count($dogs_value) -1]);
        }
        $dog_id = $this->dogs_array['dog'][$recordNumber]['dog_id'];
        $chge_string = "DELETE FROM Dogs WHERE dog_id='" . $dog_id . "';\n";
        $chge_log_file = date('mdYhis') . $this->change_log_file;
        error_log($chge_string,3,$chge_log_file); // might exceed 120 chars
}
```

This example delete method deletes one record at a time. Thus, the delete string is built outside of the loop. The update method allows for multiple records to be updated, so the update string is built inside of the loop. The insert method will also require you to build the string inside the loop.

```
private function insertRecords($records_array)
{
        $chge_string = "";
        $dogs_array_size = count($this->dogs_array["dog"]);
        for($I=0;$I< count($records_array);$I++)
        {
```

```
                $this->dogs_array["dog"][$dogs_array_size + $I] = $records_array[$I];
                $dog_id = rand(0,9999); // get a number between 0 and 9999
                while (in_array($dog_id, $this->dogs_array, true)) // in array?
                { $dog_id = rand(0,9999); // if it is get another number
    }
$chge_string .="INSERT INTO Dogs VALUES('";
                $chge_string .= $dog_id . "', '" . $records_array[$I]['dog_name'] . "', '";
                $chge_string .= $records_array[$I]['dog_weight'] . "', '";
                $chge_string .= $records_array[$I]['dog_color'] . "', '";
                $chge_string .= $records_array[$I]['dog_breed'] . "');";
        }
        $chge_log_file = date('mdYhis') . $this->change_log_file;
        error_log($chge_string,3,$chge_log_file); // might exceed 120 chars
}
```

If you review the changeRecords method, a SQL WHERE clause was built using a property named dog_id. In the XML and JSON examples you did not have this field. However, SQL UPDATE requires a where clause to determine which record(s) to update. The property used needs to be unique to identify the exact record(s). The only place the code must generate this dog_id is when a new record is created in the database (in the insertRecords method). This can be done using the PHP rand method.

The PHP rand method produces random numbers. The first parameter is the starting number (0) and the second parameter is the last number (9999). The size of this field is set to char(4) in the database, which allows up to four characters. This would allow you up to 10,000 dogs. I am sure that will be more than enough!

The while loop in the insertRecords method uses the PHP in_array method to determine if the number is already in the dogs_array (which contains all the current records in the database). A third parameter, which determines if a strict **search** (comparing data types) should occur, must be set to produce reliable results with multidimensional associate arrays. If the number does exist, the logic continues to generate a new random number until a unique one is found. The value is then placed in $dog_id, which will be inserted into the database along with the other fields (dog_name, dog_weight, dog_color, and dog_breed). Note: This code assumes that the Dogs table in the database has been created with the fields in the order shown (dog_id, dog_name, dog_weight, dog_color, and dog_breed).

The change log (which is now also a SQL script file) would now contain statements similar to the following:

```
INSERT INTO Dogs VALUES('2288', 'tester1', '19', 'Green', 'Lab');
UPDATE Dogs SET dog_name='tester1', dog_weight='19', dog_color='Green',
dog_breed='Lab' WHERE dog_id='0111';
UPDATE Dogs SET dog_name='tester2', dog_weight='19', dog_color='Green',
dog_breed='Lab' WHERE dog_id='1211';
DELETE FROM Dogs WHERE dog_id='1111';
```

This file can be run against the database when all changes have been logged. The destructor can now execute this file (instead of removing the table and inserting all the records back into a new table).

```
$mysqli = new mysqli($server, $db_username, $db_password, $database);
if ($mysqli->connect_errno)
{
        throw new Exception("MySQL connection error:" . $mysqli->connect_error);
}
```

```
$chge_log_file = date('mdYhis') . $this->change_log_file;
$sql = explode(";",file_get_contents($chge_log_file));
foreach($sql as $query)  {
        If(!$mysqli->query($query))
            {
                    throw new Exception("Dog Table Change Error: " . $mysqli->error);
            }
}
}
```

The code for the destructor becomes simpler than in the original MySQL example. The destructor does not need to format any SQL statements. It only needs to execute them. The method reads the change records from the change log, splitting each via the ; at the end of each SQL command line. Each line is placed in the array $sql. The logic then loops through the array and executes each statement via the query command. If any of the SQL statements has a problem, an exception is thrown (which will also send an e-mail to support personnel via the dog_interface program). An example program is available on the book's web site.

Note: As stated, the MySQL examples are shown to help the reader see that the overall logic of the dog_data class works well with all data types. Complete books are written on using PHP to interact with databases. It is not the intent of this book to train the user to have complete knowledge of database manipulation.

## Do It

1.  The dog_data class creates a new log file every time it is run. This could cause a lot of log files to be created in a very short period of time. Your mission is to either update the readchangelog file (download it from the book's web site) or to create your own maintenance program. The code will ask the users for the number of log files (and data files) to keep. The program will then keep the most recent number of files requested. The glob method, as shown previously, can be used to retrieve all the file names. The unlink method can be used to delete a file.

    ```
    unlink($file);
    ```

2.  The MySQL examples shown now produce different contents in the change log file. Download the readchangelog program from the book's web site and make any adjustments needed to the code to properly view and delete the change log. Assuming that the database administrator has reversed the contents of the database to the last valid set of data, adjust the program to execute the change log selected against the database. Hint: Your completed program will have less code than the example from the book's web site.

## Connecting the Data Tier

Now that a reliable, well tested, data class has been created, it is time to connect it to the business rules tier. The Dog class will use the dog_data class to store the dog information in an XML file.

```
if (method_exists('dog_container', 'create_object')) {

$this->breedxml = $properties_array[4];
```

```
$name_error = $this->set_dog_name($properties_array[0]) == TRUE ? 'TRUE,' : 'FALSE,';

$color_error = $this->set_dog_color($properties_array[2]) == TRUE ? 'TRUE,' : 'FALSE,';

$weight_error= $this->set_dog_weight($properties_array[3]) == TRUE ? 'TRUE' : 'FALSE';

$breed_error = $this->set_dog_breed($properties_array[1]) == TRUE ? 'TRUE,' : 'FALSE,';

$this->error_message = $name_error . $breed_error . $color_error . $weight_error;

$this->save_dog_data();

if(stristr($this->error_message, 'FALSE'))
{
        throw new setException($this->error_message);
}
} else
{
        exit;
}
```

The constructor of the dog class sets all the properties and throws an exception if there are problems. If no problems exist, the information is saved (via save_dog_data), and the program closes (exit).

In order to keep the data tier independent of the business rules tier, dependency injection will be used to discover the location and name of the dog_data class and to call the processRecords method from the class. You will borrow the logic from Chapter 4. Actually, you can use the dog_container from Example 4-10 without any changes. If you don't remember the details of this class, revisit Chapter 4.

The dog_container class includes the get_dog_application method, which uses the logic discussed several times to search the dog application XML file for the name of the file needed (dog_data.php). The set_app method allows you to pass the application type (dogdata) to search in get_dog_application. It also includes the create_object class that will determine the class name (dog_data), make an instance of the class, and pass the class (the address of the class in memory) back to the calling program. The class does require that a clean_input function exist in the calling program. You don't currently have one in the Dog class. However, you can create a shell (an empty function) in the class to meet this requirement.

To use the container, you can use the logic that was in the dog_interface program to make an instance of the container, find the location of dog_data, and make an instance of dog_data (without knowing the class name).

```
function clean_input() { }
private function save_dog_data()
{
if ( file_exists("e5dog_container.php")) {
        require_once("e5dog_container.php"); // use chapter 5 container w exception handling
} else {
        throw new Exception("Dog container file missing or corrupt");
}
        $container = new dog_container("dogdata"); // sets the tag name to look for in XML file
        $properties_array = array("dogdata"); // not used but must be passed into create_object
        $dog_data = $container->create_object($properties_array); // creates dog_data object
        $method_array = get_class_methods($dog_data);
        $last_position = count($method_array) - 1;
```

```
        $method_name = $method_array[$last_position];
        $record_Array = array(array('dog_name'=>"$this->dog_name", 'dog_weight'=>
        "$this->dog_weight", 'dog_color'=>"$this->dog_color", 'dog_breed'=>"$this->dog_breed"));
        $dog_data->$method_name("Insert",$record_Array);
        $dog_data = NULL;
}
```

The lines to accomplish this are the same as seen previously in the dog_interface; you create the dog_container, find the location of the dogdata file, and create an instance of the dog_data class. The only difference is that "dogdata" is passed in for the search. The PHP function get_class_methods is used to create a list of methods in the dog_data class. The last method in the class is processRecords. The name of this method is pulled and placed into $method_name. The record_Array is then built to be passed into processRecords. The method is called, passing "Insert" and the record_Array. Finally, the dog_data object is set to NULL, which causes the destructor to save the data.

This allows complete *dependency injection*. The dog object does not know the name of the dog_data class, the location of the dog_data class, or the name of the method to call until it is determined by this code. This creates a complete break between the data tier and the business rules tier, as required for three-tier design.

*Example 6-5.* The dog.php file using dog_data.php to save data

```php
<?php
class Dog
{
// -------------------------------- Properties --------------------------------
private $dog_weight = 0;
private $dog_breed = "no breed";
private $dog_color = "no color";
private $dog_name = "no name";
private $error_message = "??";
private $breedxml = "";
// -------------------------------- Constructor --------------------------------
function __construct($properties_array)
{
if (method_exists('dog_container', 'create_object')) {
$this->breedxml = $properties_array[4];

$name_error  = $this->set_dog_name($properties_array[0])  == TRUE ? 'TRUE,' : 'FALSE,';
$color_error = $this->set_dog_color($properties_array[2]) == TRUE ? 'TRUE,' : 'FALSE,';
$weight_error= $this->set_dog_weight($properties_array[3]) == TRUE ? 'TRUE' : 'FALSE';
$breed_error = $this->set_dog_breed($properties_array[1])  == TRUE ? 'TRUE,' : 'FALSE,';

$this->error_message = $name_error . $breed_error . $color_error . $weight_error;
$this->save_dog_data();
if(stristr($this->error_message, 'FALSE'))
{
        throw new setException($this->error_message);
} }
else
{ exit; }
}
```

```php
function clean_input() { }
private function save_dog_data()
{
if ( file_exists("e5dog_container.php")) {
                require_once("e5dog_container.php"); // use chapter 5 container w exception
                handling
        } else {
                throw new Exception("Dog container file missing or corrupt");
        }

        $container = new dog_container("dogdata"); // sets the tag name to look for in XML file
        $properties_array = array("dogdata"); // not used but must be passed into create_object
        $dog_data = $container->create_object($properties_array); // creates dog_data object
        $method_array = get_class_methods($dog_data);
        $last_position = count($method_array) - 1;
        $method_name = $method_array[$last_position];
        $record_Array = array(array('dog_name'=>"$this->dog_name", 'dog_weight'=>
        "$this->dog_weight", 'dog_color'=>"$this->dog_color", 'dog_breed'=>"$this->dog_breed"));
        $dog_data->$method_name("Insert",$record_Array);
        $dog_data = NULL;

}
function set_dog_name($value)
{
$error_message = TRUE;
(ctype_alpha($value) && strlen($value) <= 20) ? $this->dog_name = $value :
$this->error_message = FALSE;
return $this->error_message;
}
function set_dog_weight($value)
{
$error_message = TRUE;
(ctype_digit($value) && ($value > 0 && $value <= 120)) ? $this->dog_weight = $value :
$this->error_message = FALSE;
return $this->error_message; }
function set_dog_breed($value)
{
$error_message = TRUE;
($this->validator_breed($value) === TRUE) ? $this->dog_breed = $value :
$this->error_message = FALSE;
return $this->error_message; }
function set_dog_color($value)
{
$error_message = TRUE;
(ctype_alpha($value) && strlen($value) <= 15) ? $this->dog_color = $value :
$this->error_message = FALSE;
return $this->error_message;
}
```

```php
// --------------------------- Get Methods ----------------------------------------------
function get_dog_name()
{
return $this->dog_name;
}
function get_dog_weight()
{
return $this->dog_weight;
}
function get_dog_breed()
{
return $this->dog_breed;
}
function get_dog_color()
{
return $this->dog_color;
}
function get_properties()
{
return "$this->dog_name,$this->dog_weight,$this->dog_breed,$this->dog_color.";
}
// ---------------------------General Method----------------------------------------------
private function validator_breed($value)
{
$breed_file = simplexml:load_file($this->breedxml);
$xmlText = $breed_file->asXML();
if(stristr($xmlText, $value) === FALSE)
{
return FALSE;
}
else
{
return TRUE;
}
}

}
?>
```

The Dog application now has three complete tiers.

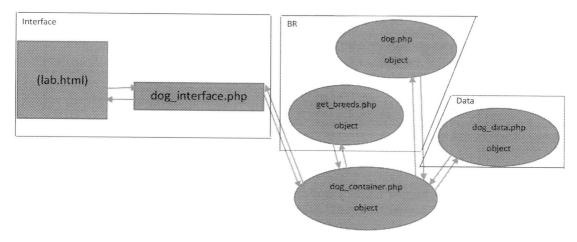

***Figure 6-3.*** *Three-tier dog application*

The interface tier contains the lab.html file and the dog_interface.php program. The business rules tier includes the dog.php class and the get_breeds class. The dog_data class is in the data tier. Any requests from the dog_interface program for communications with the business rules tier are handled by the dog_container class. Any requests for communications with the data tier (from the business rules tier) are also handled by the dog_container class. Access to the data tier is only available from or through the business rules tier. Access to the interface tier only occurs from or through the business rules tier.

The interface tier does not know the location/name of any class or method in the business rules tier. This information is discovered by using the dog_container. The business rules tier does not know the location/name of any class or method in the data tier. This information is also discovered by using the dog_container. This allows complete independence of each tier, which allows changes to occur in one tier without requiring changes in the other two tiers.

# Do It

1. Download all the files for the dog application from this chapter. Adjust file names in the dog_application XML file to discover how missing files are handled in the application. Does the application handle these problems properly? Adjust the dog_data XML file to include badly formed XML data. Run the application. Does it handle these problems properly? Empty the dog_data XML file (except for the dogs and dog tags). Run the application. Does it handle this situation properly? For any instance that causes the application to error instead of raising an exception, attempt to adjust the code to anticipate the problem and raise an exception.

# Chapter Terms

| | |
|---|---|
| Data Tier | `file_get_contents` |
| SimpleXML Data Model | `simplexml:load_string` |
| Type casting | JSON data |
| JSON Methods | associative array |
| `json_encode` | `json_decode` |
| Keywords | `new line character` |
| `file_put_contents` | `libxml:user_internal_errors(true)` |
| `libxml:get_errors` | count |
| `$this` | unset |
| Dynamic arrays | releasing an object |
| `mysqli_connect` | `mysqli_connect_errno` |
| `mysqli_fetch_assoc` | `mysqli_free_result` |
| `mysqli_close` | `SQL SELECT` |
| `SQL INSERT` | polymorphism |
| Change log file | serialize |
| unserialize | backup and recovery |
| `preg_replace` | regular expression |
| glob | embedded if then else |
| `SQL UPDATE` | SQL script file/log |
| `SQL WHERE` | rand |
| strict search | unlink |
| shell | dependence injection |

# Chapter Questions and Projects

**Multiple Choice**

1. Which of the following describes type casting?

   a. It's rarely needed in PHP

   b. It exists in most languages

   c. It's needed for serialized data

   d. All of the above

2. Which of the following describes an associative array?

   a. It has a key and value relationship (key->value)

   b. It uses numerical subscripts

   c. It does not have an index

   d. A and B

3.  Which of the following is the newline character?

    a.  &

    b.  .

    c.  ;

    d.  None of these

4.  Which of the following describes JSON data?

    a.  It has a similar format to arrays

    b.  It cannot only be used with JavaScript

    c.  It requires much more coding than when using XML data

    d.  It is more secure than XML data

5.  Which of the following describes unlink?

    a.  It can be used to release a parameter of an array

    b.  It can be used to delete a file or directory

    c.  It can be used to split apart an array

    d.  None of these

6.  Which of the following describes polymorphism?

    a.  The container that holds and secures an application

    b.  The ability to pass multiple data types into the same signature of a method

    c.  The ability to use the methods and properties of a parent class

    d.  None of these

7.  Which of the following describes rand?

    a.  It can be used to produce a random number

    b.  The first parameter is the starting number

    c.  The second parameter is the last number

    d.  All of the above

8.  When using in_array, strict search does which of the following?

    a.  It compares data types

    b.  It is the third parameter (set to true)

    c.  It should be used when searching associative arrays

    d.  All of these

9.  Which of the following describes a shell method?

    a.  It contains no data

    b.  It has no signature

    c.  It includes JSON data

    d.  All of these

10. The data tier does which of the following?

    a. Updates data

    b. Returns data

    c. Filters data

    d. All of the above

**True/False**

1. Log files are important for successful recovery of information.

2. Data is serialized to convert the data type to string.

3. After updates have been completed, all backup copies of data can be destroyed.

4. Dependency injection is necessary to keep the tiers (interface, business rules, and data) independent of each other.

5. SQL script files update all records including those that have not changed.

**Short Answer/Essay**

1. Explain the process used to correct data files that have been corrupted.

2. Why is data stored in a database usually more secure than data stored in a text file?

3. Compare and contrast the methods used to update XML data to the methods used to update MySQL data. Which is more efficient? Why?

4. When should an e-mail be sent to the system administrator when data is being updated? What should this e-mail contain? What should it not contain? Why?

5. How can a system administrator determine which data file is the last non-corrupted version?

**Projects**

1. Adjust the code from Chapter 4 project #1 or #2 to include backup and recovery ability.

2. Create a complete storage (XML or JSON format) and a backup and recovery system for one of the previous projects you have completed. The system should include the ability for the users to limit the number of recovery files, the ability to adjust contents of a selected file (update, insert, and delete), and the ability to execute the file against the most recent valid data. When the process is complete, any corrupted files should automatically be removed. The system should also keep its own log file to indicate when changes have occurred.

**Term Project**

1. Update the ABC Computer Parts Inventory program to include storage of the data (XML or JSON format) and complete backup and recovery capabilities. The application should include a change log to indicate any data changes. Additional support programs should be included to allow for easy recovery of any corrupted data. Your complete application should use logic similar to the examples shown in this chapter.

# CHAPTER 7

# Authentication

*"(To Lisa) You got the brains and talent to go as far as you want and when you do, I'll be right there to borrow money."*

—Bart Simpson

## Chapter Objectives/Student Learning Outcomes

After completing this chapter, the student will be able to:

- Define sessions and explain how they are used for authentication
- Create a PHP program that authenticates user logon
- Create a PHP program that registers users
- Create a PHP program that will allow users to change their passwords
- Create a PHP program that logs invalid login attempts
- Create a PHP program that will use current password encryption techniques

## Verification and Sessions

No discussion of security would be complete without including user ID/password authentication. The current version of PHP includes many techniques to assist developers in validating users. This chapter looks at one of the more simplistic methods.

Due to the nature of immediate verification of login credentials, the authentication process directly accesses the data source for validation (it does not pass through the business rules tier). Thus, the authentication process is considered a separate tier that is placed on top of the application to provide access. As you will see, only minor changes need to occur in the interface tier programs to restrict access. Most of the coding needed is placed in the authentication tier.

In addition to authentication, levels of access can also be determined during the sign-in process. Not every user needs full access to an application. Some users may only need read access, some may need write access to only the information that pertains to them, and some (administrators) may need full access to the complete application. Each part of the application needs to be able to determine the correct level of access without requesting additional information from the user (beyond the original login to the application).

---

**Electronic supplementary material**  The online version of this chapter (doi:10.1007/978-1-4842-1730-6_7) contains supplementary material, which is available to authorized users.

S. Prettyman. *Learn PHP 7*. DOI 10.1007/978-1-4842-1730-6_7

One login process must allow the users to verify all portions of the application. Each portion of the application needs access to common properties (such as user ID and password) that have been set by the authentication tier for verification of valid access and valid levels of access. PHP provides the ability to store information for an application in server memory by declaring a *session*. A session is considered to include the complete interaction of the user with the application (such as the complete processes of transferring money from a saving account to a checking account). A session can be established as soon as the user signs in to the application. The session can be closed after the user logs out of the system (or the application times out, or is closed). When a session is closed, all properties stored in the memory of the server are removed by the garbage collector.

While the session is active, properties can be stored and shared throughout the application. Using this process, the user ID and password can be stored in session properties. Each part of the application can then verify that the user has logged in by determining if there are values in the userid and password properties.

Before you look at the login authentication process, let's look at how to determine if a user has logged into the system. The examples in this chapter do not include verifications of security access levels. However, the process to determine these levels would use similar code as shown in these examples.

*Programming note—The* session_start *method call must be the first statement at the top of the code. There must be no spaces or code between the* <?php *tag and* session_start. *The* session_start *method produces an HTML header that would not be formed correctly if any code exists before the method call.*

```php
<?php
session_start();
if ((!isset($_SESSION['username'])) || (!isset($_SESSION['password']))) {
echo "You must login to access the ABC Canine Shelter Reservation System";
echo "<p>";
echo "<a href='login.php'>Login</a> | <a href='register.php'>Create an account</a>";
echo "</p>";
}
else {
echo "<p>Welcome back, " . $_SESSION['username'] . "</p>";
}
?>
```

Each program in the interface tier (that the user can access) would include code similar to the previous example. The session_start method, in this example, lets the operating system know that this program is part of an existing session (which is declared in the authentication tier). Each session is identified by the system using a uniquely generated ID. As long as the user (or system) has not closed the session, the session ID will be attached to any program, called by the user, which includes the session_start method. This allows the program to access all properties related to the current session.

The PHP isset method (in an if statement) can determine if values exist in the username and password properties. If values do not exist, it indicates that the user has not been authenticated. Session properties are retrieved (and set) using $_SESSION. In the previous example, if either of the properties is not set, the user is provided links to the login page (login.php) or the register page (register.php). If both properties are set, the user is welcomed to the system. The user has no choice but to log in to access the program. In addition, as mentioned in previous chapters, for more secure programs, the IP address of the user's machine, and the calling program can be determined to provide extra assurance that the user is authorized.

***Example 7-1.*** The lab.php file with user ID/password verification

```php
<?php
session_start();
if ((!isset($_SESSION['username'])) || (!isset($_SESSION['password']))) {
echo "You must login to access the ABC Canine Shelter Reservation System";
echo "<p>";
echo "<a href='login.php'>Login</a> | <a href='register.php'>Create an account</a>";
echo "</p>";
}
else
{
echo "<p>Welcome back, " . $_SESSION['username'] . "</p>";
?>
<!DOCTYPE html>
<html lan="en">
<head>
<title>Dog Object</title>
<script src="get_breeds.js"></script>
<script src="validator.js"></script>
<style type="text/css">
#JS { display:none; }
</style>
<script>
function checkJS() {
document.getElementById('JS').style.display = "inline";
}
</script>
</head>
<body onload="checkJS();">
<h1>Dog Object Creater</h1>
<div id="JS">
<form method="post" action="e5adog_interface.php" onSubmit="return validate_input(this)">
<h2>Please complete ALL fields. Please note the required format of information.</h2>
Enter Your Dog's Name (max 20 characters, alphabetic) <input type="text" pattern="[a-zA-Z]*"
title="Up to 20 Alphabetic Characters" maxlength="20" name="dog_name" id="dog_name"
required/><br /><br />
Select Your Dog's Color:<br />
<input type="radio" name="dog_color" id="dog_color" value="Brown">Brown<br />
<input type="radio" name="dog_color" id="dog_color" value="Black">Black<br />
<input type="radio" name="dog_color" id="dog_color" value="Yellow">Yellow<br />
<input type="radio" name="dog_color" id="dog_color" value="White">White<br />
<input type="radio" name="dog_color" id="dog_color" value="Mixed" checked >Mixed<br /><br />
Enter Your Dog's Weight (numeric only) <input type="number" min="1" max="120" name="dog_weight"
id="dog_weight" required /><br /><br />
<script>
AjaxRequest('e5dog_interface.php');
</script>
```

```
<input type="hidden" name="dog_app" id="dog_app" value="dog" />
Select Your Dog's Breed <div id="AjaxResponse"></div><br />
<input type="submit" value="Click to create your dog" />
</form>
</div>
<noscript>
<div id="noJS">
<form method="post" action="e5adog_interface.php">
<h2>Please complete ALL fields. Please note the required format of information.</h2>
Enter Your Dog's Name (max 20 characters, alphabetic) <input type="text" pattern="[a-zA-Z ]*"
title="Up to 20 Alphabetic Characters" maxlength="20" name="dog_name" id="dog_name"
required/><br /><br />
Select Your Dog's Color:<br />
<input type="radio" name="dog_color" id="dog_color" value="Brown">Brown<br />
<input type="radio" name="dog_color" id="dog_color" value="Black">Black<br />
<input type="radio" name="dog_color" id="dog_color" value="Yellow">Yellow<br />
<input type="radio" name="dog_color" id="dog_color" value="White">White<br />
<input type="radio" name="dog_color" id="dog_color" value="Mixed" checked >Mixed<br /><br />
Enter Your Dog's Weight (numeric only) <input type="number" min="1" max="120" name="dog_
weight" id="dog_weight" required /><br /><br />
Enter Your Dog's Breed (max 35 characters, alphabetic) <input type="text" pattern="[a-zA-Z ]*"
title="Up to 15 Alphabetic Characters" maxlength="35" name="dog_breed" id="dog_breed"
required /><br />
<input type="hidden" name="dog_app" id="dog_app" value="dog" />
<input type="submit" value="Click to create your dog" />
</form>
</div>
</noscript>
</body>
</html>
<?php
}
?>
```

In Example 7-1, the verification code is placed at the top of the program. The else statement must include all the code to execute if the user is signed into the system. Since the code for this program is HTML (and CSS) code, the if statement must be wrapped around the existing code. The closing bracket (s) of the else statement is shifted to the bottom of the code (after all HTML tags).

PHP allows you to close your PHP code (via ?>) and reopen your PHP code (via <?php) as many times as required. In this example, the PHP code is closed at the top of the program (in the else statement) just before the closing bracket. The PHP code is then reopened at the bottom of the code to include a single closing bracket, which closes the PHP else statement. This wraps the else statement around all the existing code. The users can now only access this section of the code if they are logged in.

Since PHP code is now included in the lab program, the file ending must be changed from .html to .php. Otherwise the server would not execute the PHP code.

Now let's look at how you can populate the session properties by creating a login program. First let's look at the HTML to request information from the users.

```
<form method="post" action="">
Username: <input type="text" pattern=".{8,}" title="Userid must contain eight or more
characters." name="username" id="username" required/><br />
```

```
Password: <input type="password" pattern="(?=.*\d)(?=.*[a-z])(?=.*[A-Z]).{8,}"
title="Password must contain at least one number, one uppercase and lowercase letter, and at
least 8 total characters." name="password" id="password" required /><br />
<input type="submit" value="Login">
</form>
```

HTML5 does not include a minimum length parameter. However, the pattern parameter can be used (with regular expressions) to establish a minimum size. In the username tag in the previous example, the pattern ".{8,}" requires at least eight characters be entered by the users. For password security, a more complicated pattern is needed. In the password example, in addition to the minimum requirement of eight characters, at least one number (?=.*\d), one uppercase letter (?=.*[A-Z]), and one lowercase letter (?=.*[a-z]) are required.

> *Security and performance—The HTML filtering provided is used to inform the users of any typos that may have occurred. In the login process you are not storing information; you are comparing information to what has already been stored. You don't have to be concerned with any possible harmful information being passed into the text boxes. Any harmful information would not match the valid information that's stored. The user would receive an invalid user ID/password message.*

```
// validate process not shown
$_SESSION['username'] = $_POST['username'];
$_SESSION['password'] = $_POST['password'];
 // Redirect the user to the home page
header("Location: http://www.asite.com/lab.php");
```

Assuming you have validated the information against a list of valid user IDs and passwords (you will look at that process soon), you can pass the valid user ID and password information into session variables. Then the PHP header method can be used to redirect the application to the next program to execute (lab.php). As long as lab.php includes the session_start method (as shown previously), it will have access to the session variables.

```
<?php
session_start();
if ((!isset($_POST['username'])) || (!isset($_POST['password'])))
{
?>
<form method="post" action="">
Username: <input type="text" pattern=".{8,}" title="Userid must contain eight or more
characters." name="username" id="username" required/><br />
Password: <input type="password" pattern="(?=.*\d)(?=.*[a-z])(?=.*[A-Z]).{8,}"
title="Password must contain at least one number, one uppercase and lowercase letter,
and at least 8 total characters."
 name="password" id="password" required /><br />
<input type="submit" value="Login">
</form>
<?php
} else {
// validate process not shown
  $_SESSION['username'] = $_POST['username'];
  $_SESSION['password'] = $_POST['password'];
```

```
 // Redirect the user to the home page
 header("Location: http://www.asite.com/lab.php");
 }
?>
```

Putting the pieces together requires an if statement to determine if the user has entered the user ID and password. If the user has not done so, the HTML code to request them is displayed. If the information has been entered (and is valid using the HTML5 pattern expressions shown) the else portion of the statement will execute (storing the values in the session variables and calling the lab.php program). This provides you with the basic shell of accepting the user ID and password, verifying they exist, and calling the program in the interface tier if they do exist. Of course, you need to authenticate the user ID and password before calling the program.

> *Programming note—The server variables* PHP_AUTH_USER *and* PHP_AUTH_PW *can be used for user ID and password validation, instead of using session variables.*

```
header('WWW-Authenticate: Basic realm="ABC Canine"');
    header('HTTP/1.0 401 Unauthorized');
```

> *Unauthorized header messages can be created if the user has not entered a user ID/password or a valid user ID/password. This will automatically cause the system to request the user enter a user ID/password. This technique is pretty straightforward. However, there have been some reports, in the past, of browsers not functioning properly with this technique. Besides, creating your own technique allows you to design the login screen with the same style as the rest of your web site.*

> *For more information, visit:*
> http://php.net/manual/en/features.http-auth.php

```
$valid_useridpasswords = array ("sjohnson" => "N3working");
$valid_userids = array_keys($valid_useridpasswords);
$userid = $_SESSION['username'];
$password = $_SESSION['password'];
$valid = (in_array($userid, $valid_userids)) && ($password == $valid_useridpasswords[$userid]);
If($valid) { header("Location: http://www.asite.com/lab.php");}
```

There are several ways you can authenticate user IDs and passwords. If you are creating a system that does not require user IDs and passwords to change, you could use arrays. In the previous example the $valid_useridpasswords associate array contains the combination of valid user IDs and passwords. The PHP method array_keys places all keys (in this example the user IDs) into a separate array ($valid_userids). After the session variables have been placed in $userid and $password, the PHP in_array method is used to determine if the correct combination of user ID and password exists. in_array determines if the user ID exists in the array. Then the user ID is used as the subscript to pull the password from the valid_useridpasswords array and compare it to the value in $password. If the user ID exists and the passwords are the same, then everything is valid. $valid will contain TRUE. If either (or both) are not valid, $valid will contain FALSE. If $valid is TRUE, the application redirects to the lab.php program.

Technically properties in a session are secured from any access outside the session. However, there have been reported instances, in the past, of hacker programs breaking this security and accessing session information. If the user ID and password, in this example, are stored in session variables and passed across the Internet to another program, hackers might gain access to the information.

If the user ID and password are externally stored in a file or database, the information will also travel outside the program. The program will no longer have control over the security of these items once they reside in the file or database. This could allow hackers access to the information. Security, as mentioned, has to be a team effort among the programmer, data administrator, and network administrator.

It is common practice to encrypt the password to reduce the chance that hackers will discover the authentication information (or any other secure information). Many PHP books demonstrate the use of the MD5 hash technique. However, over the last several years vulnerabilities have been discovered in this encryption style.

PHP 5.5 included the method password_hash, which will be adjusted over time to use the most secure encryption hashing techniques avaliable.

> *Programming note—Caution should be used when storing the encrypted version of the password. The size of the resulting encryption will increase with new hash versions. A size of 255 characters is likely to be large enough for the many years. The number of milliseconds needed for this hash increases with the size and type of the encryption. Advanced programmers may want to do some testing on their servers for time costs.*
>
> Visit *http://php.net/manual/en/function.password-hash.php for more information.*
>
> *Programming note—You cannot do a simple comparison with the hashed password created by PHP's password_hash method. The hash produced includes the encryption type, a salt value, and the hashed password.*

You only need to replace one line of code in the example to verify the password. You can replace

```
$valid = ((in_array($userid, $valid_userids)) && ($password == $valid_useridpasswords[$userid]));
```

with

```
$valid =( (in_array($userid, $valid_userids)) && (password_verify($password,
$valid_useridpasswords[$userid]));
```

If you placed the encypted password in the $valid_useridpasswords array, the validation technique would not require any other changes. The PHP password_verify method will encrpt the password provided by the user and compare it to the existing encyrpted password. If they match, it will return TRUE.

When using XML or JSON files, you can use the same logic used in the constructor for the dogdata.php program from Chapter 6, to retrieve the valid user ID and password information. The only changes needed are to the if statement, which determines the location of the user ID and password file, and to the last line in the constructor to place the array produced to $valid_useridpasswords instead of dogs_array.

```
<users>
<user>
<userid>Fredfred</userid>
<password>$2y$10$VosI32FejL.bOMaCjGbBp.Jre6Ipa.tLYQrVqj9kiVpef5zZ25qQK</password>
</user>
<user>
<userid>Petepete</userid>
<password>$2y$10$FdbXxIVXmVOHtaBNxB8vzupRBJFCqUyOTJXrlpNdrLOHKQ/U.jFHO</password>
</user>
</users>
```

Assuming the XML is in a similar format as the dog data XML file (as shown), you can use similar logic to retrieve the information.

```php
$valid_useridpasswords = json_decode($json,TRUE);
$userid = $_POST['username'];
$password = $_POST['password'];
    foreach($valid_useridpasswords as $users)
{
        foreach($users as $user)
        {
            $hash = $user['password'];
            if((in_array($userid, $user)) && (password_verify($password,$hash)))
            {
                $_SESSION['username'] = $userid;
                $_SESSION['password'] = $hash;
                header("Location: lab.php");
            }
        }
}
```

The array created using the json_decode method is in a similar format to the array created from the dog_data XML file. It requires two foreach loops, one to loop through the "users" array, and the other to loop through the "user" arrays. The in_array method can then be used to determine if the user ID exists in the user array. If it does, the password is compared to the hashed password using the PHP method password_verify. This method uses the first part of the hashed password to retrieve the information on the encryption technique and the salt value. The salt value is an automatically generated value that is used to produce the hashed password. If the passwords match, the user ID and hashed password ($hash) are saved as session variables. The main program is then called (see Example 7-1).

---

■ **Note**  In PHP 5.5, you could adjust the salt value. In PHP 7, this option was depreciated as it was deemed an unnecessary use of system resources.

---

*Example 7-2.* The login.phpfile with XML user ID/password verification

```php
<?php // same code as constructor from chapter 6 with some minor changes
session_start();
try {
$user_log_file = "user.log";
if ((isset($_POST['username'])) || (isset($_POST['password'])))
{
                libxml:use_internal_errors(true);
                $xmlDoc = new DOMDocument();
                if ( file_exists("e7dog_applications.xml") )
                {
                        $xmlDoc->load( 'e7dog_applications.xml' );
                        $searchNode = $xmlDoc->getElementsByTagName( "type" );
                        foreach( $searchNode as $searchNode )
                        {
                                $valueID = $searchNode->getAttribute('ID');
                                if($valueID == "UIDPASS") // changed value to UIDPASS
```

```
                            {
                            $xmlLocation = $searchNode->getElementsByTagName( "location" );
                            // change $this->dog_data_xml to dog_data_xml
                            $dog_data_xml = $xmlLocation->item(0)->nodeValue;
                            break;
                            }
        }
            }
    else
            {
                    throw new Exception("Dog applications xml file missing or corrupt");
            }
        $xmlfile = file_get_contents($dog_data_xml);
        $xmlstring = simplexml:load_string($xmlfile);
        if ($xmlstring === false) {
                $errorString = "Failed loading XML: ";
                foreach(libxml:get_errors() as $error) {
                        $errorString .= $error->message . " " ;  }
                throw new Exception($errorString); }
        $json = json_encode($xmlstring);
        // changed array name to $valid_useridpasswords
        $valid_useridpasswords = json_decode($json,TRUE);
// ...... code to verify userid and password ....
        $userid = $_POST['username'];
        $password = $_POST['password'];
            foreach($valid_useridpasswords as $users)           {
                    foreach($users as $user) {
                        $hash = $user['password'];
                    if((in_array($userid, $user)) && (password_verify($password,$hash))) {
                            $_SESSION['username'] = $userid;
                            $_SESSION['password'] = $password;
                            $login_string = date('mdYhis') . " | Login | " . $userid . "\n";
                            error_log($login_string,3,$user_log_file);
                            header("Location: e7lab.php");
            } }  } }
}
    catch(Exception $e)
    {
        echo $e->getMessage();
    }
// code below executes if the user has not logged in or if it is an invalid login.
?>
<form method="post" action="">
Userid must contain eight or more characters.<br/>
Password must contain at least one number, one uppercase and lowercase letter, and at least
8 total characters.<br />
Username: <input type="text" pattern=".{8,}" title="Userid must contain eight or more
characters." name="username" id="username" required/><br />
Password: <input type="password" pattern="(?=.*\d)(?=.*[a-z])(?=.*[A-Z]).{8,}"
title="Password must contain at least one number, one uppercase and lowercase letter, and at
least 8 total characters."
```

```
 name="password" id="password" required /><br />
<input type="submit" value="Login">
</form>
```

In addtion to the code mentioned, Example 7-2 also includes a `try catch` block to catch the exceptions thrown and a call to a user log file to record successful logs in to the system.

# JSON Data

To use JSON data instead of XML data, Example 7-2 would only need to include the changes shown in Chapter 6. The `userid` and `password` JSON data would also need to be formatted as shown.

```
{"user":
[
{"userid":"Fredfred","password":"$2y$10$VosI32FejL.bOMaCjGbBp.Jre6Ipa.tLYQrVqj9kiVpef5zZ25qQK"},
{"userid":"Petepete","password":"$2y$10$FdbXxIVXmVOHtaBNxB8vzupRBJFCqUyOTJXrlpNdrLOHKQ\/U.jFHO"}
] }
```

# MySQL Data

It is more common and usually more secure to store user ID and password information in a database. Databases can be secured using user IDs and passwords, which can also include levels of access (read only, read, and write) to the information. Even with this level of security, the password should still be encrypted.

Very few minor changes are needed to the MySQL constructor example from Chapter 6 to accomplish authentication.

```
$mysqli =mysqli_connect($server, $db_username, $db_password, $database);

if (mysqli_connect_errno())
  {
        throw new Exception("MySQL connection error: " . mysqli_connect_error());
  }

$sql="SELECT * FROM Users"; // Change the table used
$result=mysqli_query($con,$sql);

If($result===null)
{
        throw new Exception("No records retrieved from Database");
}

$valid_useridpasswords = mysqli_fetch_assoc($result); // change the array used

mysqli_free_result($result);

mysqli_close($con);
```

This example code will pull the information from a table in the database (Users) and place the information in an associate array (via the mysqli_fetch_assoc method). If the fields in the table are the same as the tag names from the XML file (userid and password), the associate array built will be similar to the array built using the code from Example 7-2. All previous code "// ...... code to verify userid and password ...." is replaced by the code shown here. No code below the statement should need adjusting.

## Do It

1. Create a conversion program to determine the encrypted version of a password using the PHP method password_hash (see http://php.net/manual/en/function.password-hash.php).

2. Download the example files from this section. Add XML records to the uidpass file that could be used for access permissions (read only or read/write) and levels (user or administrator). Test to verify that the new uidpass file works correctly with the existing code. Make any necessary code changes to make it compatible.

3. Download the example files from this section. Add code to the program to limit attempts to log in with a bad password to three. Record any invalid attempt to log in (after three tries) in the user log.

# Registration

In addition to authorizing user logons, most systems allow the users to create their own user IDs and passwords. By default, the self-created IDs are given the lowest priorities. An administrator can then go in and increase the level of privileges once the ID has been created. Some sites allow non-registered users (users who are not logged in).

Non-registered users should only be given read-only access to non-privileged information. Non-registered users are much more of a security risk because it would be difficult to determine their identity during a security breach. PHP provides the ability to retrieve the user's IP address using $_SERVER['REMOTE_ADDR']. This might provide some ability to trace the user. However, many users use free public access points, which generate random IP addresses. If the one of these points is used, it will be much more difficult to track them down.

In addition, providing the opportunity for users to create user IDs and passwords allows the program to gather additional information (such as name and e-mail) that can help with security, and also provide easy ability to promote the web site to users of the site. The success rate of selling what is offered on the site will be much higher to customers who are already familiar with the site. To encourage users to create user IDs and passwords, the site should offer them some benefit (such as access to the help desk) that is not available to visitors.

The *registration page* will, in many ways, work similarly to the login page. However, any valid user ID or password entered will be stored (instead of compared). Because the application will be updating the list of valid IDs, the application must validate the information before it is updated. You can use some of the techniques that you used previously when validating the dog class properties. First, as the user enters a user ID and password (which must pass the HTML5 validation shown previously), it is passed to a PHP program. Even though it is considered to be secure inside a session, the information will travel from the HTML form to the PHP code. The information should be validated again.

```
if ((isset($_POST['username'])) || (isset($_POST['password'])))
{
$userid = $_POST['username'];
$password = $_POST['password'];
if (!(preg_match("/^.*(?=.{8,})(?=.*\d)(?=.*[a-z])(?=.*[A-Z]).*$/", $password)) ||
(!(strlen($userid) >= 8)))
{
        throw new Exception("Invalid Userid and/or Password Format");
}
else
```

This if statement uses the PHP function preg_match to determine if the format of the password contains one uppercase letter, one lowercase letter, one number, and at least eight characters. Notice that the regular expression format is the same as used with the HTML5 code (the order of the expression has changed, but it still contains the same information). The PHP strlen method also checks the user ID to determine that it has eight or more characters.

If either validation does not pass, the program raises an Exception. If both pass, the else part of the statement executes to encrypt the password and store the information.

```
$password = password_hash($password, PASSWORD_DEFAULT);
$input = file_get_contents($dog_data_xml);
$find = "</users>";
$newupstring = "<user>\n<userid>" . $userid . "</userid>\n<password>" . $password;
$newupstring .= "</password>\n</user>\n</users>";
$find = preg_quote($find,'/');
$output = preg_replace("/^$find(\n|\$)/m","",$input);
$output = $output . $newupstring;
file_put_contents($dog_data_xml,$output);
$login_string = date('mdYhis') . " | New Userid | " . $userid . "\n";
error_log($login_string,3,$user_log_file);
header("Location: e7login.php");
```

Before inserting the password into the XML file, it must be encyrpted (hashed). The PHP method password_hash will convert the password to the format shown previously.

> *Programming note—password_hash has many different options and configurations available for the advanced developer. For more information,*
>
> *visit http://php.net/manual/en/function.password-hash.php.*

file_get_contents dumps the contents of the XML user ID/password file into $input. preg_quote will place backslashes next to any special characters in $find (such as the backslash contained in /users) to keep PHP from trying to interpret those characters as part of a regular expression. preg_replace will use the regular expression /^$find(\n|\$)/m to search for </users> with and without (\n) at the end. Since records in files are determined by the newline character, this will ensure that you find </users> at either the end of a line in the file or as part of a line in the file. When </users> is found in the file (the contents of the file are in $input), it is replaced by "" (empty string). preg_replace will also attempt to place backslashes in any string existing in the second parameter (where the "" is currently located). If the $newupstring is placed in that parameter, the encrypted password would be modified by preg_replace. This would cause the passwords to not verify, even if the one entered by the user is correct.

Therefore, the contents of $newupstring (the new user info) are appended to $output. The $output string is then used to replace all contents of the user ID/password XML file. Once this information has been saved successfully, the user log is updated to indicate the creation of a new user ID, and the user is redirected to the login screen to sign in to the application with the new user ID and password.

Alternatively, the previous process of loading the file into an associative array, updating the associative array, and then loading the associate array back into the XML file could have been used. However, it would have taken more code and is unnecessary because this process is only used once in the application. The program will not make multiple attempts to update the user ID and password file with the same user.

***Example 7-3.*** The registration.php file

```php
<?php
session_start();
$user_log_file = "user.log";
try
{
if ((isset($_POST['username'])) || (isset($_POST['password'])))
{
$userid = $_POST['username'];
$password = $_POST['password'];
if (!(preg_match("/^.*(?=.{8,})(?=.*\d)(?=.*[a-z])(?=.*[A-Z]).*$/", $password)) ||
(!(strlen($userid) >= 8)))
{
throw new Exception("Invalid Userid and/or Password Format");
 }
else
{
        libxml:use_internal_errors(true);
        $xmlDoc = new DOMDocument();
        if ( file_exists("e7dog_applications.xml") )
        {
        $xmlDoc->load( 'e7dog_applications.xml' );
        $searchNode = $xmlDoc->getElementsByTagName( "type" );
                foreach( $searchNode as $searchNode )
                {
                        $valueID = $searchNode->getAttribute('ID');

                        if($valueID == "UIDPASS")
                        {
                        $xmlLocation = $searchNode->getElementsByTagName( "location" );
                        $dog_data_xml = $xmlLocation->item(0)->nodeValue;
                        break;
                        }
                }
        }
        else
        {
                throw new Exception("Dog applications xml file missing or corrupt");
        }
} else {
        throw new Exception("Dog applications xml file missing or corrupt");
        }
```

```php
        $password = password_hash($password, PASSWORD_DEFAULT);
        $input = file_get_contents($dog_data_xml);
        $find = "</users>";
        $newupstring = "<user>\n<userid>" . $userid . "</userid>\n<password>" . $password .
        "</password>\n</user>\n</users>";
        $find_q = preg_quote($find,'/');
        $output = preg_replace("/^$find_q(\n|\$)/m",$newupstring,$input);
        file_put_contents($dog_data_xml,$output);
        $login_string = date('mdYhis') . " | New Userid | " . $userid . "\n";
        error_log($login_string,3,$user_log_file);
        header("Location: e7login.php");
        } } }
    catch(Exception $e)   {   echo $e->getMessage(); }
?>
<form method="post" action="">
Userid must contain eight or more characters.<br/>
Password must contain at least one number, one uppercase and lowercase letter, and at least
8 total characters.<br />
Username: <input type="text" pattern=".{8,}" title="Userid must contain eight or more
characters." name="username" id="username" required/><br />
Password: <input type="password" pattern="(?=.*\d)(?=.*[a-z])(?=.*[A-Z]).{8,}"
title="Password must contain at least one number, one uppercase and lowercase letter, and at
least 8 total characters."
 name="password" id="password" required /><br />
<input type="submit" value="submit">
</form>
```

# JSON Data

JSON data would require just a couple of slight changes.

```json
{"user":
[
{"userid":"Fredfred","password":"$2y$10$VosI32FejL.bOMaCjGbBp.Jre6Ipa.tLYQrVqj9kiVpef5zZ25qQK"},
{"userid":"Petepete","password":"$2y$10$FdbXxIVXmVOHtaBNxB8vzupRBJFCqUyOTJXrlpNdrLOHKQ\/U.jFHO"}
] }
```

The data ends with a combination of ]}, which does not occur anywhere else. $find can be set to this value ($set = "]}";). The $newupstring value can also be changed to:

```php
$newupstring = ',{"userid":"' . $userid . '","password":"' . $password . '"}\n]}';
```

These two changes (along with the previous changes) would update a JSON file with a new user ID/password combination.

# MySQL Data

MySQL would require a few more changes. After the password is encyrpted using password_hash, the database can be opened, the record inserted, and then the database can be closed.

```
$password = password_hash($password, PASSWORD_DEFAULT);
$mysqli =mysqli_connect($server, $db_username, $db_password, $database);

if (mysqli_connect_errno())
   {
          throw new Exception("MySQL connection error: " . mysqli_connect_error());
   }


$sql="INSERT INTO Users (userid, password) VALUES('" . $userid . "','" . $password . "');";
$result=mysqli_query($con,$sql);
If($result===null)
{
          throw new Exception("Userid/Password not added to Database");
}
mysqli_close($con);
$login_string = date('mdYhis') . " | New Userid | " . $userid . "\n";
error_log($login_string,3,$user_log_file);
header("Location: e7login.php");
```

# Logging In

In addition to providing the users with the ability to create their own user IDs and passwords, an application should also provide them the ability to change their passwords. The ability to provide a date limit to expire passwords is very beneficial to increase security. Everytime the user logs on, a comparision can be made on this value. If the current date is more than xx days older than the date saved, the user would be required to change the password.

Since password sniffer programs will try to guess passwords, it is also a good idea to limit to the number of attempts to sign in with the right user ID and password combination. This would reduce the chances that a password sniffing program could generate the correct combination. It is important not allow a valid signin for a period of time after the maximum amount of attempts have been made. Even though this is frustrating to the user, it reduces the chances that a password sniffing program would discover the right combination. If the program does not know that the attempts have timed out, it will receive invalid user ID/password messages, even if it guessed the right combination during the *timeout* period. These adjustments will require additional fields to the user ID/password file (or database).

```
<users>
<user>
<userid>Fredfred</userid>
<password>$2y$10$VosI32FejL.bOMaCjGbBp.Jre6Ipa.tLYQrVqj9kiVpef5zZ25qQK</password>
<datestamp>2015-09-03</datestamp>
<attempts>0</attempts>
<lastattempt>08052015044229</lastattempt>
<validattempt>08052015045431</validattempt>
</user>
```

```
<user>
<userid>Poppoppop</userid>
<password>$2y$10$C1jXhTlOmyamuLKhZxK5m.4X4TVcdeFbeLSBIA7l4fx6tUnC8vrg6</password>
<datestamp>2015-06-04</datestamp>
<attempts>1</attempts>
<lastattempt>08062015113200</lastattempt>
<validattempt>08062015113038</validattempt>
</user>
</users>
```

The $newupstring can be adjusted in the registration.php program (Example 7-3) to add the authentication fields.

```
$newupstring = "<user>\n<userid>" . $userid . "</userid>\n<password>" . $hashed_password .
"</password>\n";
$newupstring .= "<datestamp>" . date('Y-m-d', strtotime('+30 days')) . "</datestamp>\n";
$newupstring .= "<attempts>0</attempts>\n<lastattempt>" . date('mdYhis') . "</lastattempt>\n";
$newupstring .= "<validattempt>" . date('mdYhis') . "</validattempt>\n</user>\n</users>";
```

The PHP method strtotime will parse any standard date and time format and attempt to convert it to the UNIX date time format (which PHP uses). In this example, the method provides the ability to add 30 days to the current date, which in turn will be used to determine if a password has expired. Alternatively, an expired date (such as the day before the current date) could be placed in this field when user IDs are created in bulk (such as populating student IDs in a course management system). This would force the users to change the password the first time they sign in to the system. The expire date is stored in datestamp for use when the user logs in to the system.

The attempts tag, in the example, will record how many times the user tries to sign in with a bad user ID password combination (reset to zero when a valid login occurs). If the date and time in lastattempt are in five minutes, and the value of attempts is 3 or greater, the user must wait until more than five minutes has expired since the last attempt to log in. As with most login systems, even if the user logs in with valid information, the last invalid login must be five or more minutes ago. The last valid login date and time is also recorded in the validattempt tags. Although this is not used for authentication in this example, it is important to keep track of all valid logins.

To keep the code as simple as possible in the main section of the program, the code that looks up the location of the user ID and password file has been moved to the method retrieve_useridpasswordfile. Saving the data in the XML file has also been moved to the method saveupfile. No changes (except for the addition of more XML tags as mentioned previously) have occurred in the code for these methods.

***Example 7-4.*** The login.php file with password timeout and three tries timeout

```
<?php
session_start();
$user_log_file = "user.log";
$passed = FALSE;
function saveupfile($dog_data_xml,$valid_useridpasswords)
{
$xmlstring = '<?xml version="1.0" encoding="UTF-8"?>';
        $xmlstring .= "\n<users>\n";
      foreach($valid_useridpasswords as $users)
      {
      foreach($users as $user)
```

```
        {
        $xmlstring .="\n<userid>" . $user['userid'] . "</userid>\n";
        $xmlstring .="<password>" . $user['password'] . "</password>\n";
        $xmlstring .="<datestamp>" . $user['datestamp'] . "</datestamp>\n";
        $xmlstring .= "<attempts>" . $user['attempts'] . "</attempts>\n";
        $xmlstring .= "<lastattempt>" . $user['lastattempt'] . "</lastattempt>\n";
        $xmlstring .= "<validattempt>" . $user['validattempt'] . "</validattempt>\n</user>\n";
        }
    }
        $xmlstring .= "</users>\n";

$xmlstring .= "</users>\n";
$new_valid_data_file = preg_replace('/[0-9]+/', '', $dog_data_xml);
// remove the previous date and time if it exists
$oldxmldata = date('mdYhis') . $new_valid_data_file;
if (!rename($dog_data_xml, $oldxmldata))
        {
            throw new Exception("Backup file $oldxmldata could not be created.");
        }
file_put_contents($new_valid_data_file,$xmlstring);
}
function retrieve_useridpasswordfile()
{
$xmlDoc = new DOMDocument();
        if ( file_exists("e7dog_applications.xml") )
        {
        $xmlDoc->load( 'e7dog_applications.xml' );
        $searchNode = $xmlDoc->getElementsByTagName( "type" );
                foreach( $searchNode as $searchNode )
                {
                        $valueID = $searchNode->getAttribute('ID');
                        if($valueID == "UIDPASS")
                        {
                        $xmlLocation = $searchNode->getElementsByTagName( "location" );
                        $dog_data_xml = $xmlLocation->item(0)->nodeValue;
                        break;
                        }
                }
        }
else
        {
            throw new Exception("Dog applications xml file missing or corrupt");
        }
        return $dog_data_xml;
}
try {
if ((isset($_POST['username'])) && (isset($_POST['password'])))
{
        libxml:use_internal_errors(true);
        $dog_data_xml = retrieve_useridpasswordfile();
        $xmlfile = file_get_contents($dog_data_xml);
```

```php
        $xmlstring = simplexml:load_string($xmlfile);
        if ($xmlstring === false) {
                $errorString = "Failed loading XML: ";
                foreach(libxml:get_errors() as $error) {
                        $errorString .= $error->message . " " ;  }
                throw new Exception($errorString); }
        $json = json_encode($xmlstring);
        $valid_useridpasswords = json_decode($json,TRUE);
        $userid = $_POST['username'];
        $password = $_POST['password'];
        $I = 0;
        $passed = FALSE;
    foreach($valid_useridpasswords as $users)
        {
        foreach($users as $user)
        {
    if (in_array($userid, $user))           {
        $hash = $user['password'];
        $currenttime = strtotime(date('Y-m-d'));
        $stamptime = strtotime($user['datestamp']);
if ($currenttime > $stamptime)          {
// password expired force password change
                header("Location: e7changepassword.php");
                }
        if (($user['attempts'] < 3) || ( date('mdYhis', strtotime('-5 minutes')) >=
        $user['lastattempt']))
                        {
                        $hash = $user['password'];
                        if(password_verify($password,$hash))
                        {
                        $passed = TRUE;
                    $valid_useridpasswords['user'][$I]['validattempt'] = date('mdYhis');
                        // shows last time successful login
                        $valid_useridpasswords['user'][$I]['attempts'] = 0;
// successful login resets to zero
                        $_SESSION['username'] = $userid;
                        $_SESSION['password'] = $password;
                        saveupfile($dog_data_xml,$valid_useridpasswords);
// save changes before header call
                        $login_string = date('mdYhis') . " | Login | " . $userid . "\n";
                        error_log($login_string,3,$user_log_file);
                        header("Location: e7lab.php");
                        }

                        else {
                        $valid_useridpasswords['user'][$I]['lastattempt'] = date('mdYhis');
// last attempted login
                        } } }
                $I++;
        } }
```

```
                // drops to here if not valid password/userid or too many attempts
                if (!$passed) {
                        $I--;
                        echo "Invalid Userid/Password";
                        $valid_useridpasswords['user'][$I]['attempts'] = $user['attempts'] + 1;
                        // add 1 to attempts
                        // if not successful must save the values
                        saveupfile($dog_data_xml,$valid_useridpasswords);
                } } }
        catch(Exception $e)
        {    echo $e->getMessage(); }
?>
form method="post" action="">
Userid must contain eight or more characters.<br/>
Password must contain at least one number, one uppercase and lowercase letter, and at least
8 total characters.<br />
Username: <input type="text" pattern=".{8,}" title="Userid must contain eight or more
characters." name="username" id="username" required/><br />
Password: <input type="password" pattern="(?=.*\d)(?=.*[a-z])(?=.*[A-Z]).{8,}"
title="Password must contain at least one number, one uppercase and lowercase letter, and at
least 8 total characters."
 name="password" id="password" required /><br />
<input type="submit" value="Login">
</form>
```

In Example 7-4, an if statement checks the current date/time with the date/time saved in datestamp. If the current date/time is more than 30 days beyond the value in datestamp, the password change (changepassword) program is called. The next if statement determines if the user has had fewer than three invalid attempts to log in, and it has been more than five minutes since the last attempt. If this is the case, the PHP method password_verify will compare the password entered by the user with the password contained in the XML file. If the passwords match, the validattempts value will be updated with the date/time, the attempts will be reset to 0, and the user ID and password will be saved in session variables. The changes to the XML file are then saved. In addition, the user login is recorded in the log file. If the passwords do not match, the lastattempt value is updated with the current date/time.

Since a valid login or an expired password will cause the application to redirect to a different program with the PHP header method, the program will only drop to the last if statement if the user ID and password combo is not valid, or if there have been too many attempts in five minutes. When this occurs, the "invalid /password" message is displayed, and the number of attempts is increased by 1. The changes to the XML file are then saved. The program will then continue to display the user ID and password boxes with the "invalid userid/password" message. As noted, even a valid user ID/password combo that's has been entered in five minutes or three or more invalid entries (sequentially) is rejected.

# JSON Data

JSON data would require some changes to accommodate the additional fields.

```
{"user":[
{"userid":"Fredfred","password":"$2y$10$VosI32FejL.bOMaCjGbBp.Jre6Ipa.tLYQrVqj9kiVpef5zZ25qQK",
"datestamp":"2015-09-03","attempts":"0","lastattempt":"08052015044229","validattempt":
"08052015045431"},
{"userid":"Poppoppop","password":"$2y$10$C1jXhTlOmyamuLKhZxK5m.4X4TVcdeFbeLSBIA7l4fx6tUnC8vrg6",
"datestamp":"2015-09-04","attempts":"2","lastattempt":"08062015011347","validattempt":
"08062015113038"}
]}
```

The $newupstring would also require changes due to these new fields. The location of some of the code would also move to methods, as mentioned earlier.

```
$newupstring = ',{"userid":"' . $user['userid'] . '","password":"' . $user['password'] . '","';
$newupstring .= 'datestamp":"' . $user['datestamp'] . '","attempts":"' . $user['attempts'] . '","';
$newupstring .= 'lastattempt":"' . $user['lastattempt'] . '","validattempt":"' .
$user['validattempt'] .'"';
 $newupstring .= '"}\n]}';
```

# MySQL Data

MySQL login code requires the UPDATE statement (instead of an INSERT statement, as seen in the registration code) to update any fields that have changed. In addition, the clean_input method from Chapter 4 should to be used to remove any harmful PHP and SQL statements from the userid field. This will help reduce the chance of *SQL injection* occuring, which could cause the SQL statement to change more than just the required fields and record(s). For example, if the $user['userid'] field contained '*', all records would be updated instead of just one record with a valid user ID.

The user ID could also be validated as existing in the database before executing the UPDATE statement. This (assuming all data in the database is valid) would also reduce the chance of harmful changes.

In the following example, all possible files are updated at once. Alternatively, only those fields that change could be updated when needed. However this would require more code and not necessarily be any more efficient. Also, if the user ID is not validated as existing in the database beforehand, the SQL statement will automatically not update the fields if userid is not in the database.

```
$userid = clean_input($user['userid']);
$sql ="UPDATE Users SET(datestamp='" . $user['datestamp'] . "',attempts='";
$sql .=$user['attempts'] . "',lastattempt='" . $user['lastattempt'] . "',";
$sql .="validattempt='" . $user['validattempt'] . "') WHERE userid='" . $userid . "';";
```

Notice that the UPDATE code does not include the password field in the WHERE statement. In this example, some fields would be updated when the password is not valid, and some would be updated when the password is valid. If the SQL statement is broken into multiple statements (at least one for valid user ID/password and one for not valid user/password), then the WHERE statement for the valid information can include both the user ID and password, and the statement for non-valid information can just include the password. An example of a complete login, registration, and password-change application using a MySQL database is included on the book's web site under Chapter 7.

# Change Password

The process to change a password will require verification of the current password and then saving the new password. It will also require updating the date contained in the datestamp tag from the XML file. The program code is very similar to the login program.

```php
$userid = $_POST['username'];
$npassword = $_POST['password'];
$newpassword = password_hash($npassword, PASSWORD_DEFAULT);
$password = $_POST['oldpassword'];
$datestamp = date('Y-m-d', strtotime('+30 days'));
$I = 0;
$passed = FALSE;
// First a few properties are set for the userid, new userid, and the new datestamp.
$hash = $user['password'];
if(password_verify($password,$hash))
{
$passed = TRUE;
        $valid_useridpasswords['user'][$I]['password'] = $newpassword;
        $valid_useridpasswords['user'][$I]['datestamp'] = $datestamp;
        $valid_useridpasswords['user'][$I]['attempts'] = 0;
        saveupfile($dog_data_xml,$valid_useridpasswords); // save changes before header call
        $login_string = date('mdYhis') . " | Password Changed | " . $userid . "\n";
        error_log($login_string,3,$user_log_file);
        header("Location: e7logina.php");
}
else
{
$valid_useridpasswords['user'][$I]['lastattempt'] = date('mdYhis'); // last attempted login
}
```

If the user ID and old password are authenticated correctly then the new password, datestamp, and attempts properties are changed and updated in the XML file. Also an entry is placed in the log file. If the password is not verified, an "invalid userid/password" message is displayed.

***Example 7-5.*** The changepassword.php file

```php
<?php
session_start();
$user_log_file = "user.log";
function saveupfile($dog_data_xml,$valid_useridpasswords)
{
$xmlstring = '<?xml version="1.0" encoding="UTF-8"?>';
    $xmlstring .= "\n<users>\n";
        foreach($valid_useridpasswords as $users)
        {
        foreach($users as $user)
        {
        $xmlstring .="<user>\n<userid>" . $user['userid'] . "</userid>\n";
        $xmlstring .="<password>" . $user['password'] . "</password>\n";
        $xmlstring .="<datestamp>" . $user['datestamp'] . "</datestamp>\n";
        $xmlstring .= "<attempts>" . $user['attempts'] . "</attempts>\n";
```

243

```
        $xmlstring .= "<lastattempt>" . $user['lastattempt'] . "</lastattempt>\n";
        $xmlstring .= "<validattempt>" . $user['validattempt'] . "</validattempt>\n</user>\n";
                }
    }
        $xmlstring .= "</users>\n";
new_valid_data_file = preg_replace('/[0-9]+/', '', $dog_data_xml);
// remove the previous date and time if it exists
$oldxmldata = date('mdYhis') . $new_valid_data_file;
if (!rename($dog_data_xml, $oldxmldata))          {
            throw new Exception("Backup file $oldxmldata could not be created.");          }
file_put_contents($new_valid_data_file,$xmlstring); }
function retrieve_useridpasswordfile() {
$xmlDoc = new DOMDocument();
        if ( file_exists("e7dog_applications.xml") )
        {
        $xmlDoc->load( 'e7dog_applications.xml' );
        $searchNode = $xmlDoc->getElementsByTagName( "type" );
                foreach( $searchNode as $searchNode )
                {
                        $valueID = $searchNode->getAttribute('ID');

                        if($valueID == "UIDPASS")
                        {
                        $xmlLocation = $searchNode->getElementsByTagName( "location" );
                        $dog_data_xml = $xmlLocation->item(0)->nodeValue;

                        break;
                        }

                }
        }
else      {
                throw new Exception("Dog applications xml file missing or corrupt");
        }
        return $dog_data_xml;
}
if (!(isset($_SESSION['message']))) {
        // valid userid and password but password expired
        echo $_SESSION['message'];
}
try {
if((isset($_POST['username'])) && (isset($_POST['oldpassword'])) && (isset($_
POST['password'])) && (isset($_POST['password_confirm'])))
{
        libxml:use_internal_errors(true);
        $dog_data_xml = retrieve_useridpasswordfile();
        $xmlfile = file_get_contents($dog_data_xml);
        $xmlstring = simplexml:load_string($xmlfile);
if ($xmlstring === false) {
        $errorString = "Failed loading XML: ";
        foreach(libxml:get_errors() as $error) {
        $errorString .= $error->message . " " ;  }
```

```php
        throw new Exception($errorString); }
        $json = json_encode($xmlstring);
        $valid_useridpasswords = json_decode($json,TRUE);
        $userid = $_POST['username'];
        $npassword = $_POST['password'];
        $newpassword = password_hash($npassword, PASSWORD_DEFAULT);
        $password = $_POST['oldpassword'];
        $datestamp = date('Y-m-d', strtotime('+30 days'));
        $I = 0;

$I = 0;
$passed = FALSE;
    foreach($valid_useridpasswords as $users)        {
        foreach($users as $user)        {
            if (in_array($userid, $user))                {
                $hash = $user['password'];
                if(password_verify($password,$hash))
                {
                        $passed = TRUE;
                        $valid_useridpasswords['user'][$I]['password'] = $newpassword;
                        $valid_useridpasswords['user'][$I]['datestamp'] = $datestamp;
                        $valid_useridpasswords['user'][$I]['attempts'] = 0;
                        saveupfile($dog_data_xml,$valid_useridpasswords);
                        // save changes before header call
                        $login_string = date('mdYhis') . " | Password Changed | " . $userid . "\n";
                        error_log($login_string,3,$user_log_file);
                        header("Location: e7login.php");
                        } }
        $I++;
        } }
                // drops to here if not valid password/userid or too many attempts
                if (!$passed){
                        echo "Invalid Userid/Password";
                } } }
    catch(Exception $e) {
        echo $e->getMessage();
    }
?>
<form method="post" action="">
Userid must contain eight or more characters.<br/>
Password must contain at least one number, one uppercase and lowercase letter, and at least
8 total characters.<br />
Username: <input type="text" pattern=".{8,}" title="Userid must contain eight or more
characters." name="username" id="username" required/><br />
Old Password: <input type="password" pattern="(?=.*\d)(?=.*[a-z])(?=.*[A-Z]).{8,}"
title="Password must contain at least one number, one uppercase and lowercase letter, and
at least 8 total characters." name="oldpassword" id="oldpassword" required /><br />
New Password: <input type="password" pattern="(?=.*\d)(?=.*[a-z])(?=.*[A-Z]).{8,}"
title="Password must contain at least one number, one uppercase and lowercase letter, and
at least 8 total characters." name="password" id="password" required /><br />
```

```
Confirm Password:<input name="password_confirm" required="required" type="password"
id="password_confirm" oninput="check(this)"  />
<script language='javascript' type='text/javascript'>
function check(input) {
if (input.value != document.getElementById('password').value) {
    input.setCustomValidity('Password Must be Matching.');
} else {
    // input is valid -- reset the error message
    input.setCustomValidity('');
}
}
</script>
<input type="submit" value="submit">
</form>
```

In addition to the PHP already explained, Example 7-5 also includes JavaScript code to verify the correct format of the new password and the correct entry of the new password twice. A verification of the proper user ID and password entries in the PHP code has not been included in the example. Since the information is traveling over the Internet from the form to the PHP program, the user ID and password should also be verified in the PHP program. That coding is left as an exercise for this section.

# JSON Data

The only changes needed for the change password program to work with JSON data are indicated in the previous JSON sections of this chapter.

# MySQL Data

The UPDATE SQL statement needs to "set" the password property in the same structure as the other fields that were changed in the previous MySQL section. A complete authentication program using MySQL is included under Chapter 7 on the book's web site.

## Do It

1.  Copy the example files for this section from the book's web site. Adjust the change password program to include PHP code that verifies the correct format of the user ID, password, and new password.

2.  Copy the example files for this chapter from the book's web site. Adjust the registration program to check for a duplicate user ID before attempting to insert a new user ID/password combination. Hint: This can be done using the in_array method. If the user ID exists, display a message back to the users.

3.  Copy the example files for this section from the book's web site. Adjust the programs necessary to require the users to also enter their name, phone, and e-mail when registering. Also make sure to change the other programs to keep this information valid.

# Chapter Terms

| | |
|---|---|
| Authentication | session |
| `session_start` | `isset` |
| Session properties | `$_SESSION` |
| Verification code | `.{8,}` |
| `?=.*\d` | `?=.*[A-Z]` |
| `?=.*[a-z]` | header |
| `array_keys` | `password_hash` |
| `password_verify` | non-registered users |
| `$_SERVER['REMOTE_ADDR']` | registration page |
| `preg_match` | `strlen` |
| `file_get_contents` | `preg_quote` |
| `preg_replace` | expire passwords |
| Password sniffer programs | limited number of attempts |
| Timeout period | `strtotime` |
| SQL Injection | |

# Chapter Questions and Projects

**Multiple Choice**

1. Authentication does which of the following?
   a. Provides security for an application.
   b. Verifies user IDs and passwords.
   c. Should use encrypted passwords.
   d. All of the above.

2. Sessions do which of the following?
   a. Are created using the `session_create` method
   b. Allow the sharing of information between programs
   c. Don't provide any security benefits
   d. All of the above

3. Registration pages do which of the following?
   a. Allow the users to create their own user IDs and passwords
   b. Can be used to gather information about the users
   c. Should encrypt the password before storing it
   d. All of the above

4. Verification code does which of the following?
   a. Uses `session_start` to attach the program to a current session
   b. Verifies that a user has logged in

247

      c.    Must be attached only to programs in the interface tier

      d.    All of the above

5.    Which of these describes SQL injection?

      a.    The process of using an SQL statement to update a database

      b.    The process of inserting variables in a SQL statement for flexibility

      c.    Causes data to be corrupted

      d.    All of these

## True/False

1.    MD5 is the most up-to-date and secure encryption technique.

2.    `password_hash` should be used to create an encrypted password.

3.    Users should be notified that they have exceeded the maximum number of attempts to enter a correct user ID and password.

4.    An authentication system does not need to timeout passwords and force its users to change their passwords when they time out.

5.    `preg_replace` can be used with an encrypted password to ensure that PHP does not interpret special characters as PHP commands.

## Short Answer/Essay

1.    Explain the techniques that can be used to reduce the chances that a password sniffing program can discover the correct user ID and password combination.

2.    Explain how sessions work. Include an explanation on how they can help secure an application with user ID and password authentication.

3.    What is SQL injection? How can it be avoided?

4.    Why should passwords be encrypted? Explore the Internet and discover the latest versions of encryption. Does the most current version of PHP use the newest version of encryption?

## Projects

1.    Download log maintenance files from Chapter 6 or use your own maintenance files that you created from Chapter 6. Use the techniques shown in this chapter to secure these files with user ID and password authentication.

2.    Download the files from this chapter. Update the files and programs so users can request their passwords. A temporary password (new field in the XML file) must randomly be created (use `rand`) and e-mailed to the users. The password should have a quick expiration (one day or less). The user must be able to verify other information entered via the registration page (security question, or other personal info) to request the password. If the user signs in correctly with the temporary password, the system should make the user change the password.

## Term Project

1.    Update the ABC Computer Parts Inventory application to include user ID and password authentication as shown in this chapter. Be sure to secure any log maintenance programs related to the application.

# CHAPTER 8

■ ■ ■

# Multifunctional Interfaces

*"Hard work never killed anybody, but why take a chance."*

—Edgar Bergen (http://coolfunnyquotes.com)

## Chapter Objectives/Student Learning Outcomes

After completing this chapter, the student will be able to:

- Create a complete PHP application that deletes, updates, and inserts data

- Create a professional look to a completed application using CSS

- Use JavaScript to accept and manipulate data from another program

- Secure all programs in an application requiring user IDs/passwords

- Populate HTML objects with values from a JSON object

- Create a PHP program that will use current password encryption techniques

## The Complete Application

In this chapter, you will complete the development of the ABC Canine Shelter Reservation System. The current version of the system allows the users to insert only one dog before requiring the them to log in again to insert additional dogs. Also, the system does not allow users to update or delete dog information that exists in the system. You have already completed most of the PHP code necessary to provide update and delete ability in Chapter 6 (data objects). You now need to attach this portion of the data object (dog_data) to the business rules tier (dog). In addition you need to make some changes to the interface tier (dog_interface and lab) to call the update and delete methods and display the results. Most of the coding needed (as you will soon see) will take place in the lab.php file. So you will start with those changes.

## Data Handling Using JavaScript

The current lab.php file allows users to enter only dog information that will be inserted into the data storage (XML, JSON, or MySQL). The interface needs to be modified to allow users to indicate what activity they would like to accomplish (Insert, Update, or Delete). It also needs to allow users to pick a current dog if the process involves updating or deletion. This should, hopefully, indicate that you will need a list box that is populated with information on the dogs currently located in the shelter.

---

**Electronic supplementary material** The online version of this chapter (doi:10.1007/978-1-4842-1730-6_8) contains supplementary material, which is available to authorized users.

© Steve Prettyman 2015
S. Prettyman. *Learn PHP 7.* DOI 10.1007/978-1-4842-1730-6_8

You will look at the PHP changes necessary in later sections of this chapter. For now, let's assume that dog_interface (interface tier) will return this information, which was retrieved from dog_data (data tier) via the dog methods (business rules tier). You will also assume that similar coding to the dog_breeds program (Chapter 4) will be created to produce a dogs list box.

In addition, lab.php needs access to all the information from a particular dog that has been selected. The code will need to place all the information in the dog_name and dog_weight text boxes, the dog_breeds list box, and the dog_color radio buttons. You could accomplish this task in two ways. One is to allow the users to select the dog from the list box and then recall the dog_interface program to request the particular dog from the dog class, which in turn will request the information from the dog_data class. However, this is requiring an additional, unnecessary, call across the Internet to request the information. Instead, you can gather all the necessary information (dog_breed list box information, dogs list box information, and complete information of all dogs in the current data storage) when the user first calls the lab.php interface. You can use the current JavaScript AJAX code (Chapter 4) with just a couple of changes to retrieve all the necessary information.

You must make sure that the user indicates what type of operation is requested (at least if it is an insert or change/delete) before you populate the form objects (text boxes, list box, and radio button). You can accomplish this by not displaying the form objects until a selection has been made. You can make a slight adjustment to the combination of JavaScript code and CSS code, used in Chapter 4, to require the users to select from a dogs list box before the form is displayed.

---

▓ **Note** The process you are about to look at is a very common practice used in web applications. Many web applications return data in an array, JSON, or XML format. The interface (in this example, lab.php) then can use JavaScript to retrieve the information needed.

---

> *Programming note—Shopping carts use a similar technique. As the customers select items to purchase, the items are placed in a data object (probably a JSON object) on the client machine. When the customer begins the process of checking out, the data is transferred to the server. This allows the customer to make changes that will not cause additional calls to the server. Since the purchase information is not considered a security risk, this is usually a safe procedure. Of course, this would not be a good way to handle credit card information.*

Using the format shown in Figure 8-1, the user is forced to select NEW or a dog from list box before proceeding. Once the user has made a choice, the HTML form can be displayed with the default values (for an insert) or the current values for the dog selected. CSS code will initially turn the display of the buttons (and the form) to "none". JavaScript code (which you will look at soon) will change the display of the correct button(s) and the form to "inline" to display at the proper time.

Welcome back, Fredfred

# ABC Canine Shelter Reservation System

**Pick the dog name and breed to change from the dropdown box, then click the button. For new dog information select 'NEW'.**

Select 'NEW' or Dog's Name/Breed

| NEW          ⌄ |

| Click to select |

***Figure 8-1.*** *The lab.php file with dogs list box*

Figure 8-2 demonstrates the results when the user selects NEW. The same defaults are provided as shown in previous chapters. The only visual change is the text of the input button. The weakness of this approach occurs when the users do not have JavaScript enabled. For this example, if JavaScript is not enabled, you will require that all information be entered. You could request the individual dog information from the dog_data class (via the Dog class). While this approach is not as efficient as the JavaScript approach you are about to use, it is more customer friendly than requiring the entry of all the information.

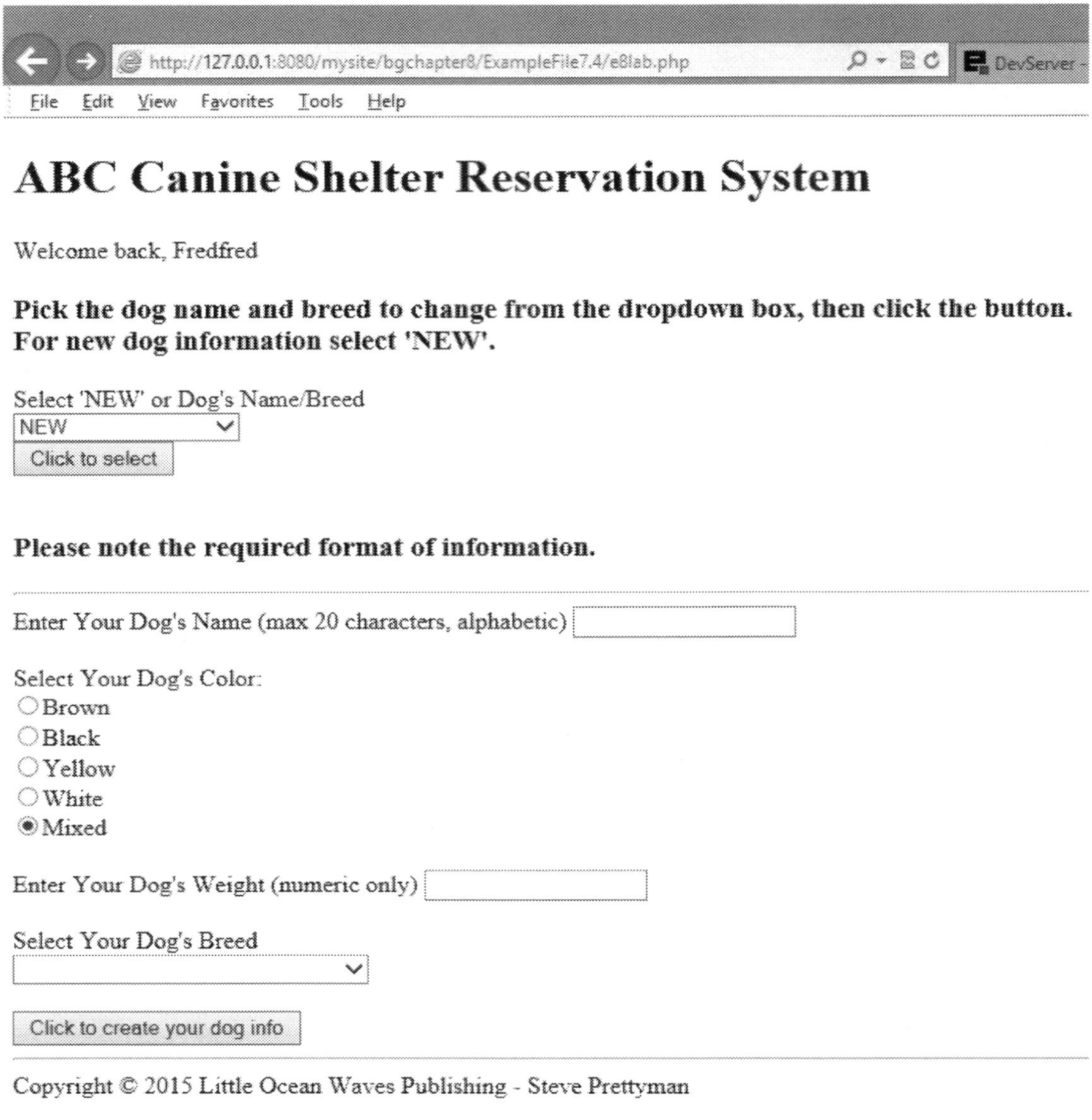
http://127.0.0.1:8080/mysite/bgchapter8/ExampleFile7.4/e8lab.php
DevServer -
File Edit View Favorites Tools Help
ABC Canine Shelter Reservation System
Welcome back, Fredfred
Pick the dog name and breed to change from the dropdown box, then click the button. For new dog information select 'NEW'.
Select 'NEW' or Dog's Name/Breed
NEW
Click to select
Please note the required format of information.
Enter Your Dog's Name (max 20 characters, alphabetic)
Select Your Dog's Color:
Brown
Black
Yellow
White
Mixed
Enter Your Dog's Weight (numeric only)
Select Your Dog's Breed
Click to create your dog info
Copyright © 2015 Little Ocean Waves Publishing - Steve Prettyman

***Figure 8-2.*** *The lab.php file with NEW selected*

Figure 8-3 displays the results when an existing dog has been selected. The list box displays the dog's name and its breed (to make it as unique as possible). In addition a dog ID could have also been provided to identify the particular dog. When the dog is selected, the dog information (`dog_name`, `dog_color`, `dog_weight`, and `dog_breed`) is populated into the form. The users then can update or delete the dog information.

# ABC Canine Shelter Reservation System

Welcome back, Fredfred

**Pick the dog name and breed to change from the dropdown box, then click the button. For new dog information select 'NEW'.**

Select 'NEW' or Dog's Name/Breed
| Pete   Basset Hound ∨ |

Click to select

**Please note the required format of information.**

Enter Your Dog's Name (max 20 characters, alphabetic) | Pete |

Select Your Dog's Color:
○ Brown
◉ Black
○ Yellow
○ White
○ Mixed

Enter Your Dog's Weight (numeric only) | 24 |

Select Your Dog's Breed
| Basset Hound    ∨ |

| Click to remove your selected dog info | Click to update your selected dog info |

Copyright © 2015 Little Ocean Waves Publishing - Steve Prettyman

***Figure 8-3.*** *The lab.php file with a dog selected*

■ **Note**  As mentioned in previous chapters, the code provided in this example does not restrict duplicate entries. Thus, in a live environment, an additional field (dog ID) will need to be used to make the dogs unique.

Previously when an `insert` occurred, the system would display a message to indicate the change was successful. The user was then required to reload the `lab.php` file if another change was required. You can fix this problem by having the `dog_interface` program set a session property with the message to be returned. The `dog_interface` can then call the `lab.php` file, which in turn can check to see if there is a message to be displayed.

Dog Sammy Insert/Update was successful

# ABC Canine Shelter Reservation System

## Pick the dog name and breed to change from the dropdown box, then click the button. For new dog information select 'NEW'.

Select 'NEW' or Dog's Name/Breed

*Figure 8-4. The lab.php file handling message from dog_interface*

You will use a combination of PHP code, JavaScript code, and CSS code to create the desired results. Let's break it down.

```php
<?php
session_start();
if ((!isset($_SESSION['username'])) || (!isset($_SESSION['password']))) {
    echo "You must login to access the ABC Canine Shelter Reservation System";
    echo "<p>";
    echo "<a href='e8login.php'>Login</a> | <a href='e8register.php'>Create an account</a>";
    echo "</p>";
}
else if(($_SERVER['HTTP_REFERER'] == 'http://127.0.0.1:8080/mysite/bgchapter8/ExampleFile8/
e8login.php') || ($_SERVER['HTTP_REFERER'] == 'http://127.0.0.1:8080/mysite/bgchapter8/
ExampleFile8/e8lab.php'))
{
if (isset($_SESSION['message'])) {
    echo $_SESSION['message'];
}
else {
    echo "<p>Welcome back, " . $_SESSION['username'] . "</p>";
}
?>
```

The PHP code at the top of the lab program will now include an additional check to determine if a message has been returned. While the if part of the statement will not require any changes, the else part has a few additional changes. Note that the new if statement checks to see if the lab program has been called by itself. The $_SERVER['HTTP_REFERER'] method returns lab.php as the calling program when dog_interface uses the header method to recall lab.php. In addition, the same if statement also checks to see if login.php has called lab. These are now the only two legitimate calls than can be made to the lab.php program.

Another if statement in the else block checks to see if a $_SESSION['message'] has been returned by using the isset method. If it has been returned, then lab.php was called by dog_interface, because login does not return a $_SESSION['message']. The lab program now displays the message. If there is no $_SESSION['message'], the welcome message is displayed.

Let's now jump to the HTML code in lab.php. Then you'll take a look at the CSS and JavaScript code.

```
<body onload="checkJS();">
<h1>ABC Canine Shelter Reservation System</h1>
<div id="JS">
<script>
AjaxRequest('e8dog_interface.php');
</script>
<h3>Pick the dog name and breed to change from the dropdown box, then click the
button.<br>For new dog information select 'NEW'.</h3>
Select 'NEW' or Dog's Name/Breed <div id="AjaxReturnValue"></div>
<input type="button" name="selected" id="selected" value="Click to select" onclick="process_
select()" /><br><br>
<div id="input_form">
<form method="post" action="e8dog_interface.php" onSubmit="return validate_input(this)">
<h3>Please note the required format of information.</h3>
<hr>
Enter Your Dog's Name (max 20 characters, alphabetic) <input type="text" pattern="[a-zA-Z]*"
title="Up to 20 Alphabetic Characters" maxlength="20" name="dog_name" id="dog_name"
required/><br /><br />
Select Your Dog's Color:<br />
<input type="radio" name="dog_color" id="dog_color" value="Brown">Brown<br />
<input type="radio" name="dog_color" id="dog_color" value="Black">Black<br />
<input type="radio" name="dog_color" id="dog_color" value="Yellow">Yellow<br />
<input type="radio" name="dog_color" id="dog_color" value="White">White<br />
<input type="radio" name="dog_color" id="dog_color" value="Mixed" checked >Mixed<br /><br />
Enter Your Dog's Weight (numeric only) <input type="number" min="1" max="120" name="dog_
weight" id="dog_weight" required /><br /><br />
<input type="hidden" name="dog_app" id="dog_app" value="dog" />
Select Your Dog's Breed <div id="AjaxResponse"></div><br />
<input type="hidden" name="index" id="index" value="-1"/>
<input type="submit" name="insert" id="insert" value="Click to create your dog info" />
<input type="submit" name="delete" id="delete" value="Click to remove your selected dog
info" />
<input type="submit" name="update" id="update" value="Click to update your selected dog
info" />
<hr>
</form>
</div>
</div>
```

In addition to some minor display message changes, a new `div` tag with an ID of `AjaxReturnValue` has been created to hold the dogs list box (which will provide the user a selection of dogs to choose). An **HTML button** (not a Submit button) follows. When clicked, it will cause a JavaScript function (`process_select`) to execute. Another `div` tag has been added which contains the HTML form. This form is to be hidden until the user clicks the button.

CSS code (`#input_form { display:none; }`) is included at the top of the program to keep the form from displaying. Additional CSS code also keeps the buttons from displaying. This code is very similar to the CSS code to keep the non-JS form from displaying if the user does not have JavaScript activated in the browser.

At the bottom of the form, a hidden property (`index`) has been created to hold the index (from the dogs array) of the dog selected. The initial value is set to -1. This property will be changed when the user selects a dog. The original Submit button is replaced by three Submit buttons (one for insert, one for delete, and one for update). Whichever button is clicked will cause a property to be created (`insert`, `delete`, or `update`) and set to a value. The property name is the ID of the button, and the contents in the property are the contents of the `value` attribute of the button selected. This will help `dog_interface` determine which type of changes the user is requesting. These buttons are also included on the non-JavaScript enabled form. Remember, in this example, non-JavaScript enabled browsers will be require users to enter all information needed to successfully accomplish an `insert`, `delete`, or `update`.

Hopefully, the changes you just looked at are pretty understandable. You are now going to look at some JavaScript code to handle this data. As mentioned, the manipulation of data by JavaScript is a common task in web applications. While this is not a JavaScript book, it is important that any web applications developer be familiar with JavaScript. I think you will see that the structure of the JavaScript language is similar to the structure of the PHP language.

First you will look at the changes to the `get_breeds.js` file (from Chapter 4). The file is renamed to `getlists.js` to reflect that it will now handle the `getBreeds` and dogs list boxes.

```
function HandleResponse(response)
{
        var responsevalues = response.split('|');
        document.getElementById('AjaxResponse').innerHTML = responsevalues[0];
        document.getElementById('AjaxReturnValue').innerHTML = responsevalues[1];
        obj = JSON.parse(responsevalues[2]);
}
```

All the code changes are in the `HandleResponse` method of the JavaScript file. Previously the values in the response property (passed to the method) were directly passed into the `div` tag with the `AjaxResponse` ID. At that point, only the list box code for the breeds was returned. Now the method will accept three types of information (the breeds list box, the dogs list box, and the dogs array). To reduce the number of calls to the web server, one AJAX call is made. It returns all the information into the `response` property. The information will be separated by using the pipeline (`|`) symbol. Soon you will see that the formation of this string will occur in the `dog_interface` program.

You will need to break the data in a similar way that you broke previous data using the PHP `explode` method. In JavaScript, the `split` method will break a string into an array using a parameter provided (`|`). In the example, this will create the array responsevalues. `var` creates this array as local to the method. It will be destroyed, because it will no longer be needed, when the method closes (hits the `}` symbol). The array now has three rows. The first row (`[0]`) contains the `getBreeds` list box code. The second row (`[1]`) contains the dogs list box code. The third row (I bet you guessed that one) contains the complete dogs array.

*Security and performance—In this application, the dogs information is not highly sensitive. Also, the information is displayed to the users. This allows the users to see and fix any data that might have been corrupted. For more sensitive information, the array should be declared using var to keep the data accessible only to the current method (function).*

The subscripts (0, 1, and 2) can now be used to pull each part of the array and release it to the proper place. responsevalues[0] is placed in AjaxResponse to display the getBreeds list. responsevalues[1] is placed in AjaxReturnValue to display the dogs list box. The dogs array, since you won't know yet which dog the user has selected, will be placed in a JSON object (obj). As you have seen, JSON data includes named indexes and values, which are very similar to associate arrays in PHP. The var statement is not used because this object must be public and available to the complete application.

If you remember from previous chapters, arrays cannot be directly formatted into strings. Arrays must be serialized. However, JSON data can also be passed in a string. You will soon see that the "array" in responsevalues[3] has been formatted as JSON data by the dog_interface program. JavaScript's JSON.parse method has the ability to look at data and, if it is valid, transform it into a JSON object. This is very similar to the PHP method json_encode.

Now let's look at how you can populate the form when the user picks a dog from the dogs list box.

The JavaScript method process_select (called by the HTML button after the user picks from the dogs list) has been placed at the top of the code in the lab.php file. It could have also been placed in its own JS file and imported in the same way as the getlists.js file. This new method use the information contained in OBJ (the JSON dogs object containing all the dogs) to populate the text boxes (dog_name and dog_weight), radio buttons (dog_color), and list box (dog_breed) with the information for the dog the user selects in the list box.

```
function process_select() {
        var colorbuttons = document.getElementsByName('dog_color');
```

First, all the color values from the radio buttons will be pulled from the HTML form and placed into an array called colorbuttons using the JavaScript method getElementsByName. dog_color (the name of each radio button) is passed into the method. This process will create an array of the radio buttons with the same indexes as the radio button subscripts for the color. For instance, the 0 position of the array will now contain brown, which is the first radio button displayed in the HTML form. This will allow you to set the proper color radio button by referencing its position (such as colorbuttons[0] to set brown).

```
if(!(document.getElementById('dogs').value == -1))
{
        index = document.getElementById('dogs').selectedIndex -1;
        document.getElementById('index').value = index;
        document.getElementById('dog_name').value = obj.dogs[index].dog_name;
        document.getElementById('dog_weight').value = obj.dogs[index].dog_weight;
```

HTML list boxes include both text and values. The text is what the user sees; the value is what it represents. This is very similar to PHP associative arrays—keys (indexes) and values. The if statement checks the dogs array to determine its current value. If the value is -1, this indicates that the users did not select anything, or they selected NEW. The JavaScript ! symbol works the same as the PHP ! symbol. The symbol changes the if portion of the statement to execute when the value for 'dogs' is not -1. Thus, the code will execute if the user has selected a dog from the dogs list box.

The selectedIndex property of a list box indicates the index selected by the user. However, the HTML list box is numbered starting at 1. JavaScript arrays and JSON objects indexes start at 0. This causes the selectedIndex to be one more than the position in a JavaScript array or JSON object. The code, in the example, subtracts 1 to balance out the relationship. This value is placed in index. It is also saved in the hidden property (on the HTML form) with the same name (index). Since index is a property and not a div tag, the JavaScript value property must be used to set the value of index.

obj is the JSON object (with all the dogs) that was created when the AJAX call occurred. Information can be retrieved from a JSON object in a very similar way as PHP associative arrays. The obj object is similar to the multidimensional dogs array shown in previous chapters. The top array is the dogs "array". In the dogs array are the "arrays" for each individual dog. These do not have an associated key name, but have a numerical index. Each dog array contains the individual elements (dog_name, dog_color, dog_breed, and dog_weight). The index property, set in the previous code line, contains the dog index selected by the user. It will be used to pull the selected dog information from obj to populate the form objects.

Since you know the exact location of the data to be retrieved (in index), loops are not needed.

obj.dogs[index].dog_name uses the JSON object name (obj), the top array name (dogs), the number of the dog array needed (index), and the name of the field required (dog_name) to access the required information. Again, the format is similar to pulling information from a PHP associative array. The dog_name and dog_weight values use this dot notation format to pull the information from the obj JSON object and place it in the appropriate text box on the HTML form.

```
dog_color = obj.dogs[index].dog_color;
if(dog_color == "Brown")
        {
                colorbuttons[0].checked = true;
        } else if (dog_color == "Black")
        {
                colorbuttons[1].checked = true;
        } else if (dog_color == "Yellow")
        {
                colorbuttons[2].checked = true;
        } else if (dog_color == "White")
        {
                colorbuttons[3].checked = true;
        }
```

Setting the color requires a little more work. The dog_color is pulled from the obj object (dog_color = obj.dogs[index].dog_color;) and placed into a property (dog_color). An if statement is then used to determine what color exists in this property. (Yes, JavaScript has a case statement that you could have also used). The if statement sets the checked property of the correct radio button to true, causing the radio button to be selected. Notice that the default value ('mixed') is not included in the if statement. If the dog is 'mixed', or somehow the color did not have a value in the object, there is no reason to change from the default value ('mixed').

```
dog_breed = obj.dogs[index].dog_breed;
document.getElementById('dog_breed').value = dog_breed;
document.getElementById('update').style.display = "inline";
document.getElementById('delete').style.display = "inline";
document.getElementById('insert').style.display = "none";
}
```

The breeds list box is set using the same code style as setting the text boxes. The value property sets the list box text viewed by the users. The users can then change the value if desired. The "update" and "delete" buttons are set to "inline" to be displayed. "Insert" is set to "none".

```
else
{
        colorbuttons[4].checked = true;
        document.getElementById('dog_name').value = "";
        document.getElementById('dog_weight').value = "";
        document.getElementById('dog_breed').value = "Select a dog breed";
        document.getElementById('insert').style.display = "inline";
        document.getElementById('update').style.display = "none";
        document.getElementById('delete').style.display = "none";
}
```

The else portion of the if statement executes if the index is -1 (NEW is selected, or nothing was selected). The defaults are set, as previously shown in other chapters, with the color set to 'mixed', the name and weight text boxes being empty, and the breeds list box set to requesting the user to Select a dog breed. The "insert" button is displayed (using "inline"). The other buttons are not displayed (using "none").

```
document.getElementById('input_form').style.display = "inline";
}
```

Finally, the display of the form itself (now called input_form') is set to 'inline', which will allow the users to see the complete form and its values, as set in the previous code. Let's take a look at the complete code.

***Example 8-1.*** The getlists.js file

```
function AjaxRequest(value)
{
  var xmlHttp = getXMLHttp();
  xmlHttp.onreadystatechange = function()
  {
    if(xmlHttp.readyState == 4)
    {
      HandleResponse(xmlHttp.responseText);
    }
  }
  xmlHttp.open("GET", value, true);
  xmlHttp.send(null);
}
function HandleResponse(response)
{
  var responsevalues = response.split('|');
  document.getElementById('AjaxResponse').innerHTML = responsevalues[0];
  document.getElementById('AjaxReturnValue').innerHTML = responsevalues[1];
  obj = JSON.parse(responsevalues[2]);
}
```

```
function getXMLHttp()
{
  var xmlHttp;
  try {
    xmlHttp = new XMLHttpRequest();
  }
  catch(e)
  {
    //Internet Explorer is different than the others
    Try {
      xmlHttp = new ActiveXObject("Msxml2.XMLHTTP");
    }
    catch(e)  {
      try {
        xmlHttp = new ActiveXObject("Microsoft.XMLHTTP");
      }
      catch(e)
{

        alert("Old browser? Upgrade today so you can use AJAX!")
        return false;
      }
    }
  }
  return xmlHttp;
}
```

***Example 8-2.*** The lab.php file with update, insert, and delete

```
<?php
session_start();
if ((!isset($_SESSION['username'])) || (!isset($_SESSION['password']))) {
  echo "You must login to access the ABC Canine Shelter Reservation System";
  echo "<p>";
  echo "<a href='elogin.php'>Login</a> | <a href='eregister.php'>Create an account</a>";
  echo "</p>";
}
else if(($_SERVER['HTTP_REFERER'] == 'http://127.0.0.1:8080/mysite/bgchapter8/login.php') ||
($_SERVER['HTTP_REFERER'] == 'http://127.0.0.1:8080/mysite/bgchapter8/lab.php'))
{

if (isset($_SESSION['message']))
{
  echo $_SESSION['message'];
}
else
{
  echo "<p>Welcome back, " . $_SESSION['username'] . "</p>";
}
?>
```

```
<!DOCTYPE html>
<html lan="en">
<head>
<title>ABC Canine Shelter Reservation System</title>
<script src="getlists.js"></script>
<script src="validator.js"></script>
<style type="text/css">
#JS { display:none; }
#insert {display: none; }
#delete {display: none; }
#update {display: none; }
#input_form { display:none; }
</style>
<script>
function checkJS() {
document.getElementById('JS').style.display = "inline"; }
function process_select() {
        var colorbuttons = document.getElementsByName('dog_color');
if(!(document.getElementById('dogs').value == -1)) {
        index = document.getElementById('dogs').selectedIndex -1;
        document.getElementById('index').value = index;
        document.getElementById('dog_name').value = obj.dogs[index].dog_name;
        document.getElementById('dog_weight').value = obj.dogs[index].dog_weight;
        dog_color = obj.dogs[index].dog_color;
        if(dog_color == "Brown") {
                colorbuttons[0].checked = true;
        } else if (dog_color == "Black")  {
                colorbuttons[1].checked = true;
        } else if (dog_color == "Yellow")  {
                colorbuttons[2].checked = true;
        } else if (dog_color == "White")  {
                colorbuttons[3].checked = true;          }
        dog_breed = obj.dogs[index].dog_breed;
        document.getElementById('dog_breed').value = dog_breed;
        document.getElementById('update').style.display = "inline";
        document.getElementById('delete').style.display = "inline";
        document.getElementById('insert').style.display = "none";
} else {
        colorbuttons[4].checked = true;
        document.getElementById('dog_name').value = "";
        document.getElementById('dog_weight').value = "";
        document.getElementById('dog_breed').value = "Select a dog breed";
        document.getElementById('insert').style.display = "inline";
        document.getElementById('update').style.display = "none";
        document.getElementById('delete').style.display = "none";}
        document.getElementById('input_form').style.display = "inline"; }
</script>
</head>
```

```
<body onload="checkJS();">
<h1>ABC Canine Shelter Reservation System</h1>
<div id="JS">
<script>
AjaxRequest('e8dog_interface.php');
</script>
<h3>Pick the dog name and breed to change from the dropdown box, then click the
button.<br>For new dog information select 'NEW'.</h3>
Select 'NEW' or Dog's Name/Breed <div id="AjaxReturnValue"></div>
<input type="button" name="selected" id="selected" value="Click to select"
onclick="process_select()" /><br><br>
<div id="input_form">
<form method="post" action="dog_interface.php" onSubmit="return validate_input(this)">
<h3>Please note the required format of information.</h3>
<hr>
Enter Your Dog's Name (max 20 characters, alphabetic) <input type="text" pattern="[a-zA-Z]*"
title="Up to 20 Alphabetic Characters" maxlength="20" name="dog_name" id="dog_name"
required/><br /><br />
Select Your Dog's Color:<br />
<input type="radio" name="dog_color" id="dog_color" value="Brown">Brown<br />
<input type="radio" name="dog_color" id="dog_color" value="Black">Black<br />
<input type="radio" name="dog_color" id="dog_color" value="Yellow">Yellow<br />
<input type="radio" name="dog_color" id="dog_color" value="White">White<br />
<input type="radio" name="dog_color" id="dog_color" value="Mixed" checked >Mixed<br /><br />
Enter Your Dog's Weight (numeric only) <input type="number" min="1" max="120" name="dog_
weight" id="dog_weight" required /><br /><br />
<input type="hidden" name="dog_app" id="dog_app" value="dog" />
Select Your Dog's Breed <div id="AjaxResponse"></div><br />
<input type="hidden" name="index" id="index" value="-1"/>
<input type="submit" name="insert" id="insert" value="Click to create your dog info" />
<input type="submit" name="delete" id="delete" value="Click to remove your selected dog info" />
<input type="submit" name="update" id="update" value="Click to update your selected dog info" />
<hr>
</form>
</div>
</div>
<noscript>
<div id="noJS">
<form method="post" action="dog_interface.php">
<h3>For Updates please enter all fields. For Deletions enter at least the dog name and
breed. Then click the button.<br>For new dog information enter the requested information,
Then click the button.<br> Please note the required format of information.</h3>
Enter Your Dog's Name (max 20 characters, alphabetic) <input type="text" pattern="[a-zA-Z ]*"
title="Up to 20 Alphabetic Characters" maxlength="20" name="dog_name" id="dog_name"
required/><br /><br />
Select Your Dog's Color:<br />
<input type="radio" name="dog_color" id="dog_color" value="Brown">Brown<br />
<input type="radio" name="dog_color" id="dog_color" value="Black">Black<br />
<input type="radio" name="dog_color" id="dog_color" value="Yellow">Yellow<br />
<input type="radio" name="dog_color" id="dog_color" value="White">White<br />
<input type="radio" name="dog_color" id="dog_color" value="Mixed" checked >Mixed<br /><br />
```

262

```
Enter Your Dog's Weight (numeric only) <input type="number" min="1" max="120" name="dog_
weight" id="dog_weight" required /><br /><br />
Enter Your Dog's Breed (max 35 characters, alphabetic) <input type="text" pattern="[a-zA-Z ]*"
title="Up to 15 Alphabetic Characters" maxlength="35" name="dog_breed" id="dog_breed"
required /><br />
<input type="hidden" name="dog_app" id="dog_app" value="dog" />
<input type="submit" name="input" id="input" value="Click to create your dog info" />
<input type="submit" name="delete" id="delete" value="Click to remove your selected dog info" />
<input type="submit" name="update" id="update" value="Click to update your selected dog info" />
</form>
</div>
</noscript>
</body>
</html>
```

The only change shown previously that was not mentioned previously is the removal of `session_
destroy` at the end of the code. Since you want the ability for `dog_interface` to recall `lab.php`, the session
needs to be active until the users complete the changes. You will create a logout routine that will close the
session later in this chapter.

## Do It

1. Explain how PHP code can be used to replace the process that the JavaScript
   code uses to display the list boxes, determine which dog was selected, and
   populate the form objects with the information from the dog selected. This
   process would be necessary for any browsers that do not have JavaScript
   enabled. Hint: The PHP code will work in a very similar way to the JavaScript
   code. What changes would be necessary to the `dog_interface.php`, `dog.php`,
   and `dog_data.php` programs to accomplish this task?

2. Download the code for this section from the book's web site. Adjust the code to
   handle dog information that will include the following additional fields: `dog_ID`
   (unique for each dog) and `dog_gender`. Assume that the `dog_interface.php`,
   `dog.php`, and `dog_data.php` file will return these fields. You won't be able to
   completely test this assignment until you read about the changes to these
   programs.

# Updating, Deleting, and Inserting in the Interface Tier

It's time to look at the changes to the programs in the interface and business rules tiers. There are very few
required changes in the data tier, since previously the `dog_data` program was created to handle display,
update, insert, and deletion of dog information. Doing this ahead of time makes the total amount of changes
necessary to the other tiers much easier.

As mentioned throughout the book, the interface tier is responsible for formatting information for
display and for requesting or processing information from the business rules tier. The `dog_interface`
program should accept the dogs array information from the data tier and, if needed, format it for use in the
`lab.php` program. It should also accept the dogs information for the dogs list box, provide any format for it,
and send it to `lab.php` for display. In addition, `dog_interface` must accept requests from `lab.php` for insert,
update, and delete of dog information and pass these requests on to the data tier for processing. This may
sound like a lot, but as you will see, most of the coding already exists in these programs.

First let's look at passing the request for insert or update to the data tier.

```
$dog_color = clean_input($_POST['dog_color']);
$dog_weight = clean_input($_POST['dog_weight']);
$dog_index = clean_input($_POST['index']);
```

The lab.php file will be sending a property ('index') to dog_interface. This property will be accepted and cleaned in the same manner as the other properties that are passed.

The type of information passed for a request to insert or update is almost exactly the same (all the dog properties plus 'index'). Thus, the processes are very similar. You do need a way to indicate to the type of request (update or insert).

```
if ((isset($_POST['insert'])) || (isset($_POST['update'])))
{
        if (isset($_POST['insert']))
        {
                $insert = TRUE;
        }
        else
        {
                $insert = FALSE;
        }
```

You can do this by creating a property. In this example, $insert will be set to TRUE if it is an insert request and FALSE if it is an update request. If the request is an update or insert, the properties array must be populated.

```
$properties_array = array($dog_name,$dog_breed,$dog_color,$dog_weight,$breedxml,$insert,$dog_index);
```

You can create the $properties_array as you have done in many examples before. Once created it will be passed into an instance of the dog class. The only real changes are the addition of $insert and $dog_index. The update procedure will use $dog_index to indicate which record to change. It will be set to -1 (by lab.php) when there is an insert because all records are inserted at the end of the data. (You could have used -1 as an indicator of an insert, instead of creating $Insert.)

```
$lab = $container->create_object($properties_array);
```

Using $container (which is an instance of dog_container already created in the code), the create_object method creates an instance of the dog class and passes the property array into it. You will make a slight change to the dog class, in a moment, to use the property array to determine if the insert or update methods from dog_data should be called to complete the request.

```
$_SESSION['message'] = "Dog $dog_name Insert/Update was successful<br />";
```

If everything was successful with the update, instead of using echo or print to display a message, the program will set $_SESSION['message'] with the message, which will then be displayed by lab.php.

```
header("Location: lab.php");
```

The application is then redirected back to lab.php. lab.php will verify that is was called from dog_interface and then display "Dog $dog_name Insert/Update was successful<br />" at the top of the page. ($dog_name is replaced with the actual dog name.)

If the request is delete, a similar process occurs.

```
else if($_POST['delete'])
        {
                $properties_array = $dog_index;
```

The dog_data delete method only needs the position in the array to determine what to remove. Thus, $properties_array is set to the value in $dog_index. Even though $properties_array is now a string and not an array, the processRecords method in dog_data uses polymorphism to accept an array or a string. This allows the code to be very similar to the update and insert code.

```
$lab = $container->create_object($properties_array);
$_SESSION['message'] = "Dog $dog_name Deletion was successful<br />";
header("Location: lab.php");
```

As seen with update and delete, $container (which is an instance of dog_container already created) calls the create_object method to create an instance of the dog class and pass $properties_array (which is really a string). If the delete is successful, $_SESSION['message'] is set with the delete message. Then the lab.php program is called. lab.php will verify that dog_container called it and then display "Dog $dog_name Deletion was successful<br />" at the top of the page. ($dog_name is replaced with the actual dog name.)

These are the only code changes needed in the dog_interface program in order to handle the request to insert, update, or delete. dog_interface must also accept the dogs list box and complete dogs array from the data tier to format and send to lab.php.

dog_interface must request the dogs array information by calling the display method in dog_data.php.

```
$container = NULL;
```

The container pointer, $container, can be reused after the request to return the breeds list has been processed. By setting it to NULL, it will free up the current container (an instance of dog_container with properties set for retrieving the breeds information).

```
$container = new dog_container("dog");
```

A new instance of the dog_container passes "dog" instead of "selectbox". This lets the container know than an instance of the dog class will be created, not an instance of the breeds class.

```
$properties = "dog";
$lab = $container->create_object($properties);
```

When an instance of the dog class is created by `create_object`, dog is again passed in to indicate that an instance of the dog class is needed.

```
$container->set_app("dog");
$dog_app = $container->get_dog_application("dog");
$method_array = get_class_methods($lab);
$last_position = count($method_array) - 1;
$method_name = $method_array[$last_position];
$returned_array = $lab->$method_name("ALL");
```

The same code that was used to call the `delete`, `insert`, and `update` methods in dog_data is used to call the display method. However, ALL is passed in instead of the properties array. ALL tells the dog_data display method to return all the dog records. All the records that are returned by dog_data are dropped into `$return_array`.

Now that the dog_interface has all the records (in `$return_array`), it can format the code to display the dogs list box. The code used is similar to the code to create the breeds list box.

```
$resultstring = "<select name='dogs' id='dogs'>";
$resultstring = $resultstring . "<option value='-1' selected>NEW</option>";
```

The property `$resultstring` will hold all the code for the list box. First the HTML select tag is created with an ID of `'dogs'`. Then the first row of the list box is created for the user to select NEW if they want to insert a new dog. Notice that the value for NEW is -1. That's also the default value for the hidden property `'index'` on the HTML form in lab.php. The code you looked at early in this chapter will determine that -1 is an indication to fill the HTML form objects with the default settings for the dog information. This is true either if the user selects NEW or does not select anything in the dogs list box.

```
foreach ($returned_array as $column => $column_value)
    {
        $resultstring = $resultstring . "<option value='$column'>" . $column_value['dog_name'];
        $resultstring .= "   " . $column_value['dog_breed'] . "</option>";
    }
$resultstring = $resultstring . "</select>";
```

A foreach loop will loop through the dogs array (contained in `$returned_array`) and build the remaining rows of the list box using the dog_name and dog_breed from each of the dog entries in the array. After all dogs have been placed in the list box, the list box is closed using the HTML `</select>` tag.

```
print $result . "|" . $resultstring . "|" . '{ "dogs" : ' . json_encode($returned_array) . "}";
```

lab.php expects to receive the breeds list box code in the first position, the dogs list box code in the second position, and the complete dogs array in the third position. `$result` already contains the complete breeds list box. `$resultstring` contains the new dogs list box. `$return_array` still contains all the dog records. lab.php expects the outer array of the dogs array to be labeled as `'dogs'`. The display method from dog_data does not pass the outer array back. The previous code will create a dogs array that holds all the individual dog arrays in it. Notice that the `$return_array` has been converted to JSON code when returned. The JavaScript code in lab.php will verify that it is properly formatted JSON code when it is received.

Let's look at the complete dog_interface program.

***Example 8-3.*** The dog_interface.php file with update, insert, and delete

```php
<?php
session_start();
const USER_ERROR_LOG = "User_Errors.log";
const ERROR_LOG = "Errors.log";
function clean_input($value)
{
 $value = htmlentities($value);
                // Removes any html from the string and turns it into &lt; format
                $value = strip_tags($value);
        if (get_magic_quotes_gpc())
        {
                $value = stripslashes($value);
                // Gets rid of unwanted slashes
        }
                $value = htmlentities($value);
                // Removes any html from the string and turns it into &lt; format
                $bad_chars = array( "{", "}", "(", ")", ";", ":", "<", ">", "/", "$" );
                $value = str_ireplace($bad_chars,"",$value);
                return $value;
}
class setException extends Exception {
    public function errorMessage() {
        list($name_error, $breed_error, $color_error, $weight_error) = explode(',',
$this->getMessage());
            $name_error == 'TRUE' ? $eMessage = '' : $eMessage = 'Name update not successful<br/>';
            $breed_error == 'TRUE' ? $eMessage .= '' : $eMessage .= 'Breed update not successful<br/>';
            $color_error == 'TRUE' ? $eMessage .= '' : $eMessage .= 'Color update not successful<br/>';
            $weight_error == 'TRUE' ? $eMessage .= '' : $eMessage .= 'Weight update not successful<br/>';
            return $eMessage;
            }
 }
function get_dog_app_properties($lab)
{
        print "Your dog's name is " . $lab->get_dog_name() . "<br/>";
        print "Your dog weights " . $lab->get_dog_weight() . " lbs. <br />";
        print "Your dog's breed is " . $lab->get_dog_breed() . "<br />";
        print "Your dog's color is " . $lab->get_dog_color() . "<br />";
}
//---------------Main Section-----------------------------------
try {
        if ( file_exists("e8dog_container.php"))
        {
                Require_once("e8dog_container.php");
        }
        else
        {
                throw new Exception("Dog container file missing or corrupt");
        }
```

```php
        if (isset($_POST['dog_app']))
        {
if ((isset($_POST['dog_name'])) && (isset($_POST['dog_breed'])) && (isset($_POST['dog_
color'])) && (isset($_POST['dog_weight'])))
        {
                $container = new dog_container(clean_input($_POST['dog_app']));
                $dog_name = clean_input(filter_input(INPUT_POST, "dog_name"));
                $dog_breed = clean_input($_POST['dog_breed']);
                $dog_color = clean_input($_POST['dog_color']);
                $dog_weight = clean_input($_POST['dog_weight']);
                $dog_index = clean_input($_POST['index']);
                $breedxml = $container->get_dog_application("breeds");
                if ((isset($_POST['insert'])) || (isset($_POST['update'])))
        {
                if (isset($_POST['insert']))
                {
                        $insert = TRUE;
                }
                                else
                                {

                                        $insert = FALSE;
                                }
                                $properties_array = array($dog_name,$dog_breed,$dog_
                                color,$dog_weight,$breedxml,$insert,$dog_index);
                                $lab = $container->create_object($properties_array);
                                $_SESSION['message'] = "Dog $dog_name Insert/Update was
                                successful<br />";

                                header("Location: e8lab.php");
                                //print "Dog $dog_name Insert/Update was successful<br />";
                                //get_dog_app_properties($lab);
                        }

            else
            {
                    $insert = FALSE;
            }
            $properties_array = array($dog_name,$dog_breed,$dog_color,$dog_
            weight,$breedxml,$insert,$dog_index);
            $lab = $container->create_object($properties_array);
            $_SESSION['message'] = "Dog $dog_name Insert/Update was successful<br />";
            header("Location: e8lab.php");
            //print "Dog $dog_name Insert/Update was successful<br />";
        }
        else if($_POST['delete'])
        {
                $properties_array = $dog_index;
                $lab = $container->create_object($properties_array);
                $_SESSION['message'] = "Dog $dog_name Deletion was successful<br />";
                header("Location: e8lab.php");
```

```php
            //print "Dog $dog_name Deletion was successful<br />";
        }
    }
    else
    {
    print "<p>Missing or invalid parameters. Please go back to the dog.php page to enter
valid information.<br />";
    print "<a href='e8lab.php'>Dog Creation Page</a>";
     }
}
else // breeds select box
{
        $container = new dog_container("selectbox");
        $properties_array = array("selectbox");
        $lab = $container->create_object($properties_array);
        $container->set_app("breeds");
        $dog_app = $container->get_dog_application("breeds");
        $method_array = get_class_methods($lab);
        $last_position = count($method_array) - 1;

        $container = NULL;
        $result = $lab->$method_name($dog_app);
        $container = NULL;
        // read dog_data array
        $container = new dog_container("dog");
        $properties = "dog";
        $lab = $container->create_object($properties);
        $container->set_app("dog");
        $dog_app = $container->get_dog_application("dog");
        $method_array = get_class_methods($lab);
        $last_position = count($method_array) - 1;
        $method_name = $method_array[$last_position];
        // return dogs from data
        $returned_array = $lab->$method_name("ALL");
        // format dogs list box
        $resultstring = "<select name='dogs' id='dogs'>";
        $resultstring = $resultstring . "<option value='-1' selected>NEW</option>";
        foreach ($returned_array as $column => $column_value)
            {
$resultstring = $resultstring . "<option value='$column'>" . $column_value['dog_name'] .
"   " ;
$resultstring = $resultstring .  $column_value['dog_breed'] . "</option>";
            }
        $resultstring = $resultstring . "</select>";
        print $result . "|" . $resultstring . "|" . '{ "dogs" : ' . json_encode($returned_
        array) . "}";
        }
}
```

```
    catch(setException $e)
    {
                echo $e->errorMessage(); // displays to the user
                $date = date('m.d.Y h:i:s');
                $errormessage = $e->errorMessage();
                $eMessage =  $date . " | User Error | " . $errormessage . "\n";
                error_log($eMessage,3,USER_ERROR_LOG); // writes message to user error log file
    }
catch(Exception $e)
    {
        echo "The system is currently unavailable. Please try again later."; // displays
        message to the user
        $date = date('m.d.Y h:i:s');
        $eMessage =  $date . " | System Error | " . $e->getMessage() . " | " . $e->getFile()
        . " | ". $e->getLine() . "\n";
        error_log($eMessage,3,ERROR_LOG); // writes message to error log file
        error_log("Date/Time: $date - Serious System Problems with Dog Application.
        Check error log for details", 1, "noone@helpme.com", "Subject: Dog Application
        Error \nFrom: System Log <systemlog@helpme.com>" . "\r\n");
        // e-mails personnel to alert them of a system problem
    }
?>
```

## Do It

1.  Download the code for this section from the book's web site. The example code
    (Example 6-3) could be broken into several methods to handle the creation of
    the list boxes and the dogs array. Create methods and move the code in these
    methods to process this information. Call the methods from the previous
    location of the code.

2.  Download the code for this section from the book's web site. Adjust the code
    to handle dog information that will include the following additional fields:
    dog_ID (unique for each dog) and dog_gender. Assume that the dog.php and
    dog_data.php files will return these fields. You won't be able to completely test
    this assignment until you read about the changes to these programs. Note: If you
    did not previously complete the earlier Do It, complete that assignment along
    with this one.

# Updating, Deleting, and Inserting in the Business Rules Tier

You are getting very close to completing the ABC Canine Shelter Reservation System. A few changes need
to be made to the Dog class to determine why the class was called (insert, delete, or update). Then the
information can be passed to the correct method in the dog_data class. As mentioned, no changes will be
needed to the dog_data class, as the methods for insert, update, and delete already exist. Also, the dog
class must retrieve all the dog records from dog_data to send to the dog_interface.

```php
<?php
class Dog
{
// ------------------------------------- Properties -----------------------------------
private $dog_weight = 0;
private $dog_breed = "no breed";
private $dog_color = "no color";
private $dog_name = "no name";
private $error_message = "??";
private $breedxml = "";
private $insert = FALSE;
private $index = -1;
```

At the top of the Dog class properties, $insert and $index are created to hold the values passed from the properties_array by the dog_interface program. $index is initially set to -1, indicating the default of assuming that the user either selected NEW or did not select a dog from the dogs list box (in lab.php).

```php
if((is_bool($properties_array[5])) && ($properties_array[6] > -1))
{ // confirms true or false and valid index or takes default
        $this->insert = $properties_array[5];
        $this->index = $properties_array[6];
}
$this->change_dog_data("Insert/Update");
}
if(is_numeric($properties_array))
{    // confirms valid index don't delete if not valid
        $this->index = $properties_array;
        $this->change_dog_data("Delete");
}
```

In the constructor, after the dog values (dog_name, dog_breed, dog_weight, and dog_color) have been validated, the insert and index values also need to be validated. The if statement shown uses the PHP method is_bool to determine if the value in $properties_array[5] is TRUE or FALSE. $properties_array[5] is the location of the value from the insert property. (It's set to TRUE if it is an insert and set to FALSE if it is an Update). The if statement also determines if the value in $properties_array[6] is greater than -1. A value greater than -1 indicates an update or deletion. A value of -1 indicates an insertion request. If valid, the values are placed into $this->insert and $this->index. Then the private method called change_dog_data is called passing in "insert/update".

The next if statement uses the PHP method is_numeric to determine if $properties_array is not actually an array and that it contains a number. If this is true, the index of the dog to be removed has been passed. If this is the case, then $property_array (containing the index to be deleted) is placed in $this->index and the private method called change_dog_data is called passing in "delete".

```php
private function change_dog_data($type)
{
if ( file_exists("e8dog_container.php")) {
        require_once("e8dog_container.php"); // use chapter 5 container w exception handling
} else        {
        throw new Exception("Dog container file missing or corrupt");
}
```

```
$container = new dog_container("dogdata"); // sets the tag name to look for in XML file
$properties_array = array("dogdata"); // not used but must be passed into create_object
$dog_data = $container->create_object($properties_array); // creates dog_data object
```

The new change_dog_data method (called in the previous code) will use code very similar to the display_dog_data method shown in a previous chapter. First the method verifies that the dog_container exists. If the container exists, an instance of the container ($container) is created passing "dogdata" which tells the container that this request will be using the dogs XML file. Next $properties_array is created with a simple array containing "dogdata". This array will not actually be used. However, the dog_data class requires that something be passed into the constructor. An instance of dog_data ($dog_data) is now created using the create_object method of the container.

```
$method_array = get_class_methods($dog_data);
$last_position = count($method_array) - 1;
$method_name = $method_array[$last_position];
```

As seen in previous code, the change_dog_data method uses the PHP get_class_methods to create an array of methods contained in the dog_data object ($dog_data). The last method in dog_data is the processRecords method, which uses a case statement to call the correct private method.

```
if (($this->index > -1) && ($type == "Delete"))
    {
    $record_Array = $this->index;
    $dog_data->$method_name("Delete",$record_Array);
    }
```

If the index is greater than -1 and the type is "delete" then the change_dog_data method calls the processRecords method of the dog_data object and passes "delete" and the index to be deleted.

```
else if (($this->index == -1) && ($type == "Insert/Update"))
    {
    $record_Array = array(array('dog_name'=>"$this->dog_name", 'dog_weight'=>"$this->
    dog_weight", 'dog_color'=>"$this->dog_color", 'dog_breed'=>"$this->dog_breed"));
    $dog_data->$method_name("Insert",$record_Array);
    }
```

If the index is -1 and the type is "insert/update" then the user has requested an "insert". An array is created containing all the dog properties (dog_name, dog_weight, dog_color, and dog_breed). Then "insert" and the array are passed into the processRecords method of the dog_object.

```
else if ($type == "Insert/Update")
    {
    $record_Array = array($this->index => array('dog_name'=>"$this->dog_name",
    'dog_weight'=>"$this->dog_weight", 'dog_color'=>"$this->dog_color",
    'dog_breed'=>"$this->dog_breed"));
    $dog_data->$method_name("Update",$record_Array);
    }
    $dog_data = NULL;
}
```

If the index is not -1 and the type is "insert/update", then the user has requested an update of information. The same array as shown with an insert is created, with one exception. The index of the array (array($this->index => ) is set to the index of the record to be updated. The array and "update" are then passed to the processRecords method of the dog_data object.

After the record has been inserted, updated, or deleted, the dog_data object ($dog_data) is set to NULL. As stated in previous chapters, the dog_data object first updates the associate array, which contains each dog's information. When the destructor of the dog_data object is called, the information is then updated to the dog_data XML file. Setting $dog_data to NULL releases the dog_data object, which calls its destructor.

That completes all the changes to the business rules tier. Let's put it all together.

***Example 8-4.*** The dog.php file with update, insert, and delete

```php
<?php
class Dog
{
// ------------------------------------ Properties ------------------------------------
private $dog_weight = 0;
private $dog_breed = "no breed";
private $dog_color = "no color";
private $dog_name = "no name";
private $error_message = "??";
private $breedxml = "";
private $insert = FALSE;
private $index = -1;
// -------------------------------- Constructor -----------------------------------------
function __construct($properties_array)
{
if (method_exists('dog_container', 'create_object')) {
if (is_array($properties_array)) {
$this->breedxml = $properties_array[4];
$name_error = $this->set_dog_name($properties_array[0]) == TRUE ? 'TRUE,' : 'FALSE,';
$color_error = $this->set_dog_color($properties_array[2]) == TRUE ? 'TRUE,' : 'FALSE,';
$weight_error= $this->set_dog_weight($properties_array[3]) == TRUE ? 'TRUE' : 'FALSE';
$breed_error = $this->set_dog_breed($properties_array[1]) == TRUE ? 'TRUE,' : 'FALSE,';
$this->error_message = $name_error . $breed_error . $color_error . $weight_error;
if(stristr($this->error_message, 'FALSE'))
{
        throw new setException($this->error_message);
}
if((is_bool($properties_array[5])) && ($properties_array[6] > -1))
{ // confirms true or false and valid index or takes default
        $this->insert = $properties_array[5];
        $this->index = $properties_array[6];
}
$this->change_dog_data("Insert/Update");
}
if(is_numeric($properties_array))
{   // confirms valid index don't delete if not valid
        $this->index = $properties_array;
        $this->change_dog_data("Delete");
}
}
}
```

```php
else
{
exit;
}
}
function clean_input() { }
function set_dog_name($value)
{
$error_message = TRUE;
(ctype_alpha($value) && strlen($value) <= 20) ? $this->dog_name = $value : $this->error_
message = FALSE;
return $this->error_message;
}
function set_dog_weight($value)
{
$error_message = TRUE;
(ctype_digit($value) && ($value > 0 && $value <= 120)) ? $this->dog_weight = $value : $this-
>error_message = FALSE;
return $this->error_message;
}
function set_dog_breed($value)
{
$error_message = TRUE;
($this->validator_breed($value) === TRUE) ? $this->dog_breed = $value : $this->error_message = FALSE;
return $this->error_message;
}
function set_dog_color($value){
$error_message = TRUE;
(ctype_alpha($value) && strlen($value) <= 15) ? $this->dog_color = $value : $this->error_
message = FALSE;
return $this->error_message; }
/ ---------------------------- Get Methods --------------------------------------------
function get_dog_name()
{
return $this->dog_name;
}
function get_dog_weight()
{
return $this->dog_weight;
}
function get_dog_breed()
{
return $this->dog_breed;
}
function get_dog_color()
{
return $this->dog_color;
}
function get_properties()
{
return "$this->dog_name,$this->dog_weight,$this->dog_breed,$this->dog_color.";
}
```

```php
// ----------------------------General Methods----------------------------------------------
private function validator_breed($value)
{
$breed_file = simplexml:load_file($this->breedxml);
$xmlText = $breed_file->asXML();
if(stristr($xmlText, $value) === FALSE)
{
return FALSE;
}
else
{
return TRUE;
}
}
private function change_dog_data($type)
{
if ( file_exists("e8dog_container.php")) {
                require_once("e8dog_container.php"); // use chapter 5 container w exception
                handling
        } else {
                throw new Exception("Dog container file missing or corrupt");
        }
        $container = new dog_container("dogdata"); // sets the tag name to look for in XML file
        $properties_array = array("dogdata"); // not used but must be passed into create_object
        $dog_data = $container->create_object($properties_array); // creates dog_data object
        $method_array = get_class_methods($dog_data);
        $last_position = count($method_array) - 1;
        $method_name = $method_array[$last_position];
if (($this->index > -1) && ($type == "Delete"))
        {
                $record_Array = $this->index;
                $dog_data->$method_name("Delete",$record_Array);
        }
         else if (($this->index == -1) && ($type == "Insert/Update"))
        {
        $record_Array = array(array('dog_name'=>"$this->dog_name", 'dog_weight'=>"$this->
        dog_weight", 'dog_color'=>"$this->dog_color", 'dog_breed'=>"$this->dog_breed"));
        $dog_data->$method_name("Insert",$record_Array);
        }
        else if ($type == "Insert/Update")
        {
        $record_Array = array($this->index => array('dog_name'=>"$this->dog_name",
        'dog_weight'=>"$this->dog_weight", 'dog_color'=>"$this->dog_color",
        'dog_breed'=>"$this->dog_breed"));
        $dog_data->$method_name("Update",$record_Array);
        }
        $dog_data = NULL;
}
```

```
function display_dog_data($record)
{
if ( file_exists("e8dog_container.php")) {
            require_once("e8dog_container.php"); // use chapter 5 container w exception handling
        } else {
            throw new Exception("Dog container file missing or corrupt");
        }
        $container = new dog_container("dogdata"); // sets the tag name to look for in XML file
        $properties_array = array("dogdata"); // not used but must be passed into create_object
        $dog_data = $container->create_object($properties_array); // creates dog_data object
        $method_array = get_class_methods($dog_data);
        $last_position = count($method_array) - 1;
        $method_name = $method_array[$last_position];
        $record_Array = $record;
        return $dog_data->$method_name("Display",$record_Array);
}
}
?>
```

As you've read, there are no required changes to the dog_data.php file because it already contains insert, update, and delete methods.

## Do It

1. Download the code for this section from the book's web site. Run the (almost) completed program. Try to "break" the program. Did you accomplish the task? If so, what broke? Attempt to fix any problems you might discover.

2. Download the code for this section from the book's web site. Adjust the code to handle dog information that will include the following additional fields: dog_ID (unique for each dog) and dog_gender. Adjust the dog.php and dog_data.php programs to return these fields. You should now be able to test the complete application. Note: If you did not previously complete the Do Its earlier in this chapter, complete these assignments along with this one.

# Final Touches

You will finish the coding of the ABC Canine Shelter Reservation System in this section (finally!). You will use some CSS code from Chapter 2 to help make the application look more professional. In addition, you will add a menu that will allow the users to read the errors logs and sign out of the application (close the session).

The CSS code from Chapter 2 uses the HTML tag (`<div id='wrapper'>`) to control the contents of the body section. This tag is therefore added directly after the body tag (and closed right before the closing body tag).

```
<body onload="checkJS();">
<div id="wrapper">
<div id="header"><h1><img src="brody.jpg"> ABC Canine Shelter Reservation System</h1>
```

The CSS code also uses the HTML tag (`<div id='header'>`) to format the header (title) of the page. The code has also been adjusted to include an image of a dog using the HTML img tag.

```
<a href="e8readerrorlog.php">Manage Error Logs</a> | <a href="e75changepassword.php">Change
Password</a> | <a href="e8lab.php?logoff=True">Log Off</a>
</div>
```

A simple menu is also included in the header section, which will allow the users to read the error log, change their passwords, or log off the application. Notice that the code to log off the system will recall the `lab.php` program and create a property "logoff" with a value of "True". You will make just a sight final adjustment to the `lab.php` code to handle this selection.

All the remaining contents of the body section are placed in the HTML tag (`<div ='contents'>`).

```
<head>
<title>ABC Canine Shelter Reservation System</title>
<link href="e8dogstylesheet.css" rel="stylesheet">
```

The CSS code from Chapter 2 will be pulled into the file in the head section. The file has been renamed. The contents of the file remain unchanged except for adding a `float: top` to the wrapper to align the display with the top of the browser and `text-align: center` to the header to center the title of the application.

These changes provide a better look and feel for the application.

The last code you need to look at in the `lab.php` program is the `logoff` routine.

```
session_start();
if (isset($_GET['logoff']))
{
session_destroy();
}
if ((!isset($_SESSION['username'])) || (!isset($_SESSION['password'])) || (isset($_GET['logoff']))) {
```

At the top of the code for `lab.php` an `if` statement is added to determine if `logoff` has been set (via GET). If it has, the session is destroyed. The `if` statement to determine if the user ID and password has not been set, and is also modified to include checking if `logoff` has been set. If it has been set, then (at this point) the user is no longer logged in to the system.

```
echo "<html><head><title>ABC Canine Shelter Reservation System</title>";
echo "<link href= 'e8dogstylesheet.css' rel='stylesheet'><style type='text/css'>img {
height: 100px; width: 140px; }</style></head><body>";
echo "<div id='wrapper'><div id='header'><h1><img src='brody.jpg'>ABC Canine Shelter
Reservation System</h1></div>";
echo "<div id='content'>";
echo "You must login to access the ABC Canine Shelter Reservation System";
echo "<p>";
echo "<a href='e74login.php'>Login</a> | <a href='e73registration.php'>Create an account</a>";
echo "</p>";
echo "</div><div id='footer'>Copyright &copy; 2015 Little Ocean Waves Publishing - Steve
Prettyman</div></div>";
echo "</body></html>";
```

The user is then redirected to either log in or create an account. Also notice that the code has been modified to include the same div tags for wrapper, header, content, and footer. This will give the page the same look as the lab.php file.

In addition, any page displayed to the users should have this look. The displayRecords method of the readerrorlog program has also been modified (as shown here) to include the same div tags.

```
echo "<html><head><title>ABC Canine Shelter Reservation System</title>";
echo "<link href=' e8dogstylesheet.css' rel='stylesheet'>";
echo "<style> table { border: 2px solid #5c744d;}";
echo "img { height: 100px; width: 140px; } </style>";
echo "</head><body>";
echo "<div id='wrapper'><div id='header'><h1><img src='brody.jpg'> ABC Canine Shelter
Reservation System</h1></div><div id='content'>";
echo "<table>";
echo "<caption>Log File: " . ERROR_LOG . "</caption>";
echo "<tr><th></th><th>Date/Time</th><th>Error Type</th><th>Error Message</th></tr><tr>";
for ($J=$row_Count; $J >= 0; $J--)
{
            echo "<td><a href='e58readlogfile.php?rn=$J'>Delete</a></td>";
            for($I=0; $I < 3; $I++)
      {
                  echo "<td> " . $error_Array[$J][$I] . " </td> ";
      }
      echo "</tr>";
}
echo "</table>";
echo "</div><div id='footer'>Copyright &copy; 2015 Little Ocean Waves Publishing - Steve
Prettyman</div></div>";
echo "</body></html>";
```

Let's look at the final version of lab.php in Example 8-5.

***Example 8-5.*** The complete lab.php file

```
<?php
session_start();
if (isset($_GET['logoff']))
{
session_destroy();
}
if ((!isset($_SESSION['username'])) || (!isset($_SESSION['password'])) || (isset($_GET['logoff']))) {
echo "<html><head><title>ABC Canine Shelter Reservation System</title>";
echo "<link href='e8dogstylesheet.css' rel='stylesheet'><style type='text/css'>img { height:
100px; width: 140px; }</style></head><body>";
echo "<div id='wrapper'><div id='header'><h1><img src='brody.jpg'>ABC Canine Shelter
Reservation System</h1></div>";
echo "<div id='content'>";
echo "You must login to access the ABC Canine Shelter Reservation System";
echo "<p>";
echo "<a href='e74login.php'>Login</a> | <a href='e73registration.php'>Create an account</a>";
echo "</p>";
```

```
echo "</div><div id='footer'>Copyright &copy; 2015 Little Ocean Waves Publishing - Steve
Prettyman</div></div>";
echo "</body></html>";
}
else if(($_SERVER['HTTP_REFERER'] == 'http://127.0.0.1:8080/mysite/bgchapter8/
ExampleFile7.4/e74login.php') || ($_SERVER['HTTP_REFERER'] == 'http://127.0.0.1:8080/mysite/
bgchapter8/ExampleFile7.4/e8lab.php'))
{
?>
<!DOCTYPE html>
<html lan="en">
<head>
<title>ABC Canine Shelter Reservation System</title>
<link href=" e8dogstylesheet.css" rel="stylesheet">
<script src="e8getlists.js"></script>
<script src="e5validator.js"></script>
<style type="text/css">
#JS { display:none; }
#input_form { display:none; }
#insert {display: none; }
#delete {display: none; }
#update {display: none; }
img { height: 100px; width: 140px; }
</style>
<script>
function checkJS() {
document.getElementById('JS').style.display = "inline";
}
function process_select() {
        var colorbuttons = document.getElementsByName('dog_color');
        if(!(document.getElementById('dogs').value == -1))
      {
    index = document.getElementById('dogs').selectedIndex -1;
    document.getElementById('index').value = index;
    document.getElementById('dog_name').value = obj.dogs[index].dog_name;
    document.getElementById('dog_weight').value = obj.dogs[index].dog_weight;
    dog_color = obj.dogs[index].dog_color;
  if(dog_color == "Brown")
  {
        colorbuttons[0].checked = true;
  } else if (dog_color == "Black")
  {
        colorbuttons[1].checked = true;
  } else if (dog_color == "Yellow")
  {
        colorbuttons[2].checked = true;
  }
else if (dog_color == "White")
  {
        colorbuttons[3].checked = true;
  }
```

```
                dog_breed = obj.dogs[index].dog_breed;
                document.getElementById('dog_breed').value = dog_breed;
                document.getElementById('update').style.display = "inline";
                document.getElementById('delete').style.display = "inline";
                document.getElementById('insert').style.display = "none";
        }
        else
        {
                colorbuttons[4].checked = true;
                document.getElementById('dog_name').value = "";
                document.getElementById('dog_weight').value = "";
                document.getElementById('dog_breed').value = "Select a dog breed";
                document.getElementById('insert').style.display = "inline";
                document.getElementById('update').style.display = "none";
                 document.getElementById('delete').style.display = "none";
        }

                document.getElementById('input_form').style.display = "inline";
}
</script>
</head>
<body onload="checkJS();">
<div id="wrapper">
<div id="header"><h1><img src="brody.jpg"> ABC Canine Shelter Reservation System</h1>
<a href="e8readerrorlog.php">Manage Error Logs</a> | <a href="e75changepassword.php">Change
Password</a> | <a href="e8lab.php?logoff=True">Log Off</a>
</div>
<div id="content">
<?php
if (isset($_SESSION['message']))
{
echo "<p>" . $_SESSION['message'] . "</p>";
}
else
{
echo "<p> Welcome back, " . $_SESSION['username'] . "</p>";
}
?>
<div id="JS">

<script>
AjaxRequest('e8dog_interface.php');
</script>
<h3>Pick the dog name and breed to change from the dropdown box, then click the
button.<br>For new dog information select 'NEW'.</h3>
Select 'NEW' or Dog's Name/Breed <div id="AjaxReturnValue"></div>
<input type="button" name="selected" id="selected" value="Click to select" onclick="process_
select()" /><br><br>
<div id="input_form">
<form method="post" action="e8dog_interface.php" onSubmit="return validate_input(this)">
<h3>Please note the required format of information.</h3>
<hr>
```

```
Enter Your Dog's Name (max 20 characters, alphabetic) <input type="text" pattern="[a-zA-Z]*"
title="Up to 20 Alphabetic Characters" maxlength="20" name="dog_name" id="dog_name"
required/><br /><br />
Select Your Dog's Color:<br />
<input type="radio" name="dog_color" id="dog_color" value="Brown">Brown<br />
<input type="radio" name="dog_color" id="dog_color" value="Black">Black<br />
<input type="radio" name="dog_color" id="dog_color" value="Yellow">Yellow<br />
<input type="radio" name="dog_color" id="dog_color" value="White">White<br />
<input type="radio" name="dog_color" id="dog_color" value="Mixed" checked >Mixed<br /><br />
Enter Your Dog's Weight (numeric only) <input type="number" min="1" max="120"
name="dog_weight" id="dog_weight" required /><br /><br />
<input type="hidden" name="dog_app" id="dog_app" value="dog" />
Select Your Dog's Breed <div id="AjaxResponse"></div><br />
<input type="hidden" name="index" id="index" value="-1"/>
<input type="submit" name="insert" id="insert" value="Click to create your dog info" />
<input type="submit" name="delete" id="delete" value="Click to remove your selected dog info" />
<input type="submit" name="update" id="update" value="Click to update your selected dog info" />
<hr>
</form>
</div> </div>
<noscript>
<div id="noJS">
<form method="post" action="e8dog_interface.php">
<h3>For Updates please enter all fields. For Deletions enter at least the dog name and
breed. Then click the button.<br>For new dog information enter the requested information,
Then click the button.<br> Please note the required format of information.</h3>
Enter Your Dog's Name (max 20 characters, alphabetic) <input type="text" pattern="[a-zA-Z ]*"
title="Up to 20 Alphabetic Characters" maxlength="20" name="dog_name" id="dog_name"
required/><br /><br />
Select Your Dog's Color:<br />
<input type="radio" name="dog_color" id="dog_color" value="Brown">Brown<br />
<input type="radio" name="dog_color" id="dog_color" value="Black">Black<br />
<input type="radio" name="dog_color" id="dog_color" value="Yellow">Yellow<br />
<input type="radio" name="dog_color" id="dog_color" value="White">White<br />
<input type="radio" name="dog_color" id="dog_color" value="Mixed" checked >Mixed<br /><br />
Enter Your Dog's Weight (numeric only) <input type="number" min="1" max="120"
name="dog_weight" id="dog_weight" required /><br /><br />
Enter Your Dog's Breed (max 35 characters, alphabetic) <input type="text" pattern="[a-zA-Z ]*"
title="Up to 15 Alphabetic Characters" maxlength="35" name="dog_breed" id="dog_breed"
required /><br />
<input type="hidden" name="dog_app" id="dog_app" value="dog" />
<input type="submit" name="input" id="input" value="Click to create your dog info" />
<input type="submit" name="delete" id="delete" value="Click to remove your selected dog info" />
<input type="submit" name="update" id="update" value="Click to update your selected dog info" />
</form>
</div>
</noscript>
</div>
```

```
<div id="footer">Copyright &copy; 2015 Little Ocean Waves Publishing - Steve Prettyman</div>
</div>
</body> </html>
<?php    } ?>
```

***Example 8-6.*** The complete readerrorlog.php file

```php
<?php
session_start();
function deleteRecord($recordNumber, &&$row_Count, &&$error_Array)
{
        for ($J=$recordNumber; $J < $row_Count - 1; $J++)
{
                for($I=0; $I < 3; $I++)
        {
                        $error_Array[$J][$I] = $error_Array[$J + 1][$I];
                }
}
unset($error_Array[$row_Count]);
$row_Count--;
}
function saveChanges($row_Count,$error_Array,$log_File)
{
        $logFile = fopen($log_File, "w");
        for($I=0; $I < $row_Count; $I++)
        {
            $writeString = $error_Array[$I][0] . " | " . $error_Array[$I][1] . " | " .
$error_Array[$I][2];
                fwrite($logFile, $writeString);
        }
        fclose($logFile);
}
function displayRecords($row_Count, $error_Array)
{
echo "<html><head><title>ABC Canine Shelter Reservation System</title>";
echo "<link href= 'e8dogstylesheet.css' rel='stylesheet'>";
echo "<style> table { border: 2px solid #5c744d;}";
echo "img { height: 100px; width: 140px; } </style>";
echo "</head><body>";
echo "<div id='wrapper'><div id='header'><h1><img src='brody.jpg'> ABC Canine Shelter
Reservation System</h1></div><div id='content'>";
echo "<table>";
echo "<caption>Log File: " . ERROR_LOG . "</caption>";
echo "<tr><th></th><th>Date/Time</th><th>Error Type</th><th>Error Message</th></tr><tr>";
echo "<tr><th></th><th>Date/Time</th><th>Error Type</th><th>Error Message</th></tr><tr>";
for ($J=$row_Count; $J >= 0; $J--)
{
                echo "<td><a href='e58readlogfile.php?rn=$J'>Delete</a></td>";
                for($I=0; $I < 3; $I++)
```

```php
                {
                        echo "<td> " . $error_Array[$J][$I] . " </td> ";
                }
        echo "</tr>";
}
echo "</table>";
echo "</div><div id='footer'>Copyright &copy; 2015 Little Ocean Waves Publishing - Steve
Prettyman</div></div>";
echo "</body></html>";
}
const ERROR_LOG = "Errors.log";
if ((!isset($_SESSION['username'])) || (!isset($_SESSION['password']))) {
echo "<html><head><title>ABC Canine Shelter Reservation System</title>";
echo "<link href='e8dogstylesheet.css' rel='stylesheet'><style type='text/css'>img { height:
100px; width: 140px; }</style></head><body>";
echo "<div id='wrapper'><div id='header'><h1><img src='brody.jpg'>ABC Canine Shelter
Reservation System</h1></div>";
echo "<div id='content'>";
echo "You must login to access the ABC Canine Shelter Reservation System";
echo "<p>";
echo "<a href='e74login.php'>Login</a> | <a href='e73registration.php'>Create an account</a>";
echo "</p>";
echo "</div><div id='footer'>Copyright &copy; 2015 Little Ocean Waves Publishing - Steve
Prettyman</div></div>";
echo "</body></html>";
}
else
{
$logFile = fopen(ERROR_LOG, "r");
$row_Count = 0;
while(!feof($logFile))
{
$error_Array[$row_Count] = explode(' | ', fgets($logFile));
                $row_Count++;
}
$row_Count--;
fclose($logFile);

if(isset($_GET['rn']))
{
deleteRecord($_GET['rn'], $row_Count, $error_Array);
saveChanges($row_Count,$error_Array,ERROR_LOG);
}
displayRecords($row_Count,$error_Array);
}
?>
```

# Do It

1.  Download the code for this section from the book's site. Also, download the displaychangelog.php program from Chapter 6 (in Example 6-4) along with a change log if you don't already have one. Update the menu provided in the lab. php program to provide a link to the displaychangelog.php program. Add code to the displaychangelog.php program to require the users to log in. Redirect the users to the choice of login or registration (as shown in the examples) if they are not logged in. Also update the HTML in the displaychangelog.php file to use the e8dogstylesheet.css file to display the change log page and the login/ registration selection page in the same format as shown in Figure 8-5.

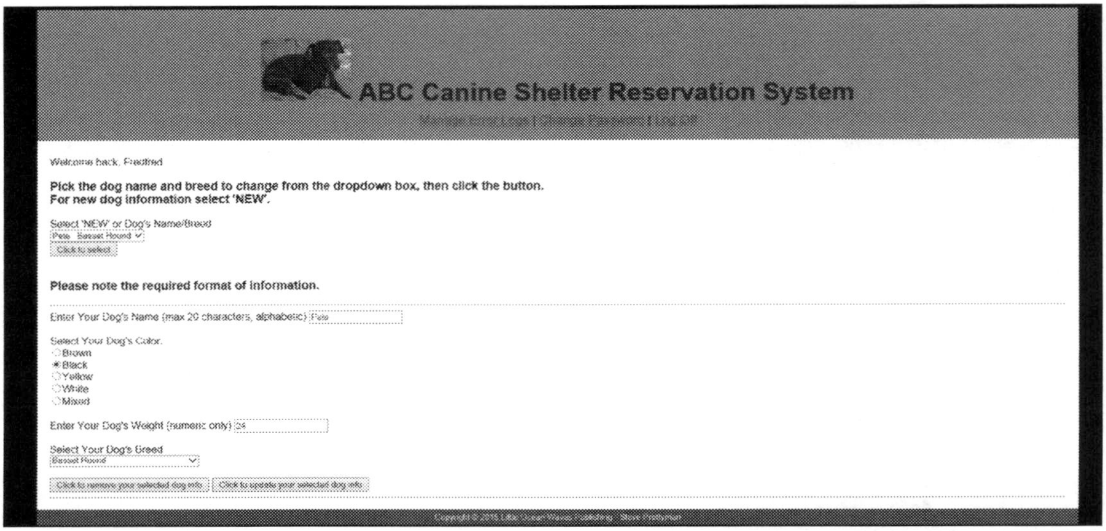

***Figure 8-5.*** *The complete lab.php file*

2.  Download the code for this section from the book's web site. Adjust the code to handle dog information that will include the following additional fields: dog_ID (unique for each dog) and dog_gender. Adjust all programs necessary (including the readerrorlog and displaychangelog (in Example 6-4)). You should now be able to test the complete application.

3.  Download the code for this section from the book's site. Add a menu for the users to return to the shelter registration page (lab.php) or log off when they are using the readerrorlog.php file. Add the code needed to the readerrorlog.php file to log off the user. If you have not already done so, include changes need to format the display of the readerrorlog.php file as shown in Figure 8-5. Also these changes in the displaychangelog.php file (if you did #1).

# ABC Canine Shelter Reservation System Logical Design

The final logical design of the ABC Canine Shelter Reservation System shows the application with four tiers (authentication, interface, business rules, and data). Additional tiers could also be used to break a large application across multiple servers.

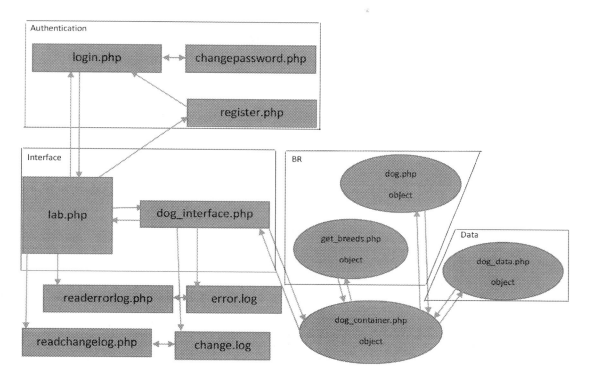

***Figure 8-6.*** *The complete ABC Canine Shelter Reservation System*

In addition to the tiers, maintenance programs (`readerrorlog` and `readchangelog`) provide the ability to tighten security, fix errors, and provide backup and recovery.

## Limitations

The ABC Canine Shelter Reservation System has been used as a teaching tool in this book. However, the system is not complete and ready for the real world. Many of the limitations of the system have been addressed in this book and used as exercises for you to gain further PHP programming skills. The changes shown next should be made to the system to improve the user experience, security, and performance. In addition, user testing is critical to ensure that the users of the system are satisfied. Users who are not happy with the design and performance of the system are not likely to use it.

lab.php

- A Dog_ID or some other type of unique field needs to be included to determine the difference between dogs with the same name and breed.

- The form for users not using JavaScript needs to use PHP to call and retrieve needed information for update and delete ability.

- A link to displaychangelog.php needs to be provided in the menu selection.

- A Dog_Gender field needs to exist. It would also be good if dog pictures existed.

- The program needs to handle and respond to users attempt to insert a dog that already exists.

dog_interface.php

- Dog_ID information (update/insert) needs to be accepted from the Dog class and passed to lab.php.

- Code is needed to return requests to lab.php for the complete dogs array and a specific dog for the non_JavaScript-enabled browsers. The information will be retrieved from dog.php.

- The Dog_Gender field needs to be pulled from dog.php and passed to lab.php.

- A session message must be passed to the lab.php program when the user attempts to enter a dog that is already in the data. The message is created in a catch block.

dog.php

- The Dog_ID information needs to be pulled from dog_data.php and passed to dog_interface.php.

- The Dog_Gender needs to be pulled from dog_data.php and passed to dog_interface.php.

dog_data.php

- The Dog_ID needs to be passed to dog.php. The ability to insert and update this field needs to be included.

- The Dog_Gender needs to be passed to dog.php. The ability to insert and updated this field needs to be included.

register.php

- This program needs to include a unique field (customerID) to determine duplicate user IDs. This field will be generated and not entered by the users.

- This program needs to detect users attempting to create a duplicate ID. Code could even make suggestions for user ID names based on what the user attempted to create (such as adding numbers to the end of the user ID).

- This program needs to require the user to also use a special symbol for the password.

- This program needs security questions in case the user forgets his password.

- Additional fields are needed, such as name, e-mail, and address.

login.php

- This program needs to be able to create a temporary password for users who forget their passwords but remember answers to their security questions.

Overall

- You need to consider moving more program (file) names to XML files for easier version changes.

- You need to consider adding levels of access and approval for new user IDs.

# Chapter Terms

| | |
|---|---|
| `$_SERVER['HTTP_REFERER']` | HTML button |
| `split` | `var` |
| `JSON object` | `JSON.parse` |
| `getElementsByName` | HTML list boxes |
| `selectedIndex` | `value` |
| dot notation format | checked property |
| `is_bool` | `img` |
| `float: top` | text-align: center |
| Four Tier Application | |

## Chapter Questions and Projects

**Multiple Choice**

1.  Which JavaScript method accomplishes a similar task as the PHP method explode?

    a.  `explode`

    b.  `slice`

    c.  `split`

    d.  None of these

2.  Which JavaScript method accomplishes a similar task as the PHP method `json_decode`?

    a.  `JSON.scan`

    b.  `JSON.parse`

    c.  `JSON.decode`

    d.  None of these

3.  A JSON object is similar to which PHP object?

    a.  An array

    b.  A multidimensional array

    c.  An associative array

    d.  None of these

4.   An HTML button can be used to do what?

    a.   Can be used to call a JavaScript method

    b.   Can submit a form

    c.   Can display a form

    d.   All of the above

5.   The `private` word is used to create a private object in PHP. What word is used in JavaScript to accomplish the same?

    a.   `private`

    b.   No additional word is needed; they are private by default

    c.   `var`

    d.   None of these

## True/False

1.   JavaScript is commonly used to retrieve and use data passed from other program languages.

2.   The CSS code `display: form` is used to display a form that has been hidden from the user.

3.   The CSS code `p {float: top }` will cause everything in all paragraph tags to float to the top of the browser window.

4.   `getElementsByName` can be used to create an array from a grouping of radio buttons.

5.   `is_numeric` could be used to determine if an object is not an array.

## Short Answer/Essay

1.   Explain why and how initially hiding a form from the users will force them to make a selection from a list box.

2.   Explain how each program in the ABC Canine Shelter Reservation System uses -1 to indicate a request for insert.

3.   Explain each tier of a four-tier application.

4.   What changes would need to occur in the ABC Canine Shelter Reservation System to convert it to a Feline Shelter Reservation System?

5.   Give an example of three algorithms (blocks of code) that have been continuously reused in the ABC Canine Shelter Reservation System.

## Projects

1.   Go back to the section entitled "Limitations" in this chapter and view the list again. Download the complete code from this chapter and fix one (or more) of these limitations. Make sure to fix the limitation in all the applicable files.

## Term Project

1.   Update the ABC Computer Parts Inventory application to provide complete `delete`, `update`, and `insert` capabilities (as shown in this chapter). Add CSS to each program in the application interface to provide a more professional display of the information. Add any code needed to ensure that the users are logged in to access any part of the application. List any limitations that still exist in this application.

# Index

© Steve Prettyman 2015
S. Prettyman. *Learn PHP 7*. DOI 10.1007/978-1-4842-1730-6

Printed in the United States
By Bookmasters